P9-AQA-710

ENHANCING HUMAN PERFORMANCE

Issues, Theories, and Techniques

Daniel Druckman and John A. Swets, Editors

Committee on Techniques for the Enhancement of Human Performance
Commission on Behavioral and Social Sciences and Education
National Research Council

NATIONAL ACADEMY PRESS
Washington, D.C. 1988

AL HARRIS LIBRARY
SOUTHWESTERN OKLA. STATE UNIV
WEATHERFORD, OK. 73096

NATIONAL ACADEMY PRESS • 2101 Constitution Avenue, NW • Washington, DC 20418

NOTICE: The project that is the subject of this report was approved by the Governing Board of the National Research Council, whose members are drawn from the councils of the National Academy of Sciences, the National Academy of Engineering, and the Institute of Medicine. The members of the committee responsible for the report were chosen for their special competences and with regard for appropriate balance.

This report has been reviewed by a group other than the authors according to procedures approved by a Report Review Committee consisting of members of the National Academy of Sciences, the National Academy of Engineering, and the Institute of Medicine.

The National Academy of Sciences is a private, nonprofit, self-perpetuating society of distinguished scholars engaged in scientific and engineering research, dedicated to the furtherance of science and technology and to their use for the general welfare. Upon the authority of the charter granted to it by the Congress in 1863, the Academy has a mandate that requires it to advise the federal government on scientific and technical matters. Dr. Frank Press is president of the National Academy of Sciences.

The National Academy of Engineering was established in 1964, under the charter of the National Academy of Sciences, as a parallel organization of outstanding engineers. It is autonomous in its administration and in the selection of its members, sharing with the National Academy of Sciences the responsibility for advising the federal government. The National Academy of Engineering also sponsors engineering programs aimed at meeting national needs, encourages education and research, and recognizes the superior achievements of engineers. Dr. Robert M. White is president of the National Academy of Engineering.

The Institute of Medicine was established in 1970 by the National Academy of Sciences to secure the services of eminent members of appropriate professions in the examination of policy matters pertaining to the health of the public. The Institute acts under the responsibility given to the National Academy of Sciences by its congressional charter to be an adviser to the federal government and, upon its own initiative, to identify issues of medical care, research, and education. Dr. Samuel O. Thier is president of the Institute of Medicine.

The National Research Council was organized by the National Academy of Sciences in 1916 to associate the broad community of science and technology with the Academy's purposes of furthering knowledge and advising the federal government. Functioning in accordance with general policies determined by the Academy, the Council has become the principal operating agency of both the National Academy of Sciences and the National Academy of Engineering in providing services to the government, the public, and the scientific and engineering communities. The Council is administered jointly by both Academies and the Institute of Medicine. Dr. Frank Press and Dr. Robert M. White are chairman and vice chairman, respectively, of the National Research Council.

Library of Congress Cataloging-in-Publication Data

Enhancing human performance : issues, theories, and techniques /
    Daniel Druckman and John A. Swets, editors.
        p.   cm.
        "Committee on Techniques for the Enhancement of Human Performance,
    Commission on Behavioral and Social Sciences and Education, National
    Research Council."
        Bibliography: p.
        Includes index.
        ISBN 0-309-03792-1.   ISBN 0-309-03787-5 (soft)
        1. Self-realization—Congresses.   2. Performance—Psychological
    aspects—Congresses.   I. Druckman, Daniel, 1939–   .   II. Swets,
    John Arthur, 1928–   .   III. National Research Council (U.S.).
    Committee on Techniques for the Enhancement of Human Performance.
    BF637.S4E56   1987
    158—dc19   87-31233
                                                                            CIP

Copyright © 1988 by the National Academy of Sciences

Printed in the United States of America

158
En 395

COMMITTEE ON TECHNIQUES FOR THE ENHANCEMENT OF HUMAN PERFORMANCE

JOHN A. SWETS, *Chair,* Bolt Beranek and Newman Inc., Cambridge, Mass.

ROBERT A. BJORK, Department of Psychology, University of California, Los Angeles

THOMAS D. COOK, Department of Psychology, Northwestern University

GERALD C. DAVISON, Department of Psychology, University of Southern California

LLOYD G. HUMPHREYS, Department of Psychology, University of Illinois

RAY HYMAN, Department of Psychology, University of Oregon

DANIEL M. LANDERS, Department of Physical Education, Arizona State University

SANDRA A. MOBLEY, Director of Training and Development, The Wyatt Company, Washington, D.C.

LYMAN W. PORTER, Graduate School of Management, University of California, Irvine

MICHAEL I. POSNER, Department of Neurology, Washington University

WALTER SCHNEIDER, Department of Psychology, University of Pittsburgh

JEROME E. SINGER, Department of Medical Psychology, Uniformed Services University of Health Sciences, Bethesda, Md.

SALLY P. SPRINGER, Department of Psychology, State University of New York, Stony Brook

RICHARD F. THOMPSON, Department of Psychology, Stanford University

DANIEL DRUCKMAN, *Study Director*

JULIE A. KRAMAN, *Administrative Secretary*

263405

265405

Contents

v

Preface

The Army Research Institute in 1984 asked the National Academy of Sciences to form a committee to examine the potential value of certain techniques that had been proposed to enhance human performance. As a class, these techniques were viewed as extraordinary, in that they were developed outside the mainstream of the human sciences and were presented with strong claims for high effectiveness. The committee was also to recommend general policy and criteria for future evaluation of enhancement techniques by the Army.

The Committee on Techniques for the Enhancement of Human Performance first met in June 1985. The 14 members of the committee were appointed for their expertise in areas related to the techniques examined. The disciplines they represent include experimental, physiological, clinical, social, and industrial psychology and cognitive neuroscience; one member is a training program director from the private sector. During the next two years, the committee gathered six times, met in toto or in part on several occasions with various representatives of the Army, conducted interviews and site visits and sent subcommittees on several others, and commissioned 10 analytical and survey papers. The committee also examined a variety of materials, including state-of-the-art reviews of relevant literature, reports commissioned by the Army Research Institute, and unpublished documents provided by institutes, practitioners, and researchers. The report that follows describes the committee's activities, findings, and conclusions. Though cast largely in terms of the sponsor's setting, this report is relevant to other settings, for example, industry. The next few paragraphs present some background.

That the United States Army should be concerned to enhance the performance of its personnel is self-evident. We know that young volunteers must become not only soldiers who do well in battle but also technicians who skillfully operate and maintain complex equipment in peace and war. We are aware, moreover, that personal skills are not enough: individuals are heavily dependent on each other within small groups, and groups of various sizes must work very effectively together to permit survival and ensure success. And, of course, all must be ready to give peak performances in situations of great hardship, uncertainty, and stress. In the face of these staggering requirements, one must realize that turnover of personnel is high and that the training time available—to impart the necessary cognitive, physical, and social skills—is brief.

So it comes as no surprise that the Army is on the lookout for techniques that can help enhance human performance. The Army Research Institute is charged with seeking out and developing such techniques: it does so by employing researchers in the human sciences and by supporting appropriate research in universities and other public and private organizations. It focuses largely on promising new techniques as they appear in the mainstream of behavioral, physiological, and social research. However, given the pressures and given a view of mainstream research as slow, narrow, and insufficiently targeted, it also comes as no surprise that some influential officers and certain segments of the Army want to cast a broader net to snare promising enhancement techniques. To do this, they look beyond traditional research organizations and practices to what are viewed as extraordinary techniques. These techniques are thought possibly to provide such unusual benefits as accelerated learning, learning during sleep, superior performance through altered mental states, better management of behavior under stress, more effective ways of influencing other people, and so on. There is also an initiative within the Army to consider techniques based on paranormal phenomena, for example, extrasensory perception to view remote sites and psychokinesis to influence the operation of distant machines.

Along with these urgings to examine, to try, or to implement extraordinary techniques come difficult new problems for those in the Army responsible for evaluation, as well as for those in the Army responsible for personnel and training practices. One issue is that proponents of such techniques are usually not content with traditional evaluation procedures or scientific standards of evidence, often giving more weight to personal experience and testimony. Furthermore, a typical technique of this kind does not arise from the usual research traditions of experiments published in refereed journals and peer review of cumulated evidence, but rather appears full-blown as a package promoted by a commercial vendor. What does the Army Training and Doctrine Command or the base commander do when the need is great, the package is ready, the claims are for miracles, some senior officers are vocally supportive, and the evaluation criteria are fluid? What do Army intelligence agencies do when the same conditions apply and other nations are said to be active in investigating paranormal effects?

The committee decided to assess a representative set of the techniques in question and resolved to address the surrounding issues in an open-minded and thorough way. We therefore divided ourselves into a number of subcommittees organized according to the behavioral processes addressed by the several techniques: accelerated learning, sleep learning, guided imagery, split-brain effects, stress management, biofeedback, influence strategies, group cohesion, and parapsychology. In addition, a subcommittee on evaluation issues was formed to examine practices and standards relevant to all the techniques. Each chapter of the report was prepared by the appropriate subcommittee, but interactions were frequent and so the report represents a collaborative effort of all the members.

Chapter 1 provides a context for the committee's task and the Army's interest in enhancing performance, characterizes some particular techniques, and introduces some general issues in evaluating them. Chapter 2 presents the committee's findings about the techniques examined and conclusions about appropriate evaluation procedures. Chapter 3 treats the relevant evaluation issues more systematically and presents the committee's philosophy of evaluation as it pertains to the matter at hand. Chapters 4 through 8 deal with particular techniques but are organized in terms of more general psychological processes. Chapter 9 considers parapsychological techniques.

The report concludes with six appendixes. Appendix A briefly summarizes the key elements of each enhancement technique. Appendix B lists the ten papers commissioned by the committee and their authors. Appendix C lists the members and activities of the subcommittees and also the activities of the committee as a whole. Appendix D lists key terms used in the research on particular techniques. Appendix E discusses the application of scientific research by the military. Appendix F contains biographical sketches of the committee members.

As committee chair, I am now in the pleasant position of recounting the several contributors to the total committee process, a process that went remarkably well. Definition and guidance for the committee's task came primarily from Edgar M. Johnson, director of the Army Research Institute. Administrative and technical liaison was ably provided by project monitor George Lawrence, who worked closely with the committee in its various activities. They were supported well by several senior Army officers, including Colonel William Darryl Henderson, Commander of the Army Research Institute; Major General John Crosby,

Assistant Deputy Chief of Staff for Personnel; and General Maxwell R. Thurman, Vice Chief of Staff. The committee met with members of a resource advisory group that included Lieutenant General Robert M. Elton, chair, Deputy Chief of Staff for Personnel; Lieutenant General Sidney T. Weinstein, Assistant Chief of Staff for Intelligence; Dr. Louis M. Cameron, Director of Army Research and Technology; Major General Maurice O. Edmunds, Commander of the Soldier Support Center; and Major General Philip K. Russell, Commander of the Medical Research and Development Command. Among the Army staff who were very helpful to the committee are Colonel John Alexander and Mr. Robert Klaus; the names of many others appear in Appendix C.

The committee's two consultants contributed special expertise: Paul Horwitz (of Bolt Beranek and Newman Inc.) joined the site visits of the subcommittee on parapsychology and advised on physical aspects of experiments in that area; James Schroeder (of Southwest Research Institute) attended the committee's meeting at Fort Benning, Georgia, and advised on the application of scientific research by the military (see Appendix E). The committee also received special expertise by commissioning papers. These papers and their authors are listed in Appendix B.

At the National Research Council, David Goslin, executive director of the Commission on Behavioral and Social Sciences and Education, once again provided wise counsel and support. Ira Hirsh, commission chair, and William Estes, also representing the commission, gave valuable advice and encouragement. Thomas Landauer, a member of the NRC's Committee on Human Factors, provided liaison in the areas of our committees' mutual interests. The reviewers of this report gave us a good measure of reinforcement along with helpful critiques. Eugenia Grohman, associate director for reports, lent experience and wisdom to this report. Special gratitude is extended to Christine McShane, the commission's editor: her skillful editing of the entire manuscript contributed substantially to its readability, and the coherence of the volume owes much to her suggestions for organizing the material. Julie Kraman, as administrative secretary to the committee, earned its considerable appreciation for setting up efficient meetings and for handling all manner of tasks graciously and smoothly.

Daniel Druckman, study director of the project, receives the committee's great appreciation for his intellectual contributions across the broad range of topics considered as well as for his logistic support. Working closely with the authors of chapters and commissioned papers, he provided an integration of the several contributions as well as much of the introductory and interstitial material. He also served on two subcommittees in areas of his expertise.

The ultimate debt of anyone who finds this report useful, and my large personal debt, is to the members of the committee. As individuals, their capabilities are broad and deep. As a group, they gave generously and productively of their time, were always engaged, responded to every challenge, and, especially, showed an exceptional talent for reaching consensus in a collegial, advised, and efficient way.

JOHN A. SWETS, *Chair*
Committee on Techniques for the
Enhancement of Human Performance

PART I

Overview

PART I CONSISTS OF THREE CHAPTERS. Chapter 1 sets the stage for the report. It describes the committee's task, provides background on the Army's interest in enhancement techniques, characterizes specific techniques examined by the committee, and identifies the main issues in evaluating the relation between techniques and human performance. Chapter 2 presents the committee's findings and conclusions. We draw general conclusions about the process of consideration given to any technique and state specific findings and conclusions for each of the areas of human performance examined.

Chapter 3 presents the committee's philosophy of evaluation as it pertains to enhancement techniques. Some of the issues involved concern the conduct of basic research; others concern the conduct of field tests. With respect to basic research, issues include the plausibility of inferences about novel concepts, causation, alternative explanations of causal relations, and the generalizability of causal relations. With respect to field tests, a number of questions are of interest: Does the enhancement program meet genuine Army needs? Is the resulting program implementable, given program design and resources? Do unintended side effects limit utility? Is the program more cost-effective than its alternatives? These questions underscore the reality that evaluation research is largely a pragmatic activity influenced by the organizational context in which it occurs.

1

Introduction

THE COMMITTEE'S TASK

At the request of the U.S. Army Research Institute, the National Research Council formed a committee to assess the field of techniques that are claimed to enhance human performance. The Institute asked the Council to evaluate the claims made by proponents of selected existing techniques and to address two general additional questions: (1) What are the appropriate criteria for evaluating claims for such techniques in the future? (2) What research is needed to advance our understanding of performance enhancement in areas related to the proposed techniques? The objectives of the committee's study are to provide an authoritative assessment of these questions for policymakers in research and development who are consumers of the techniques, as well as to consider their possible applications to Army training.

Many of the techniques under consideration grew out of the human potential movement of the 1960s, including guided imagery, meditation, biofeedback, neurolinguistic programming, sleep learning, accelerated learning, split-brain learning, and various techniques to reduce stress and increase concentration. Many of these techniques have gained popularity over the past two decades, promoted by persons eager to provide answers to problems of human performance or to prosper from them. While often using the language of science to justify their approach, these promoters are for the most part not trained professionals in the social and behavioral sciences. Nonetheless, they do appeal to basic needs for human performance, and the Army, like many other institutions, is attracted to the prospect of cost-effective procedures that can improve performance.

These institutions must evaluate the effects of such procedures, however. Issues include the appropriateness of a quick-fix approach, the distinction between the impact of an experience and actual change, and the plausibility of evidence indicating that something is happening even if the effects are not reproducible or the benefits uncertain.

A more conservative atmosphere in the 1980s is reflected in the way techniques are advanced. Motivation in the 1980s may be primarily entrepreneurial, not ideological, as it was in the 1960s. Advocates focus on relating the techniques to specific tasks, such as marksmanship, foreign language acquisition, fine motor skills, sleep inducement, and even combat effectiveness. Some techniques are in fact rooted in a scientific literature. For these reasons the various techniques have attracted the interest of institutions that have rejected, and would probably continue to reject, countercultural trends in society. Indeed, much attention has been given to these techniques by industrial, government, and military policymakers, as well as by the general public. For this reason especially, it is important to address the issues surrounding the claims made for effectiveness.

Elaborate training programs have grown, nourished by their developers' enthusiasm and salesmanship in a social context receptive to quick cures. For many of these programs, success in the marketplace is used to justify the approaches. For others, more esoteric concepts, including the role of neurotransmitters, the physics of neuromuscular programming, brain wave patterns, hemispheric laterality, high-access memory storage, preferred sensory modalities, and low-gain innervation of muscles, are used to attempt to provide scientific justification for the claims. The chapters that follow evaluate the evidence and theories used to support the claims of several popular techniques. Before turning to these evaluations, however, we provide some background on the Army's interest in these techniques, as well as a discussion of issues surrounding enhanced performance and issues in evaluating the relation between techniques and performance.

THE ARMY'S NEEDS

The Army motto, "Be all that you can be," symbolizes the current ethos of the institution, an army of excellence. Emphasis is placed on attaining certain ideals, such as fearlessness, cunning, courage, one-shot effectiveness, fatigue reversal, and nighttime fighting capabilities. These ideals are assumed to be realizable through training, even if the most effective techniques have not as yet been identified. The culture of improvement is further reinforced by the dilemma created by an all-volunteer Army and the demands of complex new computer technologies. Many civilians enter military service with only the required minimum of formal education; most of these volunteers enlist in the Army. For this reason, the Army's emphasis on skill training is well founded.

The importance of the human element in combat is recognized in the Army Science Board's 1983 report "Emerging Concepts in Human Technology," which phrases the issue in terms of high yield at relatively low investment. Human capital is considered to be the best potential source for growth in Army effectiveness, both in terms of return on investment and as a moral imperative "if we are to commit our soldiers to fight outnumbered and win." The technologies singled out in the report are those that can improve creativity and innovation, learning and training, motivation and cohesion, leadership and management, individual, crew, and unit fitness, soldier-machine interface, and the general productivity of the Army's human resources.

The Board's report largely bypasses issues of systematic evaluation of enhancement techniques within the Army context, while addressing mechanisms for integrating them with Army activities. Little concern is shown for adducing relevant criteria to determine whether implementation is feasible. The Army's ambitious goals, combined with a reluctance to deal with the complexities surrounding issues of human performance, make this institution potentially susceptible to a variety of claims made by technique developers. It would therefore seem prudent to devise criteria for evaluating those claims.

A SELLER'S MARKET

Techniques for enhancement of human performance have received much attention in the popular press. They have been actively promoted by entrepreneurs who sense a profitable market in self-improvement. The American Society for Training and Development "estimates that companies are spending an astounding $30 billion a year on formal courses and training programs for workers. And that's only the tip of the iceberg" (*Wall Street Journal*, August 5, 1986). They are also taken seriously by the U.S. military, who are at times accused of losing the "mind race" to the Soviets (see, for example, Anderson and Van Atta, *Washington Post*, July 17, 1985). The Army has shown particular interest in techniques that help people acquire, maintain, or improve such skills as classroom learning, communication and influence, creativity, and accuracy in the execution of tasks requiring motor skills. Those that are cost-effective and produce relatively rapid results are likely to receive the most attention, along with research breakthroughs that could be a basis for new training programs. What are these techniques? What claims are being made for them? Is there evidence that substantiates these claims?

Examples of techniques include biofeedback (information about internal processes), Suggestive Accelerative Learning and Teaching Techniques (a package of methods geared primarily toward classroom learning), hemispheric synchronization (a machine-aided process based on assumptions about right brain–left brain activities), neurolinguistic programming (procedures for influencing another person), and Concentrix (a procedure used to improve concentration on specific targets). Also of interest to the Army are such processes as group cohesion and stress reduction, as well as the claims for sleep learning, peak performance, and parapsychology. Together, these techniques and processes cover the major types of skills—motor, cognitive, and social. Several of them are described here briefly, along with illustrative claims found in brochures and course material.

Suggestive Accelerative Learning and Teaching Techniques (SALTT) is an approach to training that employs a combination of physical relaxation, mental concentration, guided imagery, suggestive principles, and baroque music with the intent of improving classroom performance. Some applications have included language training, typing instruction, and high school science courses. Attempts have been made to evaluate the applications, and many of these evaluations are published in the *Journal of the Society for Accelerative Learning and Teaching* (Psychology Department, Iowa State University). The following is a sampling of claims made in brochures and convention announcements: "A proven method which has broad potential application in U.S. Army training"; "It will significantly reduce training time, improve memory of material learned and introduce behavioral changes that positively affect soldier performance—self-esteem, self-confidence, and mental discipline"; and "Most students will prove to themselves that they have learned a far greater amount of material per unit of time with a greater amount of pleasure than they have ever previously done."

Neurolinguistic programming (NLP) refers to a set of procedures developed to influence and change the behaviors and beliefs of a target person. Its goals are mostly therapeutic, but its proponents also advocate the use of the techniques in advertising, management, education, and interpersonal activities. A small research literature, published primarily in the *Journal of Counseling Psychology*, has developed. Practitioners can be trained and certified at various institutes, and the National Association for Neurolinguistic Programming distributes a newsletter to its membership, currently about 500 persons. Illustrative claims and testimonials found in advertising materials include: "[NLP] has evolved a unique technology which encompasses a set of specific techniques enabling you to produce well-defined results" and "NLP . . . is clear, easy to learn, and brilliant." A typical slogan is that found in a brochure from the Potomac Institutes, Silver Spring, Maryland: "The difference that makes the difference, for education, management, psychotherapy, psychiatry, business, law, health care, and the arts.''

Hemi-Sync™, which is short for hemispheric synchronization, is a technique that consists of presenting two tones slightly differing in frequency to separate ears with stereo headphones to produce binaural beats. The long-known result is a tone that waxes and wanes at a frequency equal to the difference between the original tones. Pioneered as an enhancement technique by Robert Monroe of the Monroe Institute of Applied Science in Faber, Virginia, the technique is based on the assumption of a frequency following response (FFR) in the human brain. The FFR refers to a correspondence between sound signals heard by the ear and electrical signals recorded by an electroencephalograph (EEG). It is claimed that, by altering sound patterns, it is possible to alter states of awareness. Stated applications are in the areas of language learning, stress management, reading skills, and creativity and problem solving. Claims of effectiveness stated in the Monroe Institute's brochure are wide-ranging, covering education (e.g., ''77.8 percent of a class reported improvement in mental-motor skills''), health (early recuperation, lower blood pressure), psychotherapy (stress reduction, working with terminally ill patients, teaching autistic children), and sleep restorative training (e.g., ''forty of forty-five insomniacs reported that one-month use of Hemi-Sync™ tapes was at least as effective as medication, without the drug side effects'').

SyberVision® is a scripted videotape that presents an expert (e.g., a world-class athlete) repeatedly performing fundamental skills of his or her activity (e.g., golf) without verbal instructions. It is based loosely on principles of vicarious learning, guided imagery, and mental rehearsal. Developed and marketed by SyberVision Systems Inc., San Leandro, California, the package includes a cassette and instruction manual with an appendix on the ''simple physics of neuro-muscular programming.'' The appendix presents a scientific rationale for the technique, for example, ''the more you see and hear pure movement, the deeper it becomes imprinted in your nervous system . . . and the more likely you are to perform it as a conditioned reflex,'' and ''The decomposition of what is seen and sensorily experienced into an electromagnetic wave form is accomplished by a complex mathematical operation (Fourier Transform) by the brain'' (*Instruction Manual on Golf with Patty Sheehan*). Support for enhanced performance is, however, based on testimonials rather than experiments, for example, Killy on skiing, a Stanford tennis coach on tennis, Professional Golf Association members on golf, Peters (*In Search of Excellence*) on achievement, Salk on leadership, and a variety of corporate executives and educators on self-improvement. Claims range from sweeping statements (e.g., ''We owe these two men a large debt of gratitude'') to rather precise statements (e.g., ''In 47 days I have lost 25 pounds [191 to 166], yet I look like I lost 40'') (in the United Airlines magazine, *Discoveries*). This technique involves a significant marketing effort that builds on users' willingness to be quoted and the use of acknowledged academic experts (e.g., Stanford neuropsychologist Karl Pribram), whose role in the program is advertised as being central.

Stress management techniques are procedures designed to alleviate anxiety or tension. Catering to an age of anxiety, self-help books, groups, and clinics on managing stress proliferate. A good example of the approach is the recent book by Charlesworth and Nathan (1982), which emphasizes fitness, nutrition, managing time, general life-styles and life-cycles, as well as strategies such as progressive relaxation, autogenic training, and image rehearsal. Appendixes provide the reader with home practice charts, a guide to self-help groups, and suggested books and recordings. The groups offer their members information, emotional support, and a sense of belonging. Often stress management procedures are combined with a number of other techniques into a single package. The promoters often emphasize the total package rather than particular techniques; the packages usually combine several processes that, when acting together, are thought to produce significant effects.

The Army's needs for techniques that can improve performance make it subject to the sorts of claims illustrated above. While they and other consumers can avoid the more obvious pitfalls, the proliferation of choices and products and the lack of scientific evidence allow marketplace criteria to become the bases for decisions. But there are exceptions. Some techniques have received the attention of the scientific community, and evidence is available to be used as criteria in such areas as biofeedback, guided imagery, sleep learning, cohesion, and even for some aspects of psychic phenomena and neurolinguistic programming.

The literature has alerted us, for example, to the distinction between the effects of biofeedback on fine motor skills and on stress, to the different effects of mental and physical rehearsal, to placebo and Hawthorne effects in stress research, to the priming and repetition effects of material presented during sleep, to some dysfunctions of group cohesion, to the difficulties of replicating experiments on extrasensory perception, and to the implausibility of specialized sensory modalities as postulated by NLP (see Appendix D for key terms). These findings make evident a complex relation between technique and performance.

IMPROVED PERFORMANCE:
COMPLEX ISSUES, SIMPLE SOLUTIONS

The research literature in such traditional areas of experimental psychology as learning, perception, sensation, and motivation suggests complex relations between interventions and improved performance. Many technique promoters appear to pay little attention to this literature, preferring an alternative route to invention: rather than derive a procedure from appropriate scientific literature, they create techniques from personal experiences, sudden insights, or informal observation of "what works." Science may enter the process after the technique is developed and used, for example, to legitimize its use or to endorse methods for evaluation. Research follows rather than precedes the invention. This sequence increases the likelihood that important considerations will be missed. We highlight some of these considerations in this section.

The lack of easy avenues to improved performance may well be due to the complexity of the behavior in question. One definition of skills emphasizes the importance of the coordination of behavior: "A skilled response . . . means one in which receptor-effector-feedback processes are highly organized, both spatially and temporally. The central problem for the study of skill learning is how such organizations or patterning comes about" (Fitts, 1964:244). This definition implies that skill learning involves an orchestration of diverse processes, making the topic an interesting one to various subfields of psychology. It also makes evident a number of unresolved issues, including whether different skills are learned and retained in different ways. The research findings obtained in this literature contribute to our understanding of the necessary, if not sufficient, conditions for improved performance.

Research on skill acquisition addresses such basic questions as What are the stages of learning? and What is learned? Distinctions made between short-term and long-term memory storage and between schemas and details have contributed to our understanding of basic processes (see Welford, 1976). Other questions have more direct consequences for application: for example, what contributes to the acquisition and maintenance of skills? How can the adverse effects of stress, fatigue, and monotony be avoided? These questions are the basis for programs of research that can be divided into several parts, each defined in terms of empirical issues (Irion, 1969; see also the other chapters in Bilodeau and Bilodeau, 1969). Some examples of empirical issues are practice effects (differences due to distributed versus massed practice, long versus short rest periods, short versus long sessions), the whole-part problem (differences due to learning a task as a whole versus learning it by its constituent elements), feedback (differences due to delays in receiving knowledge of results and to type of information during the delay period), retention (differences due to whether the the task is motor or verbal), and transfer of training.

These and related considerations suggest that skill learning is an incremental process likely to differ from one type of skill to another. Whether intending to enhance motor, verbal, problem-solving, or social performances, technique designers can ill afford to ignore these lessons from the experimental literature on skill acquisition and maintenance. It is also the case, however, that the agenda of unexplored issues is much larger than the accomplishments to date, and this is recognized particularly in the rapidly growing field of cognitive psychology, in which the "information-processing revolution" is just beginning.

Practical applications are, however, not automatic. Many excellent applications do not spring from basic science; some are the result of craft and experience. More important perhaps are the indirect contributions made in both directions—from basic to applied and vice versa. A systematic approach taken in both domains serves to vitalize each, as when applied investigations reveal new phenomena that need explanation or when a new package incorporates basic principles discovered originally in the laboratory. Such an approach is likely to facilitate the design of appropriate techniques for skill acquisition. At issue is whether a particular technique can produce and sustain desired changes.

One conclusion from the research accumulated to date is that effective interventions are those that are continuous and self-regulating and take account of both context and person (see, for example, Lerner, 1984). Particularly relevant is the difference between short-term and long-term changes. Effects obtained by many techniques for performance enhancement may be short-term in their effects. This distinction is made by Back (1973, 1987) in his evaluation of the sensitivity training movement. The changes observed by sensitivity trainers and documented by evaluators may well reflect the impact of the experience per se. Such situation effects are unlikely to be sustained in different environments, an observation supported by the literatures in both developmental and social psychology (Druckman, 1971; Frederiksen, 1972). These literatures caution against hasty generalizations from observed, situation-specific effects; they also explain why long-term effects may be difficult to produce with brief exposures to "treatments." Like the sensitivity trainers of the 1960s and 1970s, many of the promoters (and consumers) of the 1980s pay little attention to issues of causality and intrinsic motivation, preferring instead to dwell on single dimensions of treatments or to offer a mixed package constructed in arbitrary ways and producing diffuse effects that reflect the experience.

The issue of expected benefits from techniques provides a bridge between research and application. Research can be designed to evaluate techniques, as well as to discover possible unintended side effects. Indeed, a research literature has developed in some of the areas examined in this book, namely biofeedback, stress, and guided imagery. For many other techniques, however, a relevant body of research does not exist; this lack applies to some of the techniques examined by the committee, as well as to those yet to appear on the market. It is these techniques that present a problem for us as evaluators. Evaluation without data is difficult, but not impossible. Our approach is to place the techniques into broader categories corresponding to the key processes being influenced, for example, learning, motor skills, and influence. By so doing, the claims can be evaluated within the frameworks of existing theories and methodologies. They can also be judged against results obtained in related areas. This approach serves as the organizing theme for the chapters that follow.

EVALUATING THE TECHNIQUES

Evaluations properly hinge on answers to a standard set of questions proposed in a paper entitled "Evaluating Human Technologies: What Questions Should We Ask?" by Hegge, Tyner, and Genser (1983) at the Walter Reed Army Institute for Research:

- What changes will the technique produce?
- What evidence supports the claims for the technique?
- What theories stand behind the technique?
- Who will be able to use the technique?
- What are the implications of the technique for Army operations?
- How does the technique fit with Army philosophy?
- What are the cost-benefit factors?

These questions served as guidelines for the committee's evaluations. Appendix A is a summary description of each technique, organized along the lines of the Hegge, Tyner, and Genser questions, covering theory, research, and application. For many of the categories, however, the desired information is either too limited to be useful or simply not available; in such cases we have considered other strategies for evaluation.

The committee faced a number of difficulties in evaluation that stem from recurrent problems posed by the technologies. One is the tendency for some promoters (and consumers) to rely primarily on testimonials or anecdotal evidence as a basis for application. Another is a general lack of strong research designs to provide evidence of effects. These problems are considered also in the context of specific techniques discussed in the chapters of Parts II and III.

Practitioners of techniques often emphasize the value of personal or clinical experience and marketplace popularity as bases for judging the techniques. They are generally less inclined to seek research evidence or to support research evaluation programs. These attitudes may be related to the fact that few practitioners are trained as researchers. For some it is sufficient to let others do the research. For others, research is viewed, in varying degrees, as a threat to their product. At one extreme, research is regarded as a debunking enterprise, engaged in by scientists who have little interest in providing human services. At another extreme, the problem is one of educating the researchers in nuance, context, and a clinical approach that emphasizes adapting techniques to changed situations and client tastes. The result is a gap in communication epitomized by two cultures—scientists searching for evidence and practitioners seeking effects and cures. A step toward bridging the gap would consist of mutual education through joint ventures. These ventures would expose scientists to the goals (and motives) of practitioners and would also make practitioners aware of the general analytical approaches used by scientists.

Experimentation is an appropriate vehicle for evaluating performance-enhancing techniques; the problem is usually defined in terms of effects of techniques (procedures) on performance (behaviors). It is also appropriate at an earlier stage in the process, when products are being developed. Products evolve in a kind of trial-and-error fashion similar in many respects to scientific discoveries. One model for integrating research with product development is engineering research and development (R&D). A strenuous applied research effort accompanies the development process in many firms, as does a quality-control program designed to evaluate products both during development and after they have been placed on the market. With a few exceptions, this model has not been adopted by firms or institutions in the field of performance enhancement.

Experimental evidence has accumulated in some areas related to techniques. Although not linked specifically to product development in the manner of an R&D operation, this work does address the question, What evidence supports the claims for the technique? In fact, so strong is the experimental tradition in some areas that a body of work has developed programmatically within a generally accepted paradigm (e.g., guided imagery). The benefits of a long research tradition can be seen in these areas. Meta-analyses have been performed and can be used as a basis for evaluation. For other areas, we are presented with the prospect of relying on scattered experiments or using other criteria as a basis for evaluation, or both (see Appendix A for summaries of the state of the science in each of the areas).

However, the benefits of experimental evidence derive primarily from the general approach rather than from the particular experiments. This idea is captured by Kelman, who noted that "an experimental finding . . . cannot very meaningfully stand by itself. Its contribution to knowledge hinges on the conceptual thinking that has produced it and into which it is subsequently fed back" (1968:161). We emphasize here the contribution of an analytical approach to thinking about behavior, as distinct from the establishment of laws about psychological processes. It is the cumulation of a series of experiments that winnows out the useful parts of treatments or techniques. It is the self-correcting progression of new experiments that refines treatments, saving those that work and discarding those that do not (or that work only under very restricted conditions). This process contributes equally well to the goals of theory development and product development.

Other evaluation criteria elucidated by Hegge, Tyner, and Genser (1983) include theories, uses, and implications for Army operations and philosophy. A problem with these criteria is that they tend to be vague and somewhat idiosyncratic, making it difficult to propose general categories on which most people would agree. Without precisely defined categories for judging techniques, it is difficult to address issues of transfer of performance from one situation to another or to evaluate newly emerging techniques. A similar problem exists with respect to developing taxonomies in broadly defined fields: there is little agreement on a set of categories for the fields of human learning, performance, motivation, perception, and social and organizational processes. More mature sub-disciplines provide an empirical basis for taxonomies, allowing for more tightly constructed systems of tasks and situations: for example, rote learning, short-term memory, concept learning, problem solving, work motivation, and team functions (see Fleishman and Quaintance, 1984). An advantage of such systems is that they capture rather precise relationships between task and performance.

This discussion serves only to introduce the issues and identifies several themes that receive more detailed attention in the chapters to follow. First, any evaluation must take into account the status of the available evidence. Confidence placed in judgments about a technique should be based on the quality of the evidence produced by researchers. Second, the evaluator cannot afford to rely exclusively on a single criterion for judging effectiveness. Theoretical and applied issues are also important, as are considerations of values served or violated by use of the technique. Third, technique development issues are not isolated from research or analytical issues. Each step in the process of product design can be regarded as an empirical issue; decisions made about procedures and packaging can be the result of experimental outcomes. Fourth, the subject of enhancing human performance is not new. It has been a topic of interest for centuries and an area of scientific work for several decades. The literatures on learning and skill acquisition should be consulted by developers, and insights derived from these literatures should be used in product design.

These themes are woven throughout the discussions of specific techniques. Each chapter discusses relevant literature, describes the specific techniques, points to directions for further research when appropriate, and notes possible applications in military and industrial settings. Despite the common coverage, however, each chapter is also unique in that each is tailored to the particular problems associated with its focus.

2

Findings and Conclusions

The committee's first major task was to evaluate the existing scientific evidence for a wide range of techniques that have been proposed to enhance human performance. This evaluation was intended by our Army sponsors to suggest guidelines for decision making on Army research and training programs. In our evaluation we draw conclusions with respect to whether more basic or applied research is warranted, whether training programs could benefit from new findings or procedures, and what, in particular, might be worth monitoring for potential breakthroughs of use to the Army. In many of the areas examined it appears feasible to pursue carefully designed programs that build on basic research; however, such programs should be monitored closely.

The committee's second major task was to develop general guidelines for evaluating newly proposed techniques and their potential application. We are aware that the use of basic and applied research in decision making is a complex issue. Although payoffs from basic research can often be realized in the long run, the value of research findings to the Army depends on developing a way of putting them into practice. With regard to applied or evaluation research, further complexities are evident: multiple, sometimes conflicting, criteria must be satisfied at each of several stages in the evaluation process, from assessing a pilot program to implementing the program in an appropriate setting. Another problem is that of choosing among alternative techniques when none of them has been subjected to a systematic evaluation. In the absence of evaluation studies, the Army needs guidelines for selecting packages and vendors.

The committee's evaluation has produced several answers to questions of how best to improve performance in specific areas. On the positive side, we learned about the possibilities of priming future learning by presenting material during certain stages of sleep, of improving learning by integrating certain instructional elements, of improving skilled performance through certain combinations of mental and physical practice, of reducing stress by providing information that increases the sense of control, of exerting influence by employing certain communication strategies, and of maximizing group performance by taking advantage of organizational cultures to transmit values. On the negative side, we discovered a lack of supporting evidence for such techniques as visual training exercises as enhancers of performance, hemispheric synchronization, and neurolinguistic programming; a lack of scientific justification for the parapsychological phenomena considered; some potentially negative effects of group cohesion; and ambiguous evidence for the effectiveness of the suggestive accelerative learning package.

The remainder of this chapter presents the committee's findings and conclusions, which are presented in two parts: general conclusions regarding the process of evaluating any technique being considered by the Army and specific findings and conclusions for each of the areas of human performance examined. Whenever appropriate, we make recommendations for research, evaluation, and practice.

GENERAL CONCLUSIONS

The committee suggests that the Army move vigorously, yet carefully and systematically, to implement techniques that can be shown to enhance performance in military settings. Such an effort would be timely because of recent developments in the relevant research areas. Moreover, the payoff is likely to be very high if techniques are selected judiciously. Although the desire for dramatic improvements in performance makes some extraordinary techniques attractive, techniques drawn from mainstream research in relevant areas of performance may be more effective. The Army's concern for enhancing human performance and its substantial resources for evaluating techniques place it in a favorable position to take advantage of developments. The Army might also consider the possibilities of transferring its findings to the civilian sector.

Collectively, the committee's conclusions call for the adoption of scientifically sound evaluation procedures; however, these procedures must be adapted to institutional needs and must take into account problems of implementation. We summarize these considerations below.

SCIENTIFIC EVIDENCE

Techniques and commercial packages proposed for consideration by the Army should be shown to be effective by adequate scientific evidence or compelling theoretical argument, or both. A technique's utility should be judged in relation to alternatives designed for similar purposes, and the estimated utility should be of significant magnitude. Specific stages of analysis can be incorporated in pilot or field testing, and such testing should be carried out by investigators who are independent of the technique's originators or promoters.

TESTIMONIALS AS EVIDENCE

Personal experiences and testimonials cited on behalf of a technique are not regarded as an acceptable alternative to rigorous scientific evidence. Even when they have high face validity, such personal beliefs are not trustworthy as evidence. They often fail to consider the full range of factors that may be responsible for an observed effect. Personal versions of reality, which are essentially private, are especially antithetical to science, which is a fundamentally public enterprise. Of course, a caution about testimonials should not be confused with a lack of openness to new and unusual ideas. Such openness is consistent with the requirement that the evidential criteria of science be satisfied.

The subject of testimonials as evidence has received considerable attention in recent research on how people arrive at their beliefs. These studies indicate that many sources of bias operate and that they can lead to personal knowledge that is invalid despite its often being associated with high levels of conviction. The committee recommends that this research be disseminated, as appropriate, in the Army. It may then be applied whenever testimony is used as the primary evidence to promote an enhancement technique.

CONDITIONS FOR IMPLEMENTATION

Two kinds of evidence should be sought to support decisions to implement a technique: successful field tests and an analysis of implementability. It would also be useful to analyze the impact of the technique or package on the larger system in which it is to be embedded. These analyses would aid in explaining why the procedures are necessary and why certain consequences are expected. In general, any description of what a technique accomplishes should be accompanied by an explanation of *why* it accomplishes what it does. Such an explanation would provide a more fundamental understanding of processes affected by exposure to the technique and permit optimal implementation.

RATIONAL DECISION MAKING

The considerations that must be entertained in selecting a technique for practical use in a military setting are different from the considerations needed to verify the existence of an enhancement effect in a scientific setting. For example, the benefits of correct decisions and the costs of incorrect decisions, that is, the risk calculus, may differ in the two settings. Furthermore, what is viewed as a timely decision will also differ. The specific differences as they apply to particular decisions should be made explicit.

MECHANISMS FOR ADVICE

It would be useful to provide valid information about useful techniques to Army commanders and other interested staff on a regular basis. Special consideration should be given to ways in which technique-related information can be transferred from scientists to practitioners. The characteristics of a transfer agent could be defined, and such a position might be established within an appropriate office.

The committee recommends that the Army Research Institute formalize the ways in which it receives and provides advice about specific techniques. A committee to review experimental designs and statistical analyses could be convened to improve the evaluation of techniques. Special and standing committees could also be used to make program recommendations and to review proposals for intramural and extramural research.

BIDDING PROCEDURES

Purchase by the Army of a commercial enhancement package should take place within the context of a set of well-defined procedures. The committee recommends that an open-bid procedure be followed, based on a full presentation of the Army's stated objectives. This would encourage competitive evaluation of techniques. The following information, presented in a standard format, should be required: the objectives of the technique, a description of its procedures, evidence that it produces the claimed effects, and the vendor's record of past achievements in relevant areas.

Lack of professional training and research experience in human performance by a designer or advocate should not preclude consideration of the proposed package; it should, however, signal the need for a more stringent analysis by the Army.

SPECIFIC FINDINGS AND CONCLUSIONS

We present below findings and conclusions for each of the areas investigated. Some statements take the form of suggested actions based on what we know; others consist of suggestions for more work or for research that has not yet been done.

LEARNING DURING SLEEP

1. The committee finds no evidence to suggest that learning occurs during verified sleep (confirmed as such by electrical recordings of brain activity). However, waking perception and interpretation of verbal material could well be altered by presenting that material during the lighter stages of sleep. We conclude that the existence and degree of learning and recall of materials presented during sleep should be examined again as a basic research problem.

2. Pending further research results, the committee concludes that possible Army applications of learning during sleep deserve a second look. Findings that suggest the possibility of state-dependent learning and retention (i.e., better recall of material when learned in the same physiological and mental state) may be applicable to fatigued soldiers. Furthermore, even presentations of material that disrupt normal sleep may be cost-effective, as may presentations that coincide with stages of light sleep.

ACCELERATED LEARNING

1. Many studies have found that effective instruction is the result of such factors as the quality of instruction, practice or study time, motivation of the learner, and the matching of the training regimen to the job demands. Programs that integrate all these factors would be desirable. We recommend that the Army examine the costs, effectiveness, and longevity of training benefits to be derived from such programs and compare them with established Army procedures.

2. The committee finds little scientific evidence that so-called super-learning programs, such as Suggestive Accelerative Learning and Teaching Techniques, derive their instructional benefits from elements outside the mainstream of research and practice. We observe, however, that these programs do integrate well-known instructional, motivational, and practice elements in a manner that is generally not present in most scientific studies.

3. We find that scientifically supported procedures for enhancing skills are not being sufficiently used in training programs and make two recommendations to remedy this problem. First, the basic research literature should be monitored to identify procedures verified by laboratory tests to increase instructional effectiveness. Second, additional basic

research should be supported to expand the understanding of skill acquisition for both noncombat and combat activities.

4. We conclude that the Army training system provides a unique opportunity for cohort testing of training regimens. The Army is in a position to create laboratory classroom environments in which competing training procedures can be scientifically evaluated.

5. The committee recommends that the Army investigate expert teacher programs by identifying and evaluating particularly effective programs within the Army. In addition, transferable elements of effective instruction can be reported to the larger instructional community.

IMPROVING MOTOR SKILLS

1. The committee concludes that mental practice is effective in enhancing the performance of motor skills. This conclusion suggests further work in two directions: (1) evaluation studies of motor skills used in the Army and (2) research designed to determine the combination of mental and physical practice that, on average, would best enhance skill acquisition and maintenance, taking into account both time and cost.

2. The committee concludes that programs purporting to enhance cognitive and behavioral skills by improving visual concentration have not been shown to be effective to date. In our judgment, these programs are not worth further evaluation at this time.

3. The committee concludes that existing data do not establish the generality of observed effects from programs that train visual capabilities to increase performance.

4. Similarly, the committee concludes that the effects of biofeedback on skilled performance remain to be determined.

5. The committee recommends additional research to establish the potential of these techniques in the domain of specific skilled performances.

ALTERING MENTAL STATES

1. Time did not allow the committee to explore the evidence for a wide variety of specific methods for relating mental states to changes in performance. Such methods include forms of self-induced hypnotic states and peak performance resulting from high levels of focused concentration and meditation. We recommend that reviews of the literature in these areas be undertaken to ascertain whether any practical results might be obtained by the use of such methods.

2. The committee finds that, while the study of mental computations in language and imagery has progressed in recent years, the effort to understand how such computations are modulated by energetic factors

such as arousal, stress, emotion, and high levels of sustained concentration has not been fully developed. For example, the claims that certain mental states produce general improvements in performance derive from the idea, supported by research, that arousal affects mental computations and that there ought to be an optimal level of arousal for the performance of such computations. We recommend this as an important area for investment of basic research funds.

3. The committee's review of the appropriate literature refutes claims that link differential use of the brain hemispheres to performance. Further evaluation of these claims depends on developing valid and reliable measures of hemispheric involvement.

4. The committee finds no scientifically acceptable evidence to support the claimed effects of techniques intended to integrate hemispheric activity, for example, Hemi-Sync™. Attempts to increase information-processing capacity by presenting material separately to the two hemispheres do not appear to be useful. We conclude that such techniques should be considered further by the Army only if scientific evidence is provided to and evaluated by the Army Research Institute.

STRESS MANAGEMENT

1. Existing data indicate that stress is reduced by giving an individual as much knowledge and understanding as possible regarding future events. In addition, giving the individual a sense of control is effective. On the basis of these findings, the committee recommends a systematic program of research and development that would address three questions: (1) How relevant is this finding for stress reduction in the Army? (2) To what extent does stress reduction realized in training transfer to combat situations? (3) What are the limitations on providing knowledge and understanding of future events and a sense of control in the Army setting? Pending the outcome of this research, we suggest that consideration be given to including the material in training programs for company grade, field grade, command, and staff officers.

2. We find that, while biofeedback can achieve a reduction of muscle tension, it does not reduce stress effectively. It is therefore not a promising research topic in that respect. We recommend that funding be directed toward investigation of more promising stress management procedures.

3. We recommend that information be gathered on the costs of stress in terms of organ breakdown, loss of efficiency, and loss of time. This information would have implications for training programs.

INFLUENCE STRATEGIES

1. The committee finds no scientific evidence to support the claim that neurolinguistic programming is an effective strategy for exerting influence.

We advise that further Army study of this aspect of NLP be made only in comparison with other techniques.

2. There are no existing evaluations of NLP as a model of expert performance. We conclude that further investigation of such models may be worthwhile and suggest that NLP be examined in comparison with several other techniques.

3. Concerning the process of technology transfer, we recommend that studies be conducted to develop training regimens for those who train others to wield social influence. The large literature on this topic in social psychology would provide a basis for such packages.

GROUP COHESION

1. We find few scientific studies that address the possible relationship between group cohesion and performance; however, such a relationship may well be found with more extensive research. There is a need for research to consider the possibility of negative effects from inducing cohesion and methods of avoiding such effects. The committee recommends continued study of cohesion and related group processes.

2. We are favorably impressed with the evaluation studies of the Army's COHORT system. We endorse the investigators' plan to proceed beyond measures of attitudes to measures of group performance.

3. We recommend that the Army, as well as independent investigators, study the possible impacts of cohesion beyond the COHORT system, for example, on intergroup performance.

PARAPSYCHOLOGY

1. The committee finds no scientific justification from research conducted over a period of 130 years for the existence of parapsychological phenomena. It therefore concludes that there is no reason for direct involvement by the Army at this time. We do recommend, however, that research in certain areas be monitored, including work by the Soviets and the best work in the United States. The latter includes that being done at Princeton University by Robert Jahn; at Maimonides Medical Center in Brooklyn by Charles Honorton, now in Princeton; at San Antonio by Helmut Schmidt; and at the Stanford Research Institute by Edward May. Monitoring could be enhanced by site visits and by expert advice from both proponents and skeptics. The research areas included would be psychokinesis with random event generators and Ganzfeld effects.

2. One possible result of the monitoring mentioned above is the proposal

of specific studies. In that situation the committee recommends the following procedures: first, the Army and outside scientists should arrive at a common protocol; second, the research should be conducted according to that protocol by both proponents and skeptics; and third, attention should be given in such research to the manipulability and practical application of any effects found to exist.

3

Evaluation Issues

Implementation of an enhancement technique, in the committee's view, should depend on two general kinds, or levels, of evaluation. The first examines primarily the scientific justification for the effectiveness of the technique and the potential of the technique for improving performance in practice. The second kind examines field tests of a pilot program incorporating the technique to determine how feasible it is and to what extent it brings about effects that Army officials consider useful.

Convincing scientific justification can come only from basic research, that is, from carefully controlled studies that usually take place in laboratory settings and that preferably are related to a body of theory. Such research can provide evidence for the existence of the causal effect on which a technique is based and can help explain, or indicate a mechanism for, the effect. Analysis in connection with basic research should go beyond scientific justification to operational potential and likely cost-effectiveness. Only field tests can assess a program's actual operations and effects, however, and for such tests a broader array of evaluative criteria are needed, related primarily to the technique's utility.

Because strong claims of support from basic research have been made for some of the techniques the committee examined, we review here what it takes to justify a scientific claim, specifically, we review some standards for evaluating basic research. We then examine in more detail some standards for evaluating field tests of pilot programs. In the third section of this chapter, we set forth briefly some of our impressions of how the Army now manages the solicitation and evaluation of new performance-enhancing techniques. This chapter concludes with a note on informal, qualitative approaches to evaluation, which are sometimes suggested as alternatives to basic research and field tests.

This chapter does not aspire to a comprehensive treatment of evaluation issues, and it barely touches on research methods. Articles, journals, books, and handbooks testify to the scope and complexity of this burgeoning field (e.g., Barber, 1976; Cook and Campbell, 1979). Our objective here is to highlight the topics that have impressed us as most germane. The various sources just mentioned would need to be consulted for even a minimal elaboration of these topics, and other committees would be required if recipes for evaluation of the Army's enhancement programs were sought as extensions of our work. Still, we believe this chapter will help the Army set general evaluation standards.

STANDARDS FOR EVALUATING BASIC RESEARCH

The purpose of basic research is to permit inferences to be drawn in accordance with scientific standards, including inferences about novel concepts, about causation, about alternative explanations of causal relations, and about the generalizability of causal relations.

For novel concepts, evidence must be gathered that both the purported enhancement technique and the relevant performance have been (1) defined in a way to highlight their critical elements, (2) differentiated from related variables that might bring about similar effects, and (3) put into operation (manipulated or measured) in ways that include the critical parts. The burden is on the evaluator to analyze how the components of each new technique differ from concepts already in the literature. The need for this standard is illustrated well by packages for accelerated learning, as discussed in Chapter 4.

Evidence needs also to be adduced that supposed cause and effect variables vary together in a systematic manner. Relevant procedures include comparison of performance before and after introduction of the technique, contrasts of experimental and control groups in an experimental design, and calculation of statistical significance. Illusory covariation can occur more easily in nonstatistical studies, which are used often to support the existence of paranormal effects, as discussed in Chapter 9.

Especially demanding is the need for evidence that the performance effect observed is due to the postulated cause and not to some other variable. Ruling out alternative explanations or mechanisms requires intimate knowledge of a research area. Historical findings and critical commentary are needed to identify alternatives, determine their plausibility, and judge how well they have been ruled out in particular sets of experiments. Common threats to the validity of any presumed cause-effect relation include effects stemming from subject selection, unexpected changes in organizational forces, the spontaneous maturation of subjects, and the sensitizing effects of a pretest measurement on a posttest assessment. Experiments with random assignment of subjects to treatments are preferred, but some of the better quasi-experimental designs are also useful. Another class of threats to validity is associated with subject reactions to such conceptual irrelevancies as experimenter expectations about how subjects should perform or subjects' performing better merely because they are receiving attention. Procedures that have evolved to reduce this sort of threat include double-blind experiments, placebo control groups, mechanical delivery of treatments, and the elimination of all communication between experimenters and subjects or among subjects. These safeguards, however, are not certain, and implementing them is not a simple matter.

Finally, for a technique to be of value, one must ascertain that a causal relation observed in one setting is likely to be observed in other settings in which the technique is to be employed. Replication of an experiment by an independent investigator is a first step. Another step is to produce the cause and effect with different samples of people, settings, and times. Systematic reviews of the literature, perhaps aided by what is referred to as meta-analysis of studies (as illustrated in Chapter 5), are also helpful. Beyond these steps, a thorough theoretical understanding of causal processes, which is a fundamental goal of science, permits increased practical control.

Our point—perhaps seeming obvious to many but nonetheless needing emphasis here—is that a planned or existing program for implementing an enhancement technique is much more likely to bear fruit if evidence for the technique's effectiveness is properly derived from basic research. A complex set of ground rules exists for conducting and drawing inferences from basic research, and waiving those rules greatly increases the chances of incorrect conclusions.

STANDARDS FOR EVALUATING FIELD TESTS OF PROGRAMS

An adequate appraisal of an actual enhancement program requires attention to three general factors. First, the organizational (i.e., political, administrative) context in which the program is embedded should be described. That context strongly influences the choice of evaluation criteria, the types of evaluations considered feasible, and the extent to which evaluation results will be used. Second, the program's consequences should be described and explained, including planned and unplanned, short-term and long-term consequences. The way the program is construed influences the claims resulting from an evaluation and the degree of confidence that can be placed in what was learned. Third, value or merit should be explicitly assigned to a program. Valuing relates an enhancement technique to an Army need and to feasible alternatives. In the following sections we comment on these three factors in turn.

THE ORGANIZATIONAL CONTEXT

A description of the broader context of an enhancement program would include an assessment both of the various constituencies with a stake in its implementation and of the priorities of the larger institution. We do not discuss stakeholder interests in general at this point because we refer to some specifically later in this chapter, in the section on the committee's impressions of current Army evaluation practices. We do comment here on the Army's institutional priorities as they may relate to scientific standards.

We understand that the Army, like other organizations in society, may have—and quite possibly should have—different standards for evaluating knowledge claims, or technique effectiveness, than science has. The scientific establishment is conservative in the tests it administers to discipline its conjectures; in particular, its goal is to reduce uncertainty as far as possible, no matter how long that takes. In the Army, by contrast, the need for timely information and decisions may lead to an acceptance of greater uncertainty and a higher risk of being wrong.

There is no Army doctrine of which we are aware concerning the degree of risk that is acceptable in evaluations of pilot programs. Yet surely one objective of evaluations of pilot programs should be to describe the costs to the Army of drawing incorrect conclusions so that inferential standards can be made commensurate with those costs. If the costs are relatively low, the riskier approach of most commercial research (as, for example, in management consulting or marketing) may be preferred to the more conservative approach of basic science.

DESCRIBING A PROGRAM'S CONSEQUENCES

In evaluating a program, it is desirable to present an analysis and defense of the questions probed and not probed, together with justification for the priorities accorded to various issues. Primary issues usually include the program's immediate effects and its organizational side effects.

Immediate Effects

A primary problem in evaluation is to decide on the criteria by which a program is to be assessed. The major sources for identifying potential criteria include program goals, interviews with interested persons, consideration of plausible consequences found in the literature, and insights gained from preliminary field work.

Such criteria specify only potential effects, however. They do not speak to the matter of whether the relation between a supposed cause and effect is truly causal. In this respect, a fundamental issue of methodology is the use of randomized experiments. Although logistic reasons abound in any practical context for not going to the trouble to use such research designs, one might nonetheless argue that the Army is in a better position to conduct randomized experiments than are organizations in such fields as education, job training, and public health. The reason for going to such trouble is that randomized experiments give a lower risk of incorrect causal conclusions than the alternatives.

Alternatives at the next level of confidence are quasi-experimental designs that include pretest measures and comparison (control) groups. Relatively little confidence can be placed either in before-after measurements of a single group exposed to a technique without an external comparison, or in comparisons of nonequivalent intact groups for which pretest measures are not available.

Side Effects

Unintended side effects include impacts on the broader organization, and these should be monitored. For example, trainers from other (non-experimental) units may copy what they think is going on, or they may simply be upset by the implementation of new instructional packages in the experimental units. Units not treated in the same way as the experimental units may be unwilling to cooperate when cooperation would seem to be in their best interest. They may also suffer by comparison, as is thought to be the case, for example, when COHORT units are introduced into a division (see Chapter 8). Evaluators should strive to see any program as fitting into a wider system of Army activities on which it may have unintended positive or negative effects.

ASSIGNING VALUE TO PILOT PROGRAMS

The described consequences of a program tell us what a program has achieved but not how valuable it is. Three other factors are important in inferring value: Does the new technique meet a demonstrable Army need to the extent that without it the organization would be less effective? How likely is it that the program can be transferred to other Army settings, either as a total package or in part? How well does the new program fare when compared with current practice and with alternatives for bringing about the same results?

Meeting Needs

Representatives of the commercial world who seek outlets for their products often confound wants with needs, enthusiasm with proof, and hope with reality. While it is axiomatic that all field tests should aim to meet genuine Army needs, it is not clear how needs are now assessed when the developers of new products approach Army personnel for permission to do general research or field tests. It is clear that a needs analysis should be part of the documentation about every field test.

What should a needs analysis look like? At the minimum, it should document the current level of performance at some task, why the level is inadequate, what reason there is to believe that performance can change, and what the Armywide impacts would probably be if the performance in question were improved. In addition, an analysis should question why a particular program is needed for solving the problem. Such an analysis would describe the program, critically examine its justification in basic research, identify the financial and human resources required to make the program work, relate the resources required to the funds available, examine other ways of bringing about the same intended results, and justify the program at hand in terms of its anticipated cost-effectiveness. To facilitate critical feedback, such reports should be independent of the persons who sponsor a program, though based on a thorough, firsthand acquaintance with the program and its developers and sponsors.

As just described, needs analysis is a planning exercise to justify mounting a pilot program. It is not a review of program achievements relative to needs, for which a description of a program's consequences is required. At that later stage in evaluation a judgment is required about whether the magnitude of a program's effects is sufficient to reduce needs to a degree that makes a practical difference. More is at stake than whether the program makes a statistically reliable difference in performance. Size of effect relative to need is the crucial concern. When the magnitude of change required for practical significance has been specified in advance, it is easy to use such a specification to probe how well a need has been met. But the level of change required to alleviate need is not usually predetermined, and there are political reasons why developers are not always eager to have their programs evaluated in terms of effect sizes they themselves have clearly promised or that others have set for them.

Needs can be specified only by Army officials, and it is vital that such officials inspect the results a program has achieved, relating them to their perception of need. Since the Army is heterogeneous, it would be naive to believe that there are no significant differences within it about how important various needs are and how far a particular effect goes in meeting a particular need. Some theorists relate needs primarily to the number of persons performing below a desired level, while others emphasize the seriousness of consequences for unit performance, for which deficiencies in only one or two persons may be crucial. Some practitioners are likely to think a deficit in skill X is worse than a deficit in skill Y, while others may believe the opposite. Evaluators who take the concept of need seriously have to take cognizance of such heterogeneity, perhaps using group approaches like the Delphi technique to bring about consensus on both the level of need and the extent to which a particular pattern of evaluative results helps meet that need.

Likelihood of Transfer

Although some local commanders may sponsor field trials for the benefit of their command alone, the more widely a successful new practice can be implemented within the Army, the more important it is likely to be. Consequently, evaluations of pilot programs should seek to draw conclusions about the likelihood that findings will transfer to populations and settings different from those studied.

In this regard, it is particularly important to probe the extent to which any findings from a pilot study might depend on the special knowledge and enthusiasm of those persons who deliver or sponsor the program. Such persons are often strongly committed to a program, treating it with a concern and intensity that most regular Army personnel could not be expected to match. While it is sometimes possible to transfer such committed persons from one Army site to another in order to implement a program, in many instances this cannot be done. Transfer is partly a question of the psychology of ownership; authorities who did not sponsor a product will sometimes reject out of hand what others have developed, including their immediate predecessors. Since Army leaders in any position turn over with some regularity due to transfers, promotions, and retirement, successors will probably not identify with a program as strongly as the original sponsors and developers did.

The likelihood of transfer also affects the degree to which program implementation is monitored. Pilot programs are likely to be more obtrusively monitored than other programs. Not only is this obtrusiveness due to developers' and evaluators' fussing over their charge, it is also due to teams of experts brought in to inspect what is novel and to responsible officers wanting to show others the unique programs they are leading (and on which the success of their careers may depend). For at least these reasons pilot programs tend to stand out more than the regular programs they may engender. Research suggests that the quality with which programs are delivered may in fact increase when outside personnel are obviously monitoring individual and group performance.

It is naive to believe that one can go confidently from a single pilot program to full-blown Armywide implementation. Even if this were feasible politically, it would not be technically advisable unless there were compelling evidence from a great deal of prior research indicating that the program was indeed built on valid substantive foundations. Given a single pilot program, decisions about transfer are best made if the program is tested again, at a larger but still restricted set of sites and under conditions that more closely approximate those that would pertain if the new enhancement technique were implemented as routine policy. Only then might serious plans for Armywide implementation be feasible.

Contrast with Alternatives

Most of the evaluation we have discussed contrasts a novel program with standard practices that are believed worth improving; yet rational models of decision making are usually predicated on managers' having to choose among several different options for performing a particular task. One would hope that every sponsor of a novel performance enhancement technique is conversant with the practical alternatives to it and has cogent arguments for rejecting them.

Many novel techniques have some components that are already in standard practice or can be clearly derived from established theories. Upon close inspection, pilot programs often turn out to be less novel than their developers and sponsors claim. Of course, the Army may often find it convenient to order complete packages in the form offered and may not have much latitude to interact with developers in order to modify package contents to emphasize what is truly a novel alternative and to downplay that which is merely standard practice.

Ultimately, alternatives have to do with costs. Although many forms of cost are at issue—including those associated with how much a new practice disrupts normal Army activities and how much stress it puts on personnel—the major cost usually considered is financial. Cost analysis is always difficult, nowhere more so than in the Army, which uses many ways to calculate personnel costs. Nonetheless, in planning an evaluation, some evidence about the total cost of a pilot program to the Army will usually be available and can be critically scrutinized. It is also useful, as far as possible, to ascribe accurate Army costs to each of the major components of such an intervention. In our view, what is called cost-effectiveness analysis lends itself better than what is called cost-benefit analysis to the comparison of different programs. The purpose of cost-effectiveness research is to express the total cost for each program in dollar terms and to relate this to the amount of effect as expressed in its original metrics—unlike cost-benefit research, in which even the effects have to be expressed in dollar terms. Sophisticated consumers of evaluation should want something akin to cost-effectiveness knowledge, for it reflects decisions they should be making. Is it not useful to know, for example, that the best available computer-assisted instruction packages are much less cost-effective than peer tutoring?

CURRENT STATUS OF ARMY EVALUATIONS

We set forth here some of our impressions of the way in which the Army currently manages the solicitation and evaluation of novel techniques to enhance performance. We must stress that these are only impressions, gained through the limited investigative capabilities of a committee such as ours, not hard conclusions based on systematic research directed at the particular question. Furthermore, although the opinions that follow are largely critical of Army procedures, they are not accompanied by much detail. As noted earlier, the focus here is on the identification of the various Army constituencies that have a stake in enhancement programs and on the role they play in evaluation.

How the Army decides which among competing proposals should be sponsored for development or for field tests is not clear. What is clear is that decision making is diffuse both geographically and institutionally. Sponsorship may come from senior managers in the Pentagon or from local personnel of varying rank. While differences in the quality of program design, implementation, or evaluation may be correlated with the source of sponsorship, such a correlation is not clear at present in the Army context.

A particular concern is that Army sponsors of pilot programs may base their judgment about the value of a program either on their own ideas about what is desirable or effective or on the persuasiveness of the arguments presented to them by program developers, who stand to gain financially if the Army adopts their program. Judgments of value should depend on broader analysis of Army needs and resources, as well as on realistic assessment of the quality of proposed ideas based on a thorough and independent knowledge of the relevant research literatures. Sponsors should examine what is being advocated at every stage: proposal, testing, and implementation.

Also of concern when pilot programs are planned is how decisions are reached about funding and about the quality of implementation expected from them. Although systematic evidence is lacking, it seemed to committee members that pilot programs are not generally implemented well and, except for fiscal accountability, are not closely monitored by their Army sponsors. Evaluations of pilot programs should try to characterize resources required by the program and the resources actually available.

We found little evidence that sponsors, advocates, or local implementers had aspirations to evaluations that use state-of-the-art methods. We found no guidelines about the standards expected for evaluative work, whether in the form of published minimal standards or published statements of preferred practices. When it comes to field trials of novel ideas for enhancing human performance, the monitoring of evaluation quality does not seem to be part of the organizational context. Given the absence of formal expectations in these regards, it is not surprising that the pilot programs we saw and the evaluation materials we read were usually disappointing in the technical quality of the research conducted. In settings in which program sponsors or advocates control an evaluation, weaker evaluations (e.g., based on testimony) will sometimes be preferred to stronger methods (e.g., experiments) because the latter are usually more disruptive when implemented and are more likely to result in effects that are disappointing, however much more accurate they may be. The weaker methods are easier to implement when few units are available, are less disruptive of ongoing activities, are easier to manipulate for self-interested ends, and need not be as expensive for data collection.

We saw little evidence that the Army requires evaluations by persons independent of the pilot program under review. Moreover, the noninde-pendent evaluations we saw did not seem to have been subjected to any of the peer review procedures to which research results (and plans) are subjected not only in academic sciences, but also in much of the corporate world, as with, say, pharmaceutical testing. While in-house evaluation is highly valuable for gaining feedback for program improvement, many experienced evaluators contend that it is inadequate for assigning overall value because in-house evaluators cannot divorce themselves from their own stake in the program under examination. Although it is not easy to specify organizational standards adequate for a high-quality field test of some novel technique, it is also not difficult to detect the inadequacies associated with local program sponsors' having few clear expectations about the desirable qualities of program operations or evaluative practices. In the absence of such expectations, program developers and evaluators may believe that few officials care about the small-scale field tests of techniques on which the developers'—and, all too often, the evaluators'—own welfare depends.

Since the organizational climate we have just described is not optimal for gaining trustworthy information about program value, future evaluators of Army field trials might do well to characterize: (1) what program managers expect in terms of the quality of the program and its evaluation; (2) who is paying attention to the trials; and (3) for what purposes they want to use any information provided by the evaluation. This kind of information, as mentioned above, contributes to a description of the organizational context of a program, which is a major part of an adequate evaluation.

QUALITATIVE APPROACHES

Alternatives to experimentation are the largely qualitative traditions, which rely mostly on direct observation, sometimes supplemented by archival data. Investigative journalists operate in this mode; so do many cultural anthropologists, political scientists, and historians. These professions use clues to suggest hypotheses about possible causes and investigate the empirical evidence in ever-greater detail in an attempt to rule out hypotheses until they are left with just one. A critical aspect of their work is the use of substantive theories and ad hoc findings from the past to help in ruling out alternative explanations. Also working in this tradition are committees of psychologists who seek to make statements about the causes of enhanced human performance. Rarely conducting studies themselves, they instead sift through historical evidence provided by reviews of the literature and make on-site observations in the manner of detectives, pathologists, investigative journalists, and cultural anthropologists.

These traditions rely strongly on personal testimony. Respondents' reports are taken seriously and, indeed, should be. Any method can, in principle, generate strong causal evidence, provided that plausible alternatives to a preferred hypothesis have been ruled out. The general issues are: Can personal testimony usually rule out all the plausible alternative interpretations? Does use of it engender the very threats to validity that militate against strong inferences? Dale Griffin, in a paper prepared for the committee (see Appendix B), suggests "no" to the first question and "yes" to the second. His analysis of biases that operate when people attempt to explain how and why they changed after an experience reveals many of the shortcomings associated with relying on testimony as a major means of testing causal hypotheses.

While testimony can be regarded as a form of confirmatory evidence, it does not provide any of the disconfirming evidence needed to reduce uncertainty. Rarely are there the kinds of comprehensive probes needed to discover why respondents believe that the effects are due to a treatment rather than to maturation, statistical regression, or the pleasant feelings aroused by the experiences. People are typically weak at identifying the range of such alternatives, however simply they may be described, and at distinguishing the different ways in which the causal forces might operate. How can people know how they would have matured over time in the absence of an intervention (technique) that is being assessed? How can people disentangle effects due to a pleasant experience, a dynamic leader, or a sense of doing something important from effects due to the critical components of the treatment per se? Much research has shown that individuals are poor intuitive scientists and that they recreate a set of known cognitive biases (Nisbett and Ross, 1980; Griffin). These include belief perseverance, selective memory, errors of attribution, and overconfidence. These biases influence experts and nonexperts alike, usually without one's awareness of them. Scientists hold these biases in partial check by using random assignment instead of testimony and by the tradition of public scrutiny to identify and analyze alternative interpretations for observed events. Such methodological traditions can be transmitted to consumers and producers of enhancement techniques through courses on statistical inference and formal decision making. These courses would have the salutary effect of calling attention to the shortcomings of testimony as evidence.

We submit that experimental methods facilitate causal inferences better than the alternatives. They reduce more uncertainty by ruling out more of the contending interpretations for observed effects. However, we refer here to the *relative* superiority of experimentation; such superiority should not be confused with either the perfection or even the adequacy of experimentation. Its problems include the facts that experiments cannot be implemented under all conditions and that experimentation has its own set of unintended side effects. Thus, experimental methods do not guarantee causal inferences and so cannot obviate the need for critical analysis that, on a case-by-case basis, is sensitive to the contexts and traditions of particular institutions or communities, such as the Army, on one hand, and the various promoters of new enhancement techniques, on the other. Moreover, well-conceived research is costly: it requires specially trained investigators, equipped facilities, and programs that may need extensive collaborations and review panels. It is also a demanding craft that requires sensitivity to detail and precision in order to ensure results that are interpretable.

On balance, the benefits derived from careful experimentation outweigh the costs just mentioned. All other things being equal, experimentation is much the preferred strategy for judging the efficacy of techniques that purport to enhance performance, and it should be used whenever possible.

PART II

Psychological Techniques

IN PART II WE DISCUSS A VARIETY of psychological and social-psychological processes. Our discussions are oriented largely toward the particular techniques chosen for evaluation, yet in each chapter we attempt to draw on a broader literature concerning the processes being influenced—learning, performance, mental states, stress, and social interactions. More detailed reviews of relevant research can be found in the papers that were prepared as background for the committee's work (see Appendix B).

By weaving insights about basic processes into the discussions of techniques, we hope to convey to the reader a larger message about techniques in general. There are, of course, many other procedures designed to influence psychological processes, and any particular technique is likely to affect more than one process. The chapters that follow are intended to suggest implications for a broad range of techniques to enhance human performance.

4

Learning

In the area of learning, the committee chose learning during sleep and accelerated learning techniques as topics for consideration. The choice of these particular topics relates to the Army's desire to reduce training time. Clearly, benefits would accrue to an organization that is able to use sleeping hours for training and to speed the learning process during waking hours. This chapter investigates these possibilities, drawing on a variety of sources for its conclusions and conveying several interesting insights that may have practical implications.

LEARNING DURING SLEEP

If one simply looks at the best available past research on learning during sleep (see Aarons, 1976, for a remarkably thorough review), it is hard to imagine a more discouraging state of affairs. The learning of verbal materials presented auditorily during sleep appears to take place only to the extent that the presentation of the material triggers alpha-wave activity (an electroencephalographic indicator of arousal or wakefulness) in the learner. When all possible criteria are applied to verify that the learner is truly asleep, there appears to be no evidence of conscious recall or recognition of materials presented during sleep. Since about the mid-1970s, in fact, research activity on sleep learning has nearly expired, at least in this country.

New developments in our knowledge of memory, however, suggest that sleep learning deserves a second look. From an applied perspective, some of the positive demonstrations of sleep learning, dating back many years, possibly deserve an effort at replication. In 1916, for example, L.L. Thurstone was reportedly (Simon and Emmons, 1955) able to shorten the Morse code training of sailors by three weeks by giving additional training during the sleeping period. Such results tend to be dismissed since no EEG recordings were taken to verify sleep, but it may be that the costs of such training during the sleep period—in terms of disrupted sleep and the negative consequences therefrom on later waking efficiency—are minor compared with the benefits of accelerated training. Soviet research on sleep learning (see the background paper by Eric Eich, Appendix B) has apparently been carried out with less concern for whether pure learning during true sleep is possible and more concern for how such training might facilitate ongoing instruction.

From a theoretical perspective, sleep learning also deserves a second look (see Tilley, 1979). Viewed in the current context of research on human memory, one should expect only certain types of learning to take place during true EEG-verified sleep, and one should only expect that learning to show up on certain types of memory tests. The past negative results, in general, were obtained with presentation procedures that were inappropriate and with testing procedures that would be insensitive to any learning that did take place.

In our discussion of learning during sleep, we first reassess the possibility in terms of modern conceptions of human memory; we then look at potential applications of sleep learning, whether pure (during true sleep) or impure (during near sleep); and we conclude with an outline of the types of research projects that merit support. We do not, however, review past research on learning during sleep. As noted above, that research consists almost entirely of two types: (1) earlier research reporting positive results but lacking appropriate controls to verify sleep and (2) later research reporting negative results given verified sleep. The few results we do cite are used as illustrations. For an excellent overview of the current state of research in the field, we direct the reader to the paper prepared for the committee by Eich.

OTHER TYPES OF LEARNING WITHOUT AWARENESS

There is an ongoing revolution in how researchers view the storage and retrieval processes that underlie learning. We have come to realize that there are different types of storage that might or might not take place as a consequence of a certain experience and that the presence of any such stored information may or may not influence later memory performance, depending on the way in which the memory is tested. Certain types of learning appear to be data-driven or stimulus-driven, that is, they do not require effort or intention or even awareness on the part of the learner, whereas other types of learning—those more familiar to us—are conceptually driven, that is they *do* require conscious effort, intention to learn, and active interpretation of the material to be learned.

In general, only conceptually driven learning is adequately measured by tests that require an active effort to recall or recognize the target information. Learning of the data-driven type may not show up at all on such tests, or it might show up in a pattern that would lead to the opposite conclusion one would draw from other, more appropriate ways of measuring it. It is learning of the data-driven type, measured in an appropriate way, that one might expect to take place during sleep, but past research on learning during sleep has focused on verbal learning of the conceptually driven variety.

Because some of the current distinctions being made in the human memory field are so critical to a reassessment of sleep learning, it is worth taking time to clarify and illustrate those distinctions in more detail.

Types of Knowledge

Although there are heated arguments about the details and about certain ambiguous cases, it has become common among researchers to distinguish among episodic, semantic, and procedural memories (see, e.g., Tulving, 1985). In brief, *episodic memory* refers to context-specific memory (What did you have for breakfast this morning? What did you do on your trip to Europe?); *semantic memory* refers to knowledge that is independent of context (What do Americans eat for breakfast? What is the capital of Switzerland? How much is 2 × 2?); and *procedural memory* refers to knowledge that underlies motor and cognitive skills, many of them automatized (such as speech, typing, bicycle riding, and possibly certain types of tacit knowledge, such as how a system works or a game is played). The important point is that these different types of memory appear to follow somewhat different rules in terms of the nature of their storage and the ways in which they are accessed. In some circumstances, in fact, there can be a complete dissociation among these types of memories. Amnesic patients, for example, often show "source amnesia," which is an inability to recall episodic information, while showing normal retention of the semantic or procedural knowledge derived from those episodes (see, e.g., Schachter and Tulving, 1982). Thus, an amnesic patient who is given practice every few days in a complex task (such as mirror drawing or solving "Tower of Hanoi" puzzles) may have no memory of the experimenter from one practice session to another, may need to have the task explained every session, but may nonetheless show a normal learning curve across practice sessions in the task itself.

There is evidence of dissociation in normal subjects as well. The spelling of a homophone such as *read* or *fairy* can be biased toward a less frequent interpretation (*reed, ferry*) by a question inserted in an earlier phase of the experiment ("Name a musical instrument that employs a reed"), or by a repeated presentation on an unattended auditory channel of an adjective-noun pair ("Catalina ferry"), even when subjects cannot demonstrate that they recognize that such a word occurred in the experiment (Eich, 1984; Jacoby and Witherspoon, 1982). Similarly, prior presentation of a word has been shown to enhance subjects' later ability to identify that word when it is briefly exposed on a tachistoscope, whether or not they recognize the word as one presented earlier (Jacoby and Dallas, 1981). Thus, an event may leave an impact on semantic memory that survives after the episode itself is apparently forgotten.

Measurement of Memory "Strength"

As the foregoing examples demonstrate, one cannot infer the effect of a given experience on memory (or the strength of the resulting memory trace) by any one measure, such as a test of recall or recognition. At least since Ebbinghaus's work in the late nineteenth century, we have known that the different traditional measures of learning (recall, recognition, time savings during relearning) do not always give the same picture of the amount of learning resulting from a given experience, but in recent years dramatic evidence has emerged that certain indirect but sensitive measures of memory may yield a picture that is entirely different than that painted by any of the traditional measures. An event in one's life that cannot itself be recalled or recognized at some later point may nonetheless change one's perceptual thresholds, may bias one's semantic or affective interpretation of a verbal item, may reinforce earlier learning (repetition effects), and may enhance later learning (priming effects).

An example, drawn from an experiment by Jacoby (1983), illustrates how one's conclusions can depend on how one measures prior learning. In the first phase of Jacoby's experiment, target words (such as COLD) were presented in one of three different ways: (1) they were generated by the subject based on a strong associate and a letter cue (HOT C _ _ _), (2) they were simply presented together with the strong associate (HOT COLD), or (3) they were presented without any such associative context (XXX COLD). On a test of later recognition, COLD was best recognized as a word that had occurred earlier if it had been generated, next best if was presented with HOT, and worst if it was presented in the absence of a semantic context. If memory was tested by looking at the effect of prior presentation on subjects' ability to identify words exposed briefly on a tachistoscope, the exact opposite ordering of conditions was obtained. Thus, in Jacoby's experiment more than one type of learning took place when a target item was presented: stimulus-driven activation of the sensory features corresponding to the item in memory and conceptually driven associations of the item with both semantically related items in memory and the experimental context. Recognition performance is sensitive primarily to the latter; perceptual identification is sensitive primarily to the former. Thus, the nature of the original learning determines what type of later test will reveal that learning. For a complete discussion of alternative measures of memory, see Richardson-Klaveher and Bjork (1988).

Remembering With and Without Awareness

The kinds of experiments summarized above illustrate a further important point. As Eich puts it, ". . . it is possible to distinguish the effects of *memory* for prior episodes or experiences on a person's current behavior from the person's *awareness* that he or she is remembering events of the past." Viewed from that perspective, people might learn something from material presented during sleep but not know that such learning took place, either in the sense of being able to recall the target information or to recognize that it had been presented.

Looked at within the conceptual framework outlined above, the failure of past experiments to find evidence for learning during EEG-verified sleep is not surprising. The types of learning one might expect to be possible during EEG-verified sleep are the following:

1. Lowering of perceptual thresholds or improved pronunciation of items presented during sleep, or both.

2. Semantic or affective biasing in postsleep interpretation of verbal items in a direction determined by the semantic or affective context in which those items were embedded when presented during sleep.

3. Repetition effects (i.e., when material studied before sleep is presented again during sleep and postsleep recall of that material is enhanced, even without the learner's being aware that the material was presented again).

4. Priming effects (i.e., when presentation during sleep of material to be learned after sleep increases the rate at which the material is learned, again without the learner's being necessarily aware that the material had ever been presented before).

POTENTIAL APPLICATIONS OF LEARNING DURING SLEEP

From a theoretical perspective, researchers agree that a rigorous demonstration of learning during sleep should have the following properties: (1) prior to sleep subjects should not be informed of the purpose of the procedures to be employed during sleep; (2) the material to be learned should be unique in that it occurs only during the sleep period; and (3) EEG recordings should be taken, both to ensure that presenting the material did not arouse wakefulness and to ensure that the material was not presented when the subject was already in a state of arousal or wakefulness.

From an applied perspective, however, these restrictions eliminate many of the procedures that would seem to hold the most promise for actually using sleep learning in practical contexts. Rather than keep people from knowing the purpose of the procedure to which they are to be subjected, for example, it may be important not only to reveal the purpose, but also to systematically administer some type of presleep training as well. As Eich points out in his review, one may need to learn how to learn during sleep. Procedures analogous to those inducing hypnotic suggestibility may be useful, training early in one's life might lead one to develop the ability to learn during sleep, and so forth. There may be presleep procedures that can prime subsequent learning during sleep. There does not, after all, seem to be much doubt that presleep events and state of mind can bias the nature and content of one's subsequent dreams.

Requirements 2 and 3 above are also, from a practical standpoint, misguided. Rather than have the material to be learned during sleep be unique to the sleep period, most of the potential applications of sleep learning involve its use to enhance the acquisition of material that is part of the waking curriculum. Similarly, the requirement that material presented during the sleep period not disrupt sleep or be presented during periods of wakefulness or arousal may exclude procedures of practical significance, as illustrated in the section below on applications of sleep-disrupted learning.

It remains to be demonstrated that certain types of stimulus-driven learning are possible during EEG-verified sleep. In the section below, we assume that such learning is possible.

Applications of Learning During Verified Sleep

As should be clear from the foregoing discussion, the type of application that does *not* make sense is to try to produce active postsleep recall of verbal materials presented only during sleep. The real potential of learning during sleep lies in reinforcing the learning that occurs during the waking hours. Such reinforcement would consist in part of re-presenting during sleep material learned earlier and in part of presenting during sleep material to be learned later (priming). The 1916 Morse code experiment discussed earlier is a good case in point. We do not know how much of the materials presented during sleep occurred during verified sleep, but the nighttime presentations no doubt did both of the above, that is, repeated prior learning and primed upcoming learning.

It is worth noting that an important aspect of learning Morse code— learning to recognize units in rapidly presented code—corresponds primarily to stimulus-driven learning. In general, vocabulary learning, broadly conceived (i.e., including coding systems as well as foreign language vocabulary), may be a fruitful domain for the application of learning during sleep. Nighttime presentations could reinforce daytime learning in the two senses specified above and might also facilitate perceptual fluency and speech production. Language learning involves an interaction of stimulus learning—building acoustic units—and conceptual learning—associating those units with semantic representations.

Another domain in which learning during verified sleep might apply is in altering attitudes, affective reactions, or mood. A study carried out by LeShan in 1942 is a good example, although we do not know how much of the learning in LeShan's study occurred during true sleep. The subjects were chronic fingernail biters. For 54 nights, without being informed of the purpose of the study, they were presented with a recording of the phrase "my fingernails taste terribly bitter" 300 times per night. According to LeShan's report, 40 percent of the subjects stopped biting their nails. The apparent change in attitude induced in those subjects is illustrative of the potential that learning during sleep might have in that domain.

Should it prove possible to influence attitudes, emotions, and other types of affective reactions via nighttime recordings, then it is not difficult to think of many applications, although some of them would be inappropriate on moral grounds. It is an intriguing possibility that some learning procedures might be *more* effective in changing subjects' attitudes during sleep than during waking hours; it seems unlikely, for example, that LeShan's procedure would have been as effective had it been carried out on awake subjects.

Applications of Disrupted-Sleep Learning

Should it turn out that learning during true sleep is not possible, there may still be some significant applications of learning procedures carried out during the night. Even if such procedures disrupt the quantity or quality of sleep, their benefits might outweigh their costs. In the Morse code study discussed above, for example, the reported benefits were a three-week reduction in the amount of time the subjects (sailors) took to reach the required level of performance (compared with sailors who did not get the additional Morse code training during sleep). The costs of the sleep-learning procedure, in terms of decreased waking productivity owing to disrupted sleep, may have been minor compared with the benefits.

Looking at sleep-learning procedures from a cost-benefit standpoint suggests potentially significant applications of dynamic sleep-learning procedures. Since an individual goes through cycles of the various stages of sleep (as indexed by the pattern of EEG activity), some of which correspond to semiwakefulness or higher arousal, or both, the presentation of material could be programmed to occur during the natural arousal cycles. Not only would the acquisition of the material to be learned be most effective, in all likelihood at such times the cost in sleep disruption would be minimized because those periods of arousal were not caused by the procedure. Such programming of sleep learning could potentially be carried out automatically. It would seem technically feasible for a single apparatus to monitor a sleeping subject's EEG and to trigger the presentation of material during periods of arousal.

In general, sleep-disrupted learning might be especially effective in terms of enhancing later retrieval of the target information when the subject is exhausted or deprived of sleep, or both. As Eich points out, one of the difficulties of demonstrating learning during sleep is that the learning that takes place may be largely state-specific. Sleep, especially the profound sleep of the deeper stages (stage IV and REM sleep), is a special state both mentally and physically. Learning that takes place in that state may not transfer well, if at all, to states of full alertness and wakefulness. The natural cycles of semiwakefulness during the night, however, must share many properties with the states of drowsiness and semisleep that accompany exhaustion and sleep deprivation. Sleep-disrupted learning might therefore enhance later memory performance in a sleep-deprived waking state. Since cognitive performance deteriorates under sleep deprivation, such potential transfer of training during sleep may help the subject when he or she needs it most. With the technical advances that facilitate nighttime fighting, sleep management and performance under sleep deprivation are going to be ever more significant problems in the round-the-clock military engagements of the future, so the potential of such an application could be quite significant. There is a need to demonstrate, however, that the specific procedural skills critical to nighttime fighting are amenable to enhancement by sleep training.

DIRECTION AND DESIGN OF FUTURE RESEARCH

The committee concludes that sleep learning as a technique to enhance or speed training deserves a second look. An appropriate second look requires both basic research, designed to clarify whether some variety of stimulus-driven learning is possible during EEG-verified sleep, and applied research, designed to explore whether the benefits of sleep-disrupted learning outweigh the costs associated with disrupted sleep.

Research on Stimulus-Driven Learning During EEG-Verified Sleep

In terms of the potential applications of learning during sleep and in terms of what other research options are most fruitful to pursue, it is of central importance to know whether there exists any type of learning during sleep. Toward that end, rigorous research should be carried out incorporating the usual EEG controls to verify that the material to be learned is presented during true sleep (without disrupting that sleep), but with a critical change from earlier experiments (see Tilley, 1979): the measures of learning should have been shown to be sensitive to stimulus-driven learning rather than to active recall or recognition. The appropriate measures are those discussed earlier: priming of postsleep learning, repetition of presleep learning, postsleep perceptual identification of logical items presented during sleep, biasing of postsleep semantic or affective interpretation of items presented in a biasing context during sleep, and so forth.

Should it prove possible to achieve such stimulus-driven learning without the subject's awareness, then a whole new domain of possible applications and additional basic research questions will arise. For example, can attitudes be altered by sleep-learning procedures? Is bone conduction a better vehicle than air conduction for presenting auditory information during sleep? (Eich suggests that it may be, because bone conduction "has the curious effect of shifting the phenomenal source of speech from the outside to the inside of one's head.") These and a variety of other questions, many of them outlined in Eich's paper, become important questions should it be possible to achieve stimulus-driven learning during verified sleep.

Research on Sleep-Disrupted Learning

Even if the outcome of the basic research recommended above were to be negative, it may be important to test the feasibility of certain applications of sleep-disrupted learning. Does sleep-disrupted learning transfer in positive ways to postsleep states of exhaustion and sleep deprivation? Can sleep-learning repetition or priming of information that is part of the normal training of a soldier facilitate that training to the extent that it offsets any detrimental effects of the sleep-learning proce-dure? Is it technically feasible to build an apparatus that would both monitor a soldier's sleep-state EEG and present, possibly via bone conduction, information to be learned when a certain specified EEG pattern is registered?

If one focuses not on the theoretical possibility of learning during true sleep but on the practical purposes it may serve to use the hours a subject is asleep (whether superficial or not) to achieve learning, then the foregoing questions and a variety of related questions merit research. The committee feels that it is important to conclude on a note of caution. The kinds of EEG-verified sleep learning that may be possible may have limited applicability to the kinds of learning that are important to the Army, and the costs of disrupted-sleep learning may outweigh the benefits. A substantial commitment of funds to an actual sleep-learning program should await clear positive results from the kinds of research programs we suggest above.

SOURCES OF INFORMATION

In addition to drawing on the relevant knowledge of its members, the subcommittee on sleep learning commissioned a review paper by Eric Eich, arranged a special briefing by LaVerne Johnson, chief scientist at the Naval Health Research Center in San Diego, and benefited from presentations given by military officers at Fort Benning, Georgia. Eich's paper provided a useful interpretation of sleep learning within the context of present-day theories of human information processing and memory. Johnson's talk provided a historical context for the research by tracing its development from the earliest known studies by Thurstone in 1916 to the present. And exposure to the varieties of training at Fort Benning alerted the committee to the special demands placed on soldiers to perform important jobs while in states of exhaustion and sleep deprivation.

ACCELERATED LEARNING

With respect to the goal of accelerating the learning process, that is, increasing the rate or depth, or both, of learning beyond that characteristic of typical training in a given task, three types of research are relevant. First, basic research on human beings as learners is crucial: knowing the basic characteristics of human attention, of the storage and retrieval processes that underlie human memory, and of the representation of knowledge and procedural skills in long-term memory provides a framework for examining practical techniques that are or are not likely to accelerate learning.

The other two areas of research are related to each other: research on the characteristics of effective instruction, and research on effective learning strategies on the part of the learner. The first of these more applied research domains focuses on the skills, techniques, and knowledge the instructor can bring to the training situation; the second focuses on the strategies the learner can bring to the training situation to accelerate the learning process. The fact that efficient learning strategies may be transmitted from the instructor to the learner is only one of the ways in which these two research domains are related.

We focus in this section on accelerated learning programs that attempt to provide a system for addressing instructor and student variables together. It is a working assumption of such programs that one must look at teacher-learner dynamics as a whole. The paper written for the committee by Robert E. Slavin, "Principles of Effective Instruction," is a good characterization of research on the instructor's contribution to the learning process, and a recent chapter by Weinstein (1986), "Assessment and Training of Student Learning Strategies," is a good treatment of the potential contribution of the learner. Textbooks such as Anderson (1981) and Glass and Holyoak (1986) do a good job of capturing the current status of basic research on human beings as processors of information.

PACKAGED PROGRAMS FOR ACCELERATED LEARNING

Accelerated learning methods are a class of techniques using unusual methods of instruction with the intent of substantially increasing the speed of learning. The techniques are referred to by the names Suggestive Accelerative Learning and Teaching Techniques (SALTT), Suggestopedia, and Superlearning. The approach employs a combination of physical relaxation exercises, guided imagery, a suggestion of efficient learning, a belief in tapping mental reserves, and an alternation of active and passive review (generally with baroque music). The techniques have been popularized in the press in *Psychology Today* (August 1977), *Parade* magazine (March 12, 1978), and a popular paperback, *SuperLearning*, by Ostrander and Schroeder (1979). Schuster and Gritton (1986) provide a textbook for SALTT procedures that includes a review of studies supporting the approach. There is an international society (Society for Accelerative Learning and Teaching), which holds an annual meeting that draws about 500 participants. The society publishes a journal, the *Journal of the Society for Accelerative Learning and Teaching*, which was begun in 1975. The journal contains testimonials, evaluation studies, and reviews of SALTT techniques and research.

The SALTT approach developed as an outgrowth of presentations and writings by Georgi Lozanov of Bulgaria. His dissertation and public presentations attracted attention in America in the early 1970s (see

Bancroft, 1976). Lozanov describes himself as a psychotherapist who was known as a hypnotist for 10 to 15 years and who has a strong interest in pedagogy. His techniques have been applied in several Eastern bloc countries. Many Western advocates of accelerated learning have studied with Lozanov and have adopted his methods of instruction.

Some proponents of the SALTT approach make wide-ranging claims of extraordinary learning rates. Lozanov (1978:27) claims "memorization in learning by the suggestopedic method is accelerated 25 times over that in learning by conventional methods." Ostrander and Schroeder (1979:15) report claims that Suggestopedia increases learning:

. . . from five to fifty times, increases retention, requires virtually no effort on the part of students, reaches retarded and brilliant, young and old alike, and requires no special equipment. And people testified not only had they learned a whole language in a month, or a semester of history in a few weeks, they rebalanced their health and awakened creative and intuitive abilities while they were learning their facts.

In a discussion of techniques, Wenger (1983:89) claims "the first dozen methods [of accelerated learning] consistently yielded a rate of apparent acquisition of conceptual learning several hundred times greater than that found from conventional methods."

With such strong endorsements, one would hope to find many studies showing impressive learning gains. However, after ten years of informal research, there is little scientific support for even the mild claims of two- to threefold improvements made by some of the more pragmatic proponents (Schuster and Gritton, 1986). Lozanov's empirical studies reported only a 20 percent improvement. In controlled experiments using the same teacher with extended study utilizing SALTT procedures, modest improvements are reported relative to controls, for example, 10 percent improvement in learning German (Gasser-Roberts and Brislan, 1984); 25 percent improvement in learning English as a second language (Zeiss, 1984). A number of quasi experiments report that students can learn comparable information in one-third the time (see Schuster and Gritton, 1986); however, most of these demonstrations suffer from a number of confounding factors (see below).

SALTT procedures exploit a number of traditional (e.g., spacing repetitions) and nontraditional (e.g., review with music) procedures in a conglomeration of techniques to improve learning. SALTT provides a packaged program with specific techniques to deal with student motivation, instructor motivation, instructor training, and presentation of material. By dealing with the multiple aspects of instruction, SALTT techniques may enhance the instructor's ability to keep students motivated to perform, to remain engaged in the task, and to provide material at an appropriate level. In his background paper, Slavin faults many traditional instruction procedures (e.g., computer-based instruction, self-study) for emphasizing presentation of material at the appropriate level while ignoring the factors of motivation, engaged time, and instructional quality. The conglomeration of techniques typical in any SALTT experiment, however, makes it difficult to distinguish between essential and nonessential aspects of SALTT.

SALTT seeks to change instructors' attitudes, expectations, and behaviors to produce better instruction. In general, it is difficult to change the behavior of practicing instructors, although the suggestion-sales techniques employed by SALTT instructors may motivate some of them to alter their teaching behavior for the better.

THE SALTT CLASSROOM

A SALTT classroom includes features that are not present in the traditional classroom. The environment is a pleasant living room–lounge atmosphere with comfortable chairs rather than rows of desks. This setting is intended to provide a relaxed, comfortable, and nonthreatening learning environment. The instructor encourages the interaction of the entire class through the use of positive reinforcement, relaxation, and confidence-building techniques.

Schuster and Gritton (1986) provide a detailed account of the components of a SALTT class session. A session includes three major components: preliminaries, presentation, and practice. Rather than focusing on content material for an entire session, a significant period of time is spent performing relaxation, suggestion, and restimulation exercises.

The preliminary phase (about 10 percent of the class time) relaxes the students and prepares them to absorb new material. This involves mild physical relaxation exercises such as stretching. Next, students perform a mental relaxation task (e.g., watching their breathing) to take their minds off their day-to-day problems and attend to the teacher. Thereafter teachers perform a "suggestive setup" to convince students that the learning will be fun, easy, efficient, and long-lasting. Students use guided imagery to recall a pleasant learning experience (e.g., Remember how you felt on your best-ever English test? Who was the teacher? How did your stomach feel?). These procedures might take three to ten minutes of an hour-long session, with more time required for the first two sessions.

The presentation phase (about 40 percent of the lesson) presents the material in a dramatic, dynamic way and then reviews it passively with background music. This phase has three components. The first, preview, gives the student the big picture, providing advanced organizers as to how the current lesson fits into the entire course and the specific behavior objectives of the lesson (Ausubel, 1960). The preview typically requires only a few minutes. The second component, dramatic presentation, presents the material in a dynamic way. Students are strongly encouraged to make vivid images relating to the material to be learned. They generate images on their own and actively deal with the material. For example, to learn programming, they imagine themselves as a computer sequentially executing instructions. This component might take 20 minutes of a class. The third component involves passive review with music. The instructor rhythmically repeats key material while playing baroque music in the background. The rhythm of the words and the sound of the music are assumed to produce a special mental condition that accelerates learning. This might encompass 15 minutes of an hour-long session.

The third phase of a SALTT session is practice, which entails 50 percent of the lesson. There are three components. The first, activation of the knowledge, involves using the knowledge described in the presentation phase. For example, in a foreign language class, there might be a choral reading of the material. The second component is elaboration, which involves having the student use the material in new and different ways. In a foreign language class, students are given foreign language names and perform interactive procedures such as ordering a meal in the new language. Error correction is often indirect (e.g., the teacher does not say that a foreign phrase was wrong but rather immediately uses the phrase correctly). The third component is the use of frequent quizzes. The questions generally assess information that has been presented several times. The students are provided the answers to the quizzes and scores are generally not used to determine class grades.

THE EVIDENCE

Assumed Theoretical Support

A variety of physiological and clinical phenomena are cited as support for SALTT (see Lozanov, 1978; Schuster and Gritton, 1986). There is an assumption that whole-brain learning produces integrated brain activity coordinating left brain, right brain, and subcortical activity. The hemispheric specialization is cited to suggest that the whole brain should be used to increase learning. Evidence is also cited that music and subjects' mental activities alter EEG activity. There is no direct evidence, however, that these brain phenomena can substantially enhance learning. Relaxation is also assumed to produce better learning; however, the psychological evidence on this is weak and better supports the view that optimal levels of relaxation occur when the subject is in a normal state (e.g., tense individuals learn better in normal tense states—Schuster and Martin, 1980). The research on expectancy effects is cited as evidence for the use of suggestion techniques. In their paper prepared for the committee, Monica J. Harris and Robert Rosenthal show that positive expectations to learn can result in more positive assessments of performance. One must be cautious, however, in assuming that these placebo techniques will work in situations in which subjects receive extended exposure to positive expectations.

Support for Traditional Instructional Components

The majority of the time in a SALTT classroom is spent in activities that are typical in the classrooms of expert teachers and have substantial psychological support. Although 10 minutes of a SALTT class session may be occupied with nontraditional tasks (relaxation exercises and review with music), perhaps 50 minutes are spent engaged in component tasks (elaboration, generation, imagery, repetition, and frequent testing) that clearly benefit instruction in standard laboratory experiments.

Generation and Elaboration. A SALTT class session typically presents fewer instructor-generated elaborations of the material and encourages more student-generated elaborations. Research in reading comprehension indicates that students benefit little from author-generated elaborations, and such elaborations may even impede the learning of facts. In contrast, student-generated elaborations enhance learning (see Reder, Charney, and Morgan, 1986). For example, in ten studies Reder and Anderson (1980, 1982) found that students who read author-elaborated chapters from college textbooks did consistently worse than students who read only the chapter summaries, which were one-fifth as long. From this perspective, the SALTT strategy of presenting a short preview, dramatic presentations and review (during the presentation phase), followed by an extensive practice phase involving student-generated images and elaborations is likely to be superior to a single presentation by the instructor with extensive instructor-generated elaborations. Study of the "generation effect" (e.g., Slamecka and Graf, 1978) has shown that students learn far more by actively generating answers (e.g., solving simple anagrams) than by passively reading or listening to material.

Spacing of Repetitions. SALTT lessons repeat material more frequently and with substantial spacing relative to typical college courses. Critical material is presented during the presentation, review, activation, elaboration, and test phases of the experiment. The literature on spacing and repetition effects (e.g., Crowder, 1976, Chapter 9; Landauer and Bjork, 1978) shows that long-term memory can be greatly increased by repeating the material under optimal spacing conditions rather than presenting it once or under massed conditions.

Imagery. SALTT procedures emphasize the use of imagery. Imagery has long been employed by mnemonists (Luria, 1969) and can generally improve long-term memory for concrete objects (Paivio, 1971; Paivio and Desrochers, 1979).

Songs and Rhythm as Mnemonic Devices. The use of song and rhythm has been shown to improve recall. In a SALTT foreign language class for lawyers, students sing the elements of a contract (Stockwell, 1986). The rhyming information embedded in such songs provides an extra cue that may facilitate learning.

Cooperative Learning. SALTT classes frequently break up into groups in which students cooperatively utilize the material. Cooperative teaching has been shown to be effective in enhancing instruction in the educational literature (Danserean, 1986; Slavin, 1983, and the paper prepared for the committee).

Advanced Organizers. SALTT instructors are encouraged to present "advanced organizers" to give students an overview of how the material to be learned relates to previous material. Advanced organizers have been shown to enhance the learning of reading material (Mayer, 1979).

Tests as Motivational Devices and Learning Events. SALTT instructors employ daily quizzes. Frequent testing has long been recognized as a factor in maintaining subject effort in animals and humans (e.g., Adams, 1980). But SALTT procedures do not overdo testing, as is frequently done with programmed instruction. When tested too often, students are encouraged to read passively, forfeiting the benefits of generation and elaboration.

Review of the SALTT Learning Literature

There is an extensive published literature on accelerated learning techniques (at least three major books and over 2,800 pages of journal articles). Unfortunately, the majority of the work involves testimonials with little quantitative data (e.g., in a review of the field, L.L. Palmer, 1985, found that only about half the studies report statistics). Testimonials can be useful to identify hypotheses, but any hypothesis must be viewed as tentative until it is verified with experimental procedures employing control groups with random assignment of subjects. The history of the use of bloodletting in early medicine illustrates the danger of accepting testimonial evidence (see also Chapter 9 and the paper prepared for the committee by Griffin).

Testimonial Evidence. Testimonial evidence is often cited to show that SALTT procedures can overcome learning barriers (Schuster and Gritton, 1986). Klockner (1984) cites as an example teaching adult Vietnamese women to learn English as a second language. In Vietnamese culture, elderly women are given a position of respect and are expected to show wisdom in their actions; they are not expected to make errors. To learn a new language, however, one *must* make errors. An unwillingness to make errors is a serious barrier to learning a language. Bringing Vietnamese women into a strange environment (e.g., relaxation exercises, classical music, performing skits, having different names) reduces the barriers, allowing the apprehensive student to practice, and through that practice, to learn the language. Musical suggestive techniques may be helpful in counteracting certain phobias (e.g., math or computer anxieties) that inhibit learning in problem populations. An individual with a strong phobia may learn little in a traditional class; treating the phobia may greatly accelerate his or her learning. Klockner reports a fivefold improvement in learning for her students. Given that a student may be unwilling to practice in a traditional classroom, and hence learning may be near zero, proportionally large improvements may occur.

Confounding Factors. Almost all the experimental studies of SALTT are confounded by the motivated teacher effect. An extensive study by Schuster and Prichard (1978) illustrates this. An experimental group of 16 teachers had enrolled in a SALTT teacher improvement workshop that required up to 120 hours of class time. The control instructors were selected from comparable (matching procedure unspecified) instructors in similar classes that did not sign up for teacher training workshops. At this point the study was already flawed. Instructors who volunteer for 120 hours of instruction are already likely to be more motivated to teach well. At the end of the first year of classroom teaching, three of the instructors did significantly better than their controls; three did worse. It is surprising and disappointing that any teacher training program involving so much instruction did not improve performance in the first year. In the second year, six of the instructors were dropped from the study, primarily because they were unwilling to put in the full effort to execute a SALTT lesson. At this point, seven of the ten remaining SALTT instructors showed significantly better teaching performance than did their controls. However, given the selection effect, one cannot attribute these results to the use of SALTT procedures.

The motivated instructor effect is also a problem when the same individual teaches with and without SALTT (e.g., Gasser-Roberts, 1985), if the instructor believes that the SALTT procedure is superior. The belief alone can produce better teaching (see the Pygmalion effect discussed by Rosenthal and Jacobson, 1968).

Studies of SALTT are also difficult to interpret because of the possibility of a Hawthorne effect, that is, when people realize that they have been chosen for observation, they typically perform better. The Hawthorne effect refers to results of a study conducted at the Hawthorne Plant of General Electric, where engineers tried to find the optimal light level for maximizing productivity. It was found that increasing the light level, decreasing the light level, or just measuring it improved performance. A study by Knibbeler (1982) suggests that the Hawthorne effect may be a confounding variable. He had seven instructors teach using either Suggestopedia or the silent way. (The silent way is almost the opposite of SALTT: students are presented the language with little chance for verbalization and few repetitions in a tense environment in which learning is expected to be hard work.) Both methods improved instruction equally, and only the instructor variable was significant.

Weak Designs and Questionable Interpretations. SALTT proponents frequently claim to have demonstrated more efficient learning by shortening class time and showing comparable performance. For example, Schuster (1976a) taught students with two hours of lectures per week compared with six hours in the control conditions. He found that the groups were not significantly different. One must be very cautious in interpreting such studies. First, the comparisons did not include nonclass study time, which, if equivalent (at the rate of two hours per original course hour), might reduce the ratio from 3:1 to 1.3:1. Second, almost all human learning is negatively accelerated, that is, the marginal utility of additional study time is reduced with practice (e.g., Newell and Rosenbloom, 1981). Hence reducing study time by 50 percent is expected to reduce performance by less than 50 percent. Third, most performance tests do not represent ratio or even interval scale data (e.g., it is generally easier to learn enough to go from 0 percent to 10 percent correct than to go from 90 percent to 100 percent correct). Hence a reduction in learning time may not be proportionately reflected in performance scores. Fourth, when trying to show no difference in learning, one must be careful to use a statistical test with sufficient power. With very few subjects or high variability, no learning manipulation will cause a significant difference. Schuster (1976*a*) interpreted his findings as nonsignificant. The results actually showed a strong trend in the opposite direction, namely, that the SALTT students performed substantially worse (t = 1.96, df = 49, p < .06 level in a two-tailed test; p < .05 in a one-tailed test). It would be prudent to assume that, had additional subjects been run, the effect would have been significant; hence the interpretation of nonsignificant differences is inappropriate.

One must be careful when extrapolating short-duration studies to long-duration training programs. For example, in a 15-minute learning study, Borden and Schuster (1976) found that SALTT-taught students recalled 2.5 times as many paired associates as controls. The experiment used students in an introductory psychology subject pool, who are required to spend several hours as subjects in order to satisfy a course requirement. They are often poorly motivated to perform well in an experiment. Unusual procedures such as SALTT can motivate them to perform well for short periods of time. However, if the same procedures are employed over many hours, as in a normal classroom, they may not maintain this superiority. In a study examining SALTT over multiple sessions, Schuster and Wardell (1978) found no benefit of Suggestopedic features after the first hour, suggesting that gains may be short-lived.

The evidence of benefits from the nontraditional components of SALTT procedure is weak. A number of experiments in which the specialized SALTT procedures were deleted showed little performance change (see reviews by Alexander, 1982; Schuster and Gritton, 1986). Schuster and Wardell (1978) removed the suggestive positive atmosphere, recall of a positive learning experience, dramatic presentation and relaxation, and imagery components of the task: only the elimination of imagery reduced performance. Lozanov (1978) has claimed that accelerated learning does not require physical relaxation. His own data show memorization is not enhanced by background music. Recent studies have found little effect of music (Alexander, 1982) or the elimination of dramatic presentation and music (Schuster, 1985). It should be noted that earlier short-duration studies (three minutes' learning time per music segment) did show an advantage for music of 15 to 24 percent during vocabulary learning (Schuster and Mouzon, 1982). Although the use of suggestion can modify the EEG activity to increase the generation of alpha activity, this does not appear to enhance learning (Schuster, 1976*b*). Reducing stress, relative to normal classroom levels, does not enhance learning in general; rather, it helps low-stress (baseline) individuals and hinders high-stress (baseline) individuals (Schuster and Martin, 1980).

Independent Evaluations

There are few independent evaluations of accelerated learning, and these do not support claims that SALTT substantially enhances performance of normal students. The SALTT Society instills in its practitioners a belief that they will change the world (this comment was frequently made by attendees of the 1986 annual meeting), and many practitioners have a commercial interest in promoting the techniques. Such zeal can bias the execution, evaluation, and reporting of results. Scientists accept results more readily when they are obtained by neutral or even skeptical investigators.

One study by non-SALTT proponents was carried out by the Army Research Institute at the Defense Language Institute Foreign Language Center (DLIFLC) (Bush, 1985). Forty students were randomly assigned to either a Suggestopedia or a traditional instructional class to learn Russian. The Suggestopedia section was taught by a Suggestopedia instructor from a commercial firm, the standard class by DLIFLC instructors. The Suggestopedia section met for 10 weeks, whereas the traditional section met for 15 weeks. The Suggestopedia group performed significantly worse on written (45 percent) and speaking (20 percent) tasks, with a weighted score that was 40 percent less than the control subjects.

In another study published by non-SALTT practitioners, Wagner and Tilney (1983) examined learning in a traditional classroom using a SuperLearning tape, with the instructor varying voice quality as suggested by SuperLearning (Ostrander and Schroeder, 1979). Students learned a 300-word German vocabulary over a five-week period. They found the SuperLearning group learned 50 percent less material than the standard classroom group, even though they had comparable class time. Schuster and Gritton (1986:40) fault this study for not utilizing all the elements of SALTT to see the interactive effects. This is a valid critique, although it is discouraging that the most unique component of SALTT (the music review) produced such poor acquisition. One must be cautious in evaluating negative instances of SALTT procedures used in SALTT experiments, for the negative results are generally also confounded by factors such as the instructor effect.

DIRECTION AND DESIGN OF FUTURE RESEARCH

Accelerated learning procedures provide packaged educational programs that incorporate traditional and nontraditional instructional elements. There is little evidence that the modest empirical benefits of SALTT instruction are derived from the nontraditional elements. Accelerated learning approaches deal with multiple aspects of instruction, including teacher motivation, student motivation, material presentation, elaboration, and assessment. This attempt to deal with the whole range of instructional issues is not typical for most instructional interventions (e.g., computer-assisted instruction).

The evidence available, however, does not suggest that the application of packaged accelerated learning programs will greatly benefit Army training. The nontraditional elements (e.g., relaxed environment with very positive instruction) are somewhat at odds with traditional instructional styles.

The Army can, however, distill components of cognitive psychology and accelerated learning to apply them to Army training. It should monitor and support research to identify procedures that reliably enhance learning. Additional basic research is needed to produce guidelines for instruction (e.g., how often should a component skill be practiced, with what spacing and elaboration, to be useful a year after the training course ends?). It is important that new procedures evaluate the interaction of quality of instruction, practice, study time, motivation of the learner, and matching of the training paradigm to the job demands. In addition, the Army should evaluate its own training programs to identify the transferrable elements of effective instruction to other instructors and training procedures.

The formal evaluation of competing training programs is an expensive procedure and should generally not be undertaken unless: (1) there is reliable laboratory evidence that the new techniques produce a benefit; (2) the techniques can be taught to Army instructional personnel; (3) there is reason to believe the techniques can be cost-effective; and (4) the evaluation is done with sufficient care to either significantly enhance our understanding of the approach or provide decision makers information that allows them to determine the applicability of the approach based on the new data. Nonlaboratory evaluations should be carried out by researchers who are not promoters of the techniques. The relative effectiveness and benefits of new training techniques should be made available to the providers of instructional material and to instructors.

This information should be presented in a manner that can directly influence training activities (e.g., guidelines for different types of lessons, computer procedures that can directly influence pedagogy, spacing, and repetition of new material).

It is unlikely that new techniques will increase learning rates by a factor of ten, as some approaches suggest, but careful application and extension of cognitive science and instructional principles could bring about a substantial enhancement of training effectiveness.

SOURCES OF INFORMATION

The subcommittee on accelerated learning focused its work largely on a particular learning package referred to as Suggestive Accelerative Learning and Teaching Techniques (SALTT). Our conclusions are based on reviews of the SALTT literature (published in the *Journal of the Society for Accelerative Learning and Teaching*) and on basic research in the area of effective instruction. Additional information about SALTT was obtained from practitioners and researchers at the annual meeting of the Society for Accelerative Learning and Teaching in April 1986. Two papers prepared for the committee (see Appendix B) were very useful: Slavin provided a thorough review of literature on the teacher's contribution to effective instruction, and Harris and Rosenthal provided an evaluation of the likely contribution of expectations to learning in a SALTT environment.

5

Improving Motor Skills

Many strategies can be employed to enhance human motor performance. The Army has already incorporated into military instruction many proven psychological techniques, such as demonstration or modeling, feedback, and reinforcement. The research basis for some of the newer techniques, however, has not been clearly established, although the sponsors of these techniques make claims of extraordinary improvements in performance.

Three strategies are discussed in this chapter: mental practice, visual concentration, and biofeedback. Of the three, mental practice appears to be the most promising. It has been shown to produce impressive gains in performance, gains that are even larger when combined with physical practice. The evidence on visual training exercises is less impressive. While improving vision in general, the exercises have not been shown to enhance performance; however, these results are based on a relatively small research literature, and further investigation may reveal a relation. A larger research literature exists with regard to biofeedback. While the promise of enhancement remains, research on biofeedback to date has largely failed to demonstrate clear effects.

MENTAL PRACTICE

According to Richardson (1967), "mental practice refers to the symbolic rehearsal of a physical activity in the absence of any gross muscular movements" (p. 95). In real life, mental practice is evident, for example, when a golfer closes his eyes and in imagination goes through the motions of putting (Richardson, 1967). In research studies, to create similar

61

conditions, demonstration of a skill to subjects (or having subjects perform the skill a few times) is usually followed by asking students to mentally practice the skill a specified number of times or as many times as possible within an allotted period. Beyond this, the type of symbolic activity is largely unspecified. Some subjects may therefore employ visual imagery of the skill, others may talk their way through the skill, and still others may use a combination of both strategies. The diffuse nature of this construct not only makes it difficult to control experimentally, but also results in the same topic's being investigated under a variety of other names—for example, symbolic rehearsal, imaginary practice, implicit practice, mental rehearsal, conceptualizing practice, and mental preparation.

Most experiments on skill acquisition have been variants of a research design that employs four groups of subjects randomly selected from a homogeneous population or equated on initial levels of performance. These groups are (1) mental practice, (2) physical practice, (3) combined physical and mental practice, and (4) no physical or mental practice (control). Most studies have compared the performances (before and after) of subjects who had previous mental practice to a control group that had not received instructions on mental practice. In the mental practice group, the subjects rehearse the skill in imagination for a set amount of time. Subjects in the control group are instructed not to practice the skill physically or mentally during the interval. A more appropriate control would require subjects in the no-practice group to participate in the same number of practice sessions as the mental and physical practice groups, but with activity that was irrelevant to the task. In many studies, mental practice and control groups are contrasted to a physical practice group and a group receiving combined mental and physical practice. The practice period instituted varies considerably in the number of trials in each practice session and in the total number and spacing of trials. In the combined mental and physical practice groups, practice periods usually involve having subjects either alternate mental and physical practice trials, mentally practice a number of trials and then physically practice, or physically practice a number of trials and then mentally practice. Following this practice period, the subjects' skills were tested under standard conditions to determine whether their performance scores differed as a result of the practice condition administered.

PREVIOUS REVIEWS

Several people have reviewed research examining the effects of mental practice on motor learning and skilled performance on a selective basis. The reviews by Richardson (1967) and Corbin (1972) included 22 to 56 studies and provided contradictory conclusions. Richardson (1967) reviewed studies of three types: (1) those that focused on how mental practice could facilitate the initial acquisition of a perceptual motor skill, (2) those that focused on aiding the continued retention of a motor skill, and (3) those that focused on improving the immediate performance of a skill. He concluded that in a majority of the studies reviewed, mental practice facilitated the acquisition of a motor skill. At that time there were not enough studies to draw any conclusions regarding the effect of mental practice on retention or immediate performance of a task.

Five years later, Corbin (1972) reviewed many other factors that could affect mental practice and was much more cautious in his interpretation of the effects of mental practice on acquisition and retention of skilled motor behavior. In fact, he maintained that the studies were inconclusive and that a host of individual, task, and methodological factors used with mental practice produced different results.

In a 1982 review of "mental preparation," Weinberg reviewed 27 studies dealing with mental practice. Although Weinberg noted the equivocal nature of this literature, he maintained that the following consistencies were apparent: (1) physical practice is better than mental practice; (2) a minimum skill proficiency is needed in order for mental practice to be effective; and (3) mental practice combined and alternated with physical practice is more effective than either physical or mental practice alone. The latter conclusion is similar to Richardson's (1967) cautious inference that the combined practice group is as good as or better than the physical practice trials only.

The most comprehensive review of the mental practice literature to date is that of Feltz and Landers (1983). This study used meta-analysis techniques proposed by Glass (1977). (For a review of these techniques see the paper prepared for the committee by Deborah L. Feltz, Daniel M. Landers, and Betsy J. Becker, Appendix B.) A search of published and unpublished literature yielded 60 studies in which mental practice was contrasted to a simple or placebo control. Collectively, mental practice effects were examined across 50 different tasks, ranging from dart throwing to maze learning. Analysis of the resulting 146 effect sizes yielded an overall average effect size for mental practice of 0.48. Except for the conclusion reached by Corbin (1972), Feltz and Landers's overall findings supported the conclusions of other reviewers that "mentally practicing a motor skill influences performance somewhat better than no practice at all" (Feltz and Landers, 1983:25).

Feltz and Landers also examined several variables believed to moderate the effects of mental practice. Results from these comparisons indicated that larger effect sizes were found: (1) in published compared with unpublished studies; (2) when the posttest was given a longer time after mental practice rather than immediately after; and (3) in studies employing cognitive tasks as opposed to motor and strength tasks. Subsequent polynomial regression analysis revealed that this latter, highly robust finding was dependent on the time or number of trials subjects were allowed to mentally practice. Motor tasks having a substantial cognitive component (i.e., card sorting, pegboard test, maze learning, symbol digit test) benefited from only a few trials or a few minutes' engagement in mental practice. By contrast, when tasks that primarily involved strength or motor components were examined, larger effects were evident only when subjects mentally practiced for 10 or more minutes or 20 or more trials. The results also showed no differences in effect sizes for sex, age, self-paced versus reactive tasks, and type of research design.

Based on their comprehensive review, Feltz and Landers concluded that "mental practice effects are primarily associated with cognitive-symbolic rather than motor elements of the task" and that these effects "are not just limited to early learning—they are found in early and later stages of learning and may be task specific" (1983:45–46). This latter conclusion does not support Weinberg's (1982) conclusion that for mental practice to be effective individuals must achieve a minimal skill proficiency.

The most recent review of the mental practice literature is the paper by Feltz, Landers, and Becker. The majority of the studies (69 percent) reviewed were the same as in the 1983 review, with 14 additional studies. They examined: (1) learning effects by means of effect sizes for pretest-to-posttest differences, (2) mental practice effects compared with no practice, physical practice, and mental and physical practice, and (3) effect sizes using more modern meta-analytic procedures recommended by Hedges and Olkin (1985). Only studies containing complete data for pretest and posttest comparisons were included in the review: as a result, 48 studies for 223 separate samples were reviewed.

The results revealed that the average difference in effect size from pretest to posttest across all types of practice treatments was 0.43 standard deviations and that this differed significantly from zero ($p < .05$). The mean change for all practice conditions was significantly greater than zero, with physical practice showing the greatest change effects (0.79), followed by the combined physical and mental practice group (0.62), and the control group showing the smallest change effects (0.22). The average weighted pretest–posttest effect size for mental practice groups (0.47) was very close to the 0.48 unweighted effect size reported by Feltz and Landers (1983). Contrary to what has been previously theorized in the literature (Corbin, 1972; Weinberg, 1982), combined mental and physical practice does not appear to be more effective than either mental or physical practice alone.

When the overall effects were broken down to examine the moderating variables of task type and type of dependent measure, most of the variation was found in dependent measures of accuracy and time-on-target or time-in-balance and in tasks that were essentially motor (versus cognitive or strength). The failure to find differences for cognitive tasks as well as for speed, distance, and form-dependent measures was due to the insufficient number of samples (N < 3) having these characteristics.

Although the physical practice group generally had the highest effect sizes, those of the combined physical and mental practice group were relatively close. For task measures of time-on-target or time-in-balance, the combined practice group actually had a larger difference score effect size than either the physical or mental practice groups. However, this finding is of questionable significance due to the relatively small number of samples and a much larger standard error of measurement.

The fact that many of the tasks in the studies reviewed were gross motor tasks involving accuracy of dart throwing, basketball foul shooting, ball striking, golf chip shots, bowling, and so on lends greater assurance that these findings would generalize to tasks of significance to military performance (e.g., marksmanship). The merging of mental practice with varying combinations of physical practice may lend itself to military applications. For some tasks for which actual physical practice may either be expensive, time-consuming, or physically or mentally fatiguing, the combined practice may be advantageous, since the effects are nearly as good as physical practice with only half the number of physical practice trials. It might be useful in future research to find out whether the gap between physical and combined physical and mental practice could be decreased by increasing physical practice relative to mental practice trials (e.g., a 60:40 or 70:30 ratio of physical to mental practice trials).

THEORETICAL EXPLANATIONS FOR MENTAL PRACTICE

There are two main theories to explain the effects of mental practice. The first explanation, termed symbolic learning (Sackett, 1934), posits that mental practice gives a performer the opportunity to rehearse the sequence of movements as symbolic components of the task. Most real-life tasks include components of symbolic (verbalizable) and nonsymbolic (perceptual-motor) activity. Given an opportunity for mental practice, covert rehearsal of the symbolic components of the task can occur, and overt practice can strengthen these activities. Thus, according to this theory, mental practice facilitates performance only to the extent that symbolically encoded components are relatively important.

A second type of theory, termed the neuromuscular theory (Jacobson, 1932), posits that it is possible to inhibit peripheral motor activity. This theory suggests that minimal, or low-gain, neuromuscular efferent patterns during imagined movement should be identical (in timing and in muscles used) to those patterns generated during overt movement, but reduced in magnitude. Although no overt movement takes place, this minute innervation, as indicated by electromyography (EMG), is presumed to transfer to the physical practice situation. According to the theory, only a small, localized efferent from imagery is required for visual and kinesthetic feedback to the motor cortex and thus for the motor schema to be further improved (Hale, 1981) or for the corresponding muscle movement nodes to be primed (Mackay, 1981). Conceivably, then, mental practice involves virtually all the neural activity of the overt performance.

There are a number of problems with the neuromuscular theory. The evidence provided in support of it (see Feltz and Landers, 1983, for a review) does not demonstrate that the low-gain EMG activity during mental practice is similar (i.e., in timing and in muscles used) to the EMG associated with overt performance of the skill, and it does not indicate that the presence of low-gain muscle activity during mental practice is related to subsequent task performance. In essence, investigators testing this theory to date have not measured EMG activity during overt task performance and have not measured performance following assessments of EMG activity during mental practice trials (e.g., Harris and Robinson, 1986).

Furthermore, the idea that mental practice involves "virtually all of the neural activity" related to the overt performance is called into question by studies examining regional cerebral blood flow (rCBF) during overt and covert finger movements (Roland, Larsen, et al., 1980; Roland, Skinhoj, et al., 1980). With the assumption that rCBF indicates which part of the brain is being activated, Roland et al. found that, compared with the rCBF associated with programming and control during the actual execution of finger movements, mental practice of the same sequence resulted in some brain regions' not being activated (i.e., primary sensorimotor hand area), and the rCBF in the supplementary motor area's being only 60 percent of the increase observed during actual execution. Thus, it appears that the programming during mental practice is qualitatively and quantitatively different from the programming that takes place during physical practice.

Perhaps the low-gain muscle activity that is commonly observed during mental practice may have nothing to do with programming. It may simply be an artifact associated with "priming" for the upcoming activity (e.g., arousal-attention set, Schmidt, 1982) or the idiosyncratic tendency through imagination of movement for some subjects to produce muscular impulses that correspond to the overtly produced motion (so-called Carpenter effect, Cratty, 1973).

Finally, examination of key experiments (Johnson, 1982; Kohl and Roenker, 1983; Mackay, 1981; Ryan and Simons, 1983) has led reviewers to conclude that the locus of mental practice effects are cognitive-symbolic rather than motor (Annett, 1985; Feltz and Landers, 1983). As summarized by Annett (1985:194):

What seems to be emerging is that the representations which are most effective in mental practice are of a rather abstract kind, such as spatial context in Johnson's experiments, core meaning in Mackay's experiments, and control rules rather than specific movements in the tracing experiment. If each of these rather different skills is thought of as being controlled by a motor plan then it would appear that rehearsal of critical and invariant elements of the plan which may be represented in imagery is the source of mental practice effects. The executive details of the plan, which may in any case have to be varied from time to time to meet variable conditions, probably contribute little and may not be laid down in a permanent store.

The idea that mental practice effects derive from "rehearsal of critical and invariant elements of the plan" is not the only cognitive explanation for mental practice. Other investigators (Tversky and Kahneman, 1973) suggest an "availability idea," that is, that well-rehearsed images are stored in easily retrievable places in the brain. Greater rehearsal would then allow the image to "spring to mind more quickly" and produce the belief that the image is more likely to occur as a consequence. This latter idea is similar to the idea of "images of achievement," which is currently being promoted as a central concept in a marketed self-improvement program dealing with the "neuropsychology of achievement." This self-help program has been singled out for discussion since it is the most highly developed and influential mental practice program currently being marketed, and it purports to provide a breakthrough in scientific under-standing of how and why mental practice and imagery occurs. The general achievement program as well as videotape programs for a variety of sport skills are products of SyberVision® Systems, Inc., Newark, California. A description and evaluation of the scientific bases for these products are presented in the next section.

SYBERVISION®

On August 29, 1986, two committee members visited SyberVision® Systems headquarters and interviewed Stephen DeVore, founder and president, and Karl Pribram, head of Stanford University's Neuropsy-chology Research Laboratory and director of research for SyberVision® Systems. The discussion centered on a series of audiotapes called "The Neuropsychology of Achievement" (1986) and a set of videotapes (1981) that concentrates on such sport skills as golf (men's, women's, putting, and driving), skiing (downhill and cross-country), tennis, bowling, racquetball, and baseball batting. The videotape packages include a 60-minute videotape of a well-known professional athlete (e.g., Stan Smith, Al Geiberger, Rod Carew), a personal training guide designed to accelerate learning, and four companion audiotapes: (1) an explanation of how SyberVision® works, (2) teaching tips from the professional athlete, (3) psychological characteristics of winners, and (4) the musical score from the videotape for use in imagery recall.

The tapes are of professional quality, showing a performer repeating the skill over and over. The viewing angle and speed (regular and slow motion) repeatedly change so as to reduce habituation. Occasionally the fundamental movement is amplified and simplified through computer graphics, illustrating the biomechanics of the movement. "Synchronized high performance music" is played throughout the tape; the tempo, rhythm, and timing of the music accentuate the ideal tempo, rhythm, and timing associated with optimal performance of the skill.

The videotapes are designed for three levels of use: (1) casual, recreational viewing, (2) biomechanical reinforcement, and (3) neuromuscular programming. Of particular relevance is their use in neuromuscular programming—a "scientifically formulated" procedure for transferring the high performance skills modeled on the tape into the nervous system of the observer. To do this, the instructional manual recommends: (1) relaxing by using breathing and imagery techniques; (2) watching the tape while emphasizing a whole-body, lower, upper, then whole-body focus; (3) upon completion of the tape, turning it off and with eyes closed imagining each motion about ten times in slow motion or in the computerized graphics mode; and (4) reinforcing the learning by repeated viewing of the fundamental skill. Following this sequence of steps is supposed to facilitate the development of "a fluid and graceful rhythm" in synchrony with the skilled movement on the tape.

The "simple physics of neuromuscular programming" is presented in an appendix to the instruction manual, and there is a more complete description on the first audiotape of "The Neuropsychology of Achievement" program, entitled "Your Holographic Brain: The Power of Three-Dimensional Visualization." According to the audiotape, Karl Pribram has proposed that the hologram "provides the long sought after model of how visual sensory information is received, distributed, stored and recalled by the brain." The tape goes on to say that "there is enough laboratory evidence available to demonstrate physiological, biological and mathematical bases for the model."

The evidence presented points to similar parallels between the holographic model and brain function: (1) memory is distributed throughout the brain in a way similar to a holographic image that is spread over the entire surface of a film plate; (2) a single holographic plate comes closest to matching the storage capacity of the human brain (1 cubic centimeter holds 10 billion bytes of information); and (3) both holograms and the brain can construct three-dimensional images.

According to Pribram's theory of brain functioning, the brain and the nervous system act as a holographic processor by having an equivalent object beam (i.e., the eye, since it represents 95 percent of object reality) and reference beam (i.e., the remaining senses) that interact and create interference patterns (waveforms) of nerve impulses. These nerve impulses are transformed by the brain into electromagnetic waveforms with a unique frequency that represents the exact movement specifications. The decomposition of what is seen and sensorily experienced is accomplished mathematically by the brain's ability to perform a Fourier transform (Instruction Manual, 1981). Once the transformation is completed, the electrical frequency (timing, rhythm, and tempo) associated with the movement is distributed and stored throughout the brain. To recall this stored information, the particular reference beam associated with the object beam is needed to trigger the stored motion frequency, "bring it to the surface of memory and neurally reconstruct the stored memory event" (Instruction Manual, 1981, p. 17). Thus, activities such as looking at old photographs may trigger certain emotions that can act as sensory reference beams to evoke vivid three-dimensional images.

Also included in Pribram's analysis of imagery are principles derived from quantum physics and electromagnetic energy. According to the law of quantum physics, images exist in reality because they are waveforms that possess energy and matter. Thus, the more one visualizes the image along with sensory detail and emotion, the greater the electromagnetic force will be, and the more it will mimic concrete reality.

During the interview, DeVore and Pribram confirmed what a search of the literature had already revealed: that no research could be found testing the efficacy of the SyberVision® tapes. Thus, the sole basis for the relationship of tapes to performance is anecdotal accounts and personal testimony of satisfied customers. Although both DeVore and Pribram wished to encourage research into the use of the tapes for neuromuscular programming, this type of research was not compatible with Pribram's research program, and DeVore was not willing to provide much funding for research.

On the basis of the extensive research literature on mental practice, it is conceivable that programs like SyberVision® could improve performance. However, SyberVision® is a broad-based package that includes elements of modeling and imagery, a training guide, tips from professional athletes, and common psychological characteristics of winners. If performance gains were observed, they could not be attributed to mental practice.

The available research literature on mental practice is consistent enough to support a recommendation for the Army to conduct evaluation studies on operational military tasks. However, packages like SyberVision® should not be evaluated apart from the types of mental practice training that already have an established research base. They should be evaluated only within the traditional mental practice paradigm so their pre-post performance effects can be directly compared with physical, mental, combined physical and mental, and placebo-control practice conditions.

Research evidence for neuromuscular programming via holograms and Fourier transforms is elusive. Other than the claims in the SyberVision® videotapes and audiotapes, no direct scientific evidence was found that the brain acts like a holographic processor or performs Fourier transforms. The research to which Pribram referred us (Pribram, Sharafat, and Beekman, 1984) discusses the possible interpretation of research results in light of the holographic model, but the data did not provide any direct support for the model. At the present time, therefore, the cognitive-symbolic theory still remains the most viable explanation for mental practice effects.

CONCLUSIONS

The research generally indicates that mental practice accounts for about half a standard deviation in performance gain over what is observed for controls. When mental practice is examined for motor tasks having significant cognitive components or when it is combined with physical practice, the performance gains are much greater. The explanation for mental practice effects appears to be related to symbolic rehearsal of critical and invariant elements (i.e., control rules) of the motor plan. The research does not indicate support for either Jacobson's neuromuscular theory or Pribram's holographic model as explanations for mental practice.

The overall effectiveness of mental practice supports future research in at least two directions: one is evaluation studies by the Army on operational military tasks; the other is research designed to determine which combinations of mental and physical practice (e.g., 60:40 or 70:30 ratios of physical to mental practice) would best enhance skill acquisition and maintenance, taking into account time, efficiency, and cost.

VISUAL CONCENTRATION

Many military tasks would be enhanced if concentration were improved. Although there are numerous experimental techniques to assess concentration (e.g., the dual-task paradigm and the probe technique), there are so far no concentration- and attention-training techniques derived from experimental research. The training programs designed to develop concentration fall into two categories: (1) cognitive-behavioral techniques (Meichenbaum, 1977) to focus attention better and (2) visual training to develop the eye muscles.

COGNITIVE-BEHAVIORAL TECHNIQUES

According to Schmid and Peper (1986), concentration is "the ability to focus one's attention on the task and thereby not be disturbed or affected by irrelevant external or internal stimuli." Within a cognitive-behavioral framework, Nideffer (1976, 1979, 1981, 1985, 1986) has developed what he has called attentional control training. The training consists of cognitive-behavioral techniques such as breathing–muscle relaxation (to control arousal) and mental rehearsal–positive self-talk (to shut out negative self-thoughts).

In this literature (Nideffer, 1985, 1986), attention is conceived as requiring at least two dimensions: width (broad or narrow) and direction of focus (internal or external). Table 1 illustrates four types of activities that would be performed best with a given attentional style. The idea is that, by knowing the types of attentional focus required by the task, attention can be trained and performance improved (Zaichkowsky, 1984).

There are two major problems with this approach: (1) research or evaluation studies comparing the performances of subjects receiving attentional control training and subjects not receiving training have not been conducted, and (2) other than for the broad-narrow dimension (Reis and Bird, 1982), the questionnaire used to distinguish types of attentional focus (i.e., the Test of Attentional and Interpersonal Style, TAIS) has poor validity—both with respect to factorial validity (Dewey, Brawley, and Allard, in press; Rubl, 1983; Vallerand, 1983; Van Schoyck and Grasha, 1981) and construct validity (Aronson, 1981; Jackson, 1980;

TABLE 1   Activities as a Function of Attentional Style

Width of Focus	Direction	
	Internal	External
Broad	Used to analyze and plan	Used to rapidly assess a situation
Narrow	Used to systematically mentally rehearse a performance situation or to monitor and/or control physical arousal	Used to focus in a nondistractible way on one or two external cues

Turner and Gilliland, 1977; Vallerand, 1983; Zaichkowsky, Jackson, and Aronson, 1982). In addition, it has not discriminated between skilled and unskilled performers (e.g., Jackson, 1980; Landers, Boutcher, and Wang, 1986; Zaichkowsky, Jackson, and Aronson, 1982).

Although some people persist in the belief that it may work, there is no scientific evidence that attentional control training and the concepts underlying it help in any way to improve performance. At this point, this approach to improving concentration does not appear to be promising.

VISUAL TRAINING PROGRAMS

Other programs designed to improve attentional skills assume that concentration is a combined visual and mental skill. The basic rationale is that, for those who are free of inherent visual abnormalities, exercises for the muscles surrounding the eye will improve visual abilities and thus enhance performance. It is claimed that, by training visual abilities, efficient eye movements and tracking abilities can be learned, even while the body is in motion (Revien and Gabor, 1981; Seiderman and Schneider, 1983).

The visual training programs have been designed by optometrists. The most prominent names in this field are W. Harrison, L. Revien, P. Irion, A. Seiderman, S. Schneider, C. Farnesworth, and A. Sherman. Some of these programs are designed for specific skills, whereas others have more widespread applications. One committee member who is also a member of the Visual Performance and Safety Committee of the U.S. Olympic Committee was briefed (March 7 and October 25–26, 1986) by L. Revien, C. Farnesworth, and P. Irion on techniques designed to improve visual skills. What follows are descriptions of some representative approaches to training visual skills with the intent of helping people concentrate or attend to a performance task.

These programs begin with a visual screening or testing. For example, comprehensive visual screenings of athletes have occurred at the 1985 and 1986 Sports Festivals, which are national competitions sponsored by the U.S. Olympic Committee. Included are tests for visual acuity (static and dynamic), contrast sensitivity, saccadic fixation, convergence, accommodation, refraction, eye health, depth perception, phoric-tropic posture, central-peripheral visual recognition, visual reaction time (central and peripheral), eye-body-hand coordination, and vision-balance. A detailed description of the visual tests given at the Sports Festival is given in Coffey and Reichow (1986).

The enhancement or training part of the program usually follows the screening or testing. Proponents maintain that, through a program of exercises, eye muscles and perceptual abilities will be improved. This improvement is usually assessed by retesting.

There are several programs designed to improve marksmanship skills. Information on these types of programs was obtained from Craig Farnesworth, who has worked with one of the creators of one such program, Concentrix. Farnesworth provided specific information on the procedures used in these types of programs.

The programs generally have three parts. The first consists of basic visual training. While keeping their heads still, subjects perform tasks involving eye pursuits and tracking, visual accommodation and convergence, saccades, and binocularity (i.e., phorias).

The second part of such programs is called "advanced visual skills." Numbers are flashed on a screen by a tachistoscope, and the subject must locate those numbers by pointing to a position on the screen. Also included in the advanced skills training is mental imagery and practice of the skill in which improvement is desired (e.g., marksmanship).

The final part of such programs is called "enhancement." The primary intent at this point is to produce a sensory overload so that the subject is forced to adapt quickly to the changing visual conditions. Prism lenses are used to provide visual flexibility in adapting to spatial and lighting conditions. For example, while wearing prism lenses subjects are required to throw bean bags at a target on the wall. Although the prism initially produces throws to the left of the target, subjects eventually learn to adjust so that they begin to consistently hit the target. When the prism glasses are removed, the subjects overcompensate and throw to the right of the target. The idea is that with practice on varied tasks, they will be able to adjust more quickly to changing spatial and lighting conditions.

Another type of sensory overload often provided is the performance of visual tasks while the body is undergoing dynamic movement in space. Subjects are required to read eye charts or fire laser guns at targets on the wall while they are doing feet, knee, and seat drops on a trampoline.

The ProVision Training Program

The ProVision Training Program, developed by L. Revien (Visual Skills, Inc., Great Neck, New York), consists of a set of techniques and exercises on an interactive laser videodisc. ProVision involves basic visual training and some, but not all, of the training in advanced visual skills. The training program is designed to improve (1) speed and span of recognition, (2) stereopsis under stress conditions, (3) spatial awareness and judgment, (4) response to visual stimuli, (5) visual concentration, and (6) visual performance in speed situations. For instance, an exercise for improving visual acuity involves focusing on a rotating spiral after which a tennis ball appears on the screen. If the viewer maintains concentration on the spiral, the ball should appear bigger and to move toward one. There is also a three-dimensional version (with 3-D glasses) of the laser videodisc to magnify this illusion. There are other tests for response time, speed of recognition, and hand-eye coordination.

In its promotional material, ProVision is said to improve the "quality, accuracy, magnitude, speed, and smoothness of visual impulses transmitted to the brain." The material also states that ProVision is the "product of many hours of research, experimentation and successful application by hundreds of professionals and athletes who, in every case, found a decided improvement in their visual skills and in their physical and mental performance." The claimed benefits are supported by the testimonials of fighter pilots and the batting averages of professional baseball players. None of this information is presented in a way that is amenable to scientific evaluation. The fighter pilots, known as the Aggressor Group, are from the 64th Fighter Weapons Squadron at Nellis Air Force Base in Nevada; they were given ten training sessions. Their letters evaluating the training program state that the visual performance of all pilots improved on the ProVision tests. Some pilots felt that they had benefited from the training; however, only three thought that their performance in the air had improved, and all but one pilot recommended how future research should be done in order to clearly demonstrate a relation to pilot performance.

In his October 25, 1986, presentation, Revien mentioned that ten members of the New York Yankees baseball team had received ProVision training. The training sessions ended in June 1980. Revien presented performance statistics before (1979) and after (1980) visual training for seven of the ten players (see Table 2). Six of the seven ballplayers showed improvement in batting averages. Between 1979 and 1980, the players receiving visual training improved their batting averages by 14 points, had six more runs batted in, and had two more home runs. Although data on individuals were not available, Revien reported that the batting averages of all other players not given visual training was .239 in 1980.

There are several problems in interpreting these data as a performance enhancement resulting from visual training. No mention is made of whether random assignment was employed. In addition, the number of subjects in the control group is unclear, and there was no control for a Hawthorne effect. To be able to more clearly attribute this performance enhancement to visual training, the performance measures for the control and the experimental groups should be examined before, during, and immediately following the training period. It is also necessary to demonstrate a training effect for specific visual abilities. Thus, given the incomplete presentation of data and the lack of experimental control, it

TABLE 2   Performance Measures Before and After Visual Training for Seven Members of the New York Yankees Baseball Team

Player	1979				1980			
	AVE	AB	RBI	HR	AVE	AB	RBI	HR
Soderman	.262	357	53	10	.287	257	35	11
Dent	.230	431	32	2	.262	489	52	5
Randolph	.270	574	61	5	.294	513	46	7
Watson	.288	475	71	16	.307	469	68	13
Brown	.250	68	3	2	.260	412	47	14
Cerone	.239	469	61	7	.277	519	85	14
Spencer	.288	295	53	23	.236	259	43	13
Means	.261	432	48	9	.275	419	54	11

NOTE: AVE = batting average, AB = at bats, RBI = runs batted in, HR = home runs.

cannot be concluded that the visual training program was responsible for the observed increases in batting averages.

Research Literature on Visual Training

There is a substantial body of scientific knowledge on visual training. In relation to sports performance, 40 studies have been reviewed by Stine, Arterburn, and Stern (1982). Although the review was published in 1982, inspection of the studies since then supports the following conclusions of these authors: (1) good athletes have better visual abilities than poorer athletes; (2) visual abilities (i.e., span of visual field, recognition, motion perception; depth perception; dynamic visual acuity; convergence; heterophoria; and simultaneous vision) are trainable; and (3) visual training has not been conclusively demonstrated to enhance an athlete's ability to perform.

Although studies demonstrate that many visual abilities are trainable, the transfer to real-world tasks that are relevant to sports or the military has not been demonstrated. Stine, Arterburn, and Stern's final comment is germane: "there are no valid, controlled studies that prove a positive relationship between visual training and athletic performance, nor are there any studies that disprove a relationship" (1982:633).

Direction and Design of Future Research

It is intuitively appealing to think that a relation between visual training and performance might be established. Vision is one of the more important senses in task performance, and training of visual abilities related to a task would seem likely to benefit performance. Visual abilities are trainable, but it is not clear whether training can transfer to tasks relevant to the military. A research study should be conducted to investigate whether visual training exercises can benefit military performance. A secondary research problem could be how long (or how frequently) the training needs to be given to affect performance.

Several considerations should be taken into account in the design of such a study. It is first necessary to screen people for inherent visual abnormalities (e.g., astigmatism) that would not be amenable to training. It is also important to identify a specific task (e.g., marksmanship) for which visual abilities are relevant. Relevant visual abilities might be inferred from comparative studies of good and poor performers. Once the relevant visual abilities are known, visual tests should be designed to closely approximate the characteristics of the criterion task (e.g., marksmanship). Too often the visual test bears no relation to the task to which generalization is desired. According to the long-standing principle of specificity of motor skills (Henry, 1968), the visual training tests must be very similar to the criterion task if transfer is to occur.

It is also important that the criterion task be chosen to provide reliable, sensitive measures of performance. Tasks with subjective performance ratings should be avoided in favor of objective scoring on an interval or ratio scale. For example, target shooting could be used as a criterion task if the target size were adjusted to avoid floor and ceiling effects and scored in millimeter deviations from the center of the target. In addition, to avoid Hawthorne effects, it would be advisable to give the control group something that they believe will help their performance and that occupies the same amount of time. Of course, other than varying visual training versus attentional (placebo) control, all other factors should be held constant (e.g., amount of practice, instruction in marksmanship, testing environment, and conditions).

The U.S. Olympic Committee has recently appropriated $43,000 to conduct a visual training and enhancement program with athletes. Some of this money has been earmarked for a research study on the effects of visual training on the performance of shooters and team handball players. The request for proposals is similar to a 1985 proposal developed by P. Vinger. The study was scheduled to begin in February 1987.

CONCLUSIONS

With regard to improving visual concentration, cognitive-behavioral techniques do not have a research basis to support the relation between training and improved performance. Nideffer's (1985, 1986) bipolar model, which combines width and direction of focus, has received considerable attention because of its heuristic value in purporting to explain individual differences in attentional style. Research studies using Nideffer's measure of attention (Test of Attentional and Interpersonal Style) have found that it lacks both construct and factorial validity. Thus, the scientific basis for what Nideffer calls attentional control training is severely compromised. At this point, the approach does not appear promising, and further evaluation is not recommended.

By contrast, there does appear to be a research basis for the association between visual training exercises and improved vision. A variety of visual abilities can be improved with training of the muscles controlling the eyes. Because of this association, it is often assumed that skilled performance improves as a result of visual training, but there is no satisfactory scientific evidence to show any relation between visual training and performance. It is conceivable, however, that such a relation could be established, and we therefore recommend that research studies be designed to examine the potential of these techniques for skilled performance.

BIOFEEDBACK

In contrast to the literature on visual concentration, the literature on biofeedback includes numerous studies that lend themselves to scientific scrutiny. Our review of this vast literature is restricted to cognitive and motor performances that might have potential military applications.

Biofeedback is essentially the providing of information about an individual's biological functions. In practice, it consists of training individuals to use instruments, such as polygraphs, computers, and physiological equipment, to provide themselves with feedback on their physiological state so they can *learn* "to make voluntary changes in whatever process is being monitored" (Danskin and Crow, 1981). The goal of this training, often with very expensive equipment, is to eventually allow the trainee to regulate the desired bodily changes without instrumentation.

Although there has been considerable biofeedback research dealing with human performance, it has generally failed to clearly demonstrate biofeedback effects, because (1) the effects of biofeedback are often confused with broader therapeutic techniques, such as progressive muscle relaxation or mental imagery (Benson, Dryer, and Hartley, 1978; DeWitt, 1980; French, 1978, 1980; Gillette, 1983; Peper and Schmid, 1983; Powers, 1980; Wilson, Willis, and Bird, 1981), and (2) the specific performance to be enhanced by means of biofeedback is often poorly described, and therefore only diffuse effects (such as general stress reduction) are anticipated. Research on biofeedback used as an approach to stress management is included in Chapter 7.

A major research thrust is the use of biofeedback for the voluntary control of specific cortical or autonomic responses that are assumed or known to be directly related to specific behaviors. For example, knowing that the tachycardia accompanying exercise causes pain in angina pectoris patients suggests that such patients can be taught to lower heart rate so they can tolerate more strenuous exercise before reporting pain (McCroskery et al., 1978). Examination of studies with known links between cortical-autonomic responses and specific behaviors has revealed much more promising results. Lawrence (1984) has reviewed the biofeedback research in areas such as rifle shooting, playing stringed instruments, problem solving, sensory thresholds, learning (reaction time), sleep, manual dexterity in cold environments, and motion sickness. With the exception of problem solving and sensory thresholds, in which EEG biofeedback was employed, Lawrence's review revealed that, compared with a control group, subjects trained in biofeedback techniques performed better. He concluded that for military applications "some promise exists in learned control of specific internal events for specific performances."

A problem with the evidence presented in Lawrence's review is that most of the research consists of single studies that have not been replicated. And in some instances, the authors' subsequent reports (Daniels and Landers, 1981; Finley, Karimian, and Alberti, 1979; Finley et al., 1978; Ford et al., 1980; Landers and Christina, 1986; Sheer, 1977, 1984) failed to replicate initial findings. In what follows, we update many of the topics previously reviewed (Lawrence, 1984; Lawrence and Johnson, 1977; Rockstroh et al., 1984), and include topics not presented in the previous reviews. We discuss the research that has been conducted on each of the following types of feedback: electromyography (EMG), EEG, heart rate (HR), respiration, thermal self-regulation, and multiple autonomic responses.

ELECTROMYOGRAPHY

Several studies have been designed to improve performance by decreasing muscular tension. It is assumed that, by reducing general bodily tension or tension in specific muscle groups to "desirable levels," greater economy of muscular energy would be evident and performance would be enhanced. By providing information about tension that individuals cannot normally perceive, it is maintained that EMG biofeedback can supplement normal proprioceptive mechanisms until they become sufficiently sensitive to provide voluntary control over tension (Basmajian, 1974).

EMG biofeedback training has been used to enhance musical skills, increase hip flexibility to prevent hamstring injury, improve sprinting performance, and improve hand-eye tracking and lateral balancing performance (see Table 3). With few exceptions (Cummings, Wilson, and Bird, 1984; Griffiths et al. 1981; Wilson and Bird, 1981), these studies have shown that EMG levels in the targeted muscle group were reduced more in persons receiving feedback than in controls; however, these results must be viewed cautiously, since feedback effects were not significantly different from those of placebo controls (i.e., relaxation-meditation) (Cummings, Wilson, and Bird, 1984; Griffiths et al., 1981; Wilson and Bird, 1981). In this research it does not appear that EMG biofeedback training has any greater tension-reducing benefits than variants of Jacobson's (1938) progressive muscle relaxation training.

The performance results were equally unimpressive. Only two of the ten studies showed limited support for biofeedback effects on performance. Wilson and Bird (1981) found that improvement in hip flexibility occurred more readily with biofeedback compared with controls, but they were unable to replicate this in a second experiment. Sabourin and Rioux (1979) found that subjects trained in "active" biofeedback (i.e., producing different levels of tension) performed better on memorizing nonsense syllables, rotary pursuit, and simple reaction time. However, subjects undergoing the usual EMG biofeedback procedure of lowering tension levels (called "passive") had significantly lower reaction time performance than controls. Even more revealing were the nonsignificant correlations between EMG levels and performance scores (Blais and Vallerand, 1986; Cummings, Wilson, and Bird, 1984; French, 1980; Morasky, Reynolds, and Sowell, 1983). These findings basically confirm the conclusion derived from Lawrence and Johnson's (1977) review of studies supported by the Defense Advanced Research Project Agency (Smith, 1975; Stoyva and Budzynski, 1973; Tebbs et al., 1974), which found that EMG biofeedback offers little promise for performance enhancement in stressful situations.

This conclusion applies to the existing research in general, which is based on the assumption that lowering muscle tension to a previously undefined level will enhance performance. As Lawrence and Johnson (1977) point out, this is a naive assumption, since muscle relaxation may be maladaptive in many situations requiring a sudden and vigorous physical response.

Surprisingly, none of the investigators cited in Table 3 determined a priori what the desirable level of muscular tension should be for the specific performance task examined. For example, the Morasky et al. studies of musical performance did not compare advanced versus beginning musicians to determine muscular differences that might suggest

TABLE 3 Electromyography Feedback (EMG FDBK) Training and Its Effect on Various Performance (PERF) Measures

Primary Investigator	Subjects	Experimental Conditions	Site Trained	Training Duration	Performance Measure	Results
Morasky et al. (1981)	9 stringed instrument players	(a) FDBK (b) No FDBK	Left forearm extensors	Four 2-hour sessions	None	None
Morasky et al. (1983)	8 clarinet players	(a) FDBK (b) No FDBK	Left forearm extensors	Four 1-hour sessions	Trills/scales	No PERF differences
Wilson et al. (1981) Study I	10 gymnasts	(a) FDBK (b) Self-RELAX	Hip extensors (biceps femoris)	9 sessions over 3 weeks	Hip flexibility	PERF improved in both groups, but was quicker in FDBK group
Study II	18 gymnasts	(a) RELAX + FDBK (b) RELAX (c) Control	Hip extensors (biceps femoris)	8 sessions over 3 weeks	Hip flexibility	No flexibility differences among groups
Cummings et al. (1984)	30 sprinters	(a) FDBK (b) RELAX (c) Control	Hip extensors (biceps femoris)	Eight 10-minute sessions over 4 weeks	Hip flexibility, 50-meter sprint	FDBK and RELAX groups had more hip flexibility than control subjects during retention; no group differences in sprinting PERF
Blais (1986)	20 boys ages 10-13	(a) FDBK (b) Placebo	Frontalis muscle	6 sessions over 2 weeks	Stabilometer lateral balancing task	No PERF differences

Study	Subjects	Conditions	Muscle	Sessions	Task	Results
French (1978)	30 college men	(a) FDBK during training and posttest (b) FDBK during training (c) No FDBK	Frontalis muscle	Nine 20-minute sessions[a]	Stabilometer lateral balancing task	No FDBK effects on PERF (group A = group B)
French (1980)	30 college students	(a) FDBK during training and posttest (b) FDBK during training (c) No FDBK	Frontalis muscle	Nine 20-minute sessions[a]	Rotary pursuit, tracking task	No FDBK effects on PERF (group A = group B)
Sabourin and Rioux (1979)	18 female volunteers	(a) "active" FDBK (b) "passive" FDBK (c) Control	—	Five 30-minute sessions	Nonsense syllables, simple reaction time, rotary pursuit, tracking task	Active FDBK better than control for all PERF tasks; passive FDBK only better than control for rotary pursuit
Griffiths et al. (1981)	50 college students	(a) FDBK (b) Meditation (c) Control	Frontalis muscle	Six 20-minute sessions over 3 weeks	Puzzle assembly task performed underwater	No PERF differences among groups

[a] These sessions included, in addition to auditory EMG biofeedback, progressive relaxation and autogenic training methods. In order to demonstrate a biofeedback effect on PERF, the group receiving feedback during training and posttest (group A) would have had to perform significantly better than the group receiving feedback only during the training sessions (group B).

specific types of feedback training (Morasky, Reynolds, and Sowell, 1983; Morasky, Reynolds, and Clarke, 1981). Earlier work by Basmajian and White (1973) established that, compared with expert trumpet players, beginning players have greater tension in the upper lip than in the lower. Although it has not been investigated, the implication is that improved performance may result from feedback training to suppress the difference in lip tension. Unfortunately, such preliminary EMG comparisons of experts and novices prior to feedback training are not found in this research. As a result, determining which muscle or combination of muscles should be trained and what the criteria should be before training is completed is pure guesswork. Under such circumstances, it is not surprising that this research has yielded very little to suggest a performance enhancement due to EMG biofeedback.

ELECTROENCEPHALOGRAPHY

This section provides an overview of the research on cerebral self-regulation via biofeedback training. We address the behavioral significance of self-regulation of electrocortical parameters, namely, spontaneous EEG activity, event-related potentials, and slow potentials.

Spontaneous EEG Activity

Spontaneous EEG activity refers to signals elicited without a specific eliciting event or stimulus. Early feedback research on an EEG band, referred to as alpha (8 to 12 hertz), showed positive results (Kamiya, 1969; Mulholland, 1962). Initial enthusiasm led investigators to suggest that alpha enhancement facilitated task performance (Nowlis and Kamiya, 1970), improved delayed recall (Green, Green, and Walters, 1969), raised pain thresholds (Gannon and Sternbach, 1971), and shortened the time needed for sleep (Regestein, Buckland, and Pegram, 1973).

Following the first positive results, however, careful methodological examinations of alpha biofeedback (e.g., Paskewitz and Orne, 1975) dampened much of the initial enthusiasm (for reviews see Johnson, 1977; Lawrence and Johnson, 1977; Rockstroh et al., 1984; Yates, 1980). Although subjects could be trained to change the amount of alpha time or amplitude, this rarely produced changes above the prefeedback baseline. It appears that the previous reports of alpha increases were simply a return to baseline after (arousing) attention had been withdrawn from experimental procedures or the feedback display. According to Lynch and Paskewitz (1971:213), "alpha activity occurs in the feedback situation when an individual ceases to pay attention to any number of stimuli which normally block his activity."

The basic question of interest has been whether alpha enhancement will affect behavioral responses. A connection between alpha enhancement through biofeedback and performance has not been consistently demonstrated (for reviews see Johnson, 1977; Lawrence and Johnson, 1977). Enhanced alpha activity has not been related to performance in a short-term memory task or a choice reaction-time task (Beatty, 1973; Kamiya, 1972), nor has it been related to maze learning and perceptual-motor coordination (Levi, 1976). Similarly, alpha training was not related to performance on more complex cognitive tasks requiring any degree of effort (Orne et al., 1975). Finally, alpha enhancement does not prevent sleep loss or substitute for sleep (Hord et al., 1975; Hord et al., 1976), does not provide a recuperative break period (Kamiya, 1972), and does not result in significant pain reduction (Melzack and Perry, 1975).

Based on this evidence, the conclusion reached by Lawrence and Johnson (1977) that training in alpha enhancement does not seem to enhance performance is convincing. It may be that alpha activity represents electrophysiological background activity that is either unrelated to behavioral processes or regulated independently of them (Rockstroh et al., 1984).

An alternative explanation is that the effects of alpha enhancement have been masked by methodological inadequacies or the inability to find relevant behavioral variables. For example, some preliminary data indicate that greater success in solving arithmetic problems has been achieved by feedback on alpha wave *suppression* (Jackson, 1978). Alpha feedback has also been shown to be related to verbal or spatial task changes by localized training of the appropriate cerebral hemisphere. Murphy, Lakey, and Maurek (1976), for example, found that right-handed subjects trained to increase left brain EEG and decrease right brain frequency produced an enhancement in verbally solved arithmetic problems. The relation between right brain alpha and spatial task enhancement was also positive but not significant.

In order for such an approach to be effective, it must be studied further using more sophisticated methodology. One of the problems in studies of hemispheric function is that tasks should not be differentiated on the basis of crude vernacular descriptions of complex psychological processes. According to Gale and Edwards, "mental arithmetic may be seen to be verbal (because the subject has to make calculations) but it may also be seen to be spatial (because the subject may move the digits about in his mind's eye on an imaginary piece of paper)" (1983:120).

Specifying tasks that are appropriate to the psychological processes of interest would solve one methodological problem in EEG biofeedback; other methodological problems must also be addressed. Reviews by Plotkin (1976) and Yates (1980) emphasize the need for better understanding of the oculomotor characteristics (e.g., eyes open–eyes closed, ambient illumination), instructions to subjects about strategies of control, and several issues regarding measurement of alpha. In summarizing the existing research, Yates indicated that "alpha research is, methodologically speaking, in a state of considerable disarray. Rarely can so much effort have been expended for so little result" (Yates, 1980:309).

Another EEG band, occipital theta (3.5 to 7.0 hertz), has been related to an ability to maintain vigilance (Beatty et al., 1974). Such a relation would be important for processing information during monotonous, repetitive tasks in unstimulating environments (e.g., industrial inspection and radar monitoring). In vigilance tasks, a performance decrement usually occurs as a function of time spent continuously monitoring. With one exception (Daniel, 1967), early correlational investigations (Groll, 1966; Williams et al., 1962) showed that, during monotonous monitoring, more theta was observed in the period preceding misses than in the period preceding correct detections. Since the amount of theta activity generally present was found to be unrelated to reaction-time performance (Williams et al., 1962), it might be indirectly related to performance by reflecting changes in arousal level. Beatty and O'Hanlon suggested an activation hypothesis that predicts "that performance should deteriorate as the level of nervous system activation declines over time in the task" (1979:247).

Beatty et al. (1974) provided experimental support for the activation hypothesis. Using operant procedures to regulate occipital theta of college students, these investigators found that suppression of theta enhanced monitoring efficiency, whereas theta augmentation resulted in a deterioration in monitoring efficiency over a two-hour period. These initially very favorable results were not totally supported in subsequent experiments. In a later study using a one-hour vigilance task, Beatty and O'Hanlon (1979) found that subjects trained to reduce theta performed no better than a nonfeedback group. Although the theta-suppressing subjects did detect signals more rapidly than the theta-augmenting subjects, the magnitude of these effects was greatly reduced. Beatty and O'Hanlon (1979) suggested that the monitoring task may not have been long enough to produce a performance decrement, which could be lessened by a suppression of theta. Their results implied that suppression of theta does not increase the level of performance beyond one's capabilities under alerted conditions, but rather retards any existing vigilance decrement.

Other studies (see Lawrence and Johnson, 1977, for a review) conducted in operational environments found either weakened effects (Beatty and O'Hanlon, 1975) or no effects at all (Hord et al., 1975; Morgan and Coates, 1975; Beatty and O'Hanlon, 1975). Considering that many of these studies examined trained naval radar observers, air controllers, and sonar operators, the findings cast considerable doubt on the benefits of this research for performance in situations relevant to the military.

The conclusion reached by Lawrence and Johnson is appropriate (1977:169):

. . . theta suppression may prevent or lessen performance decrements that are typically found in vigilance tasks of long duration. A performance decrement may be a necessary condition for the observation of theta effect, and there are no data to suggest that theta suppression can lead to performance enhancement above initial levels.

This may be the only performance benefit accruing from theta suppression. However, this optimistic appraisal must be viewed with caution until further work is done to establish better reliability and robustness in operational environments.

Event-Related Potentials

Several investigators have studied the relationship between operant control of various event-related potentials (ERPs) and behavior. ERPs refer to common features of brain potentials that are time-locked to an evoking or eliciting event. These potentials are usually labeled with regard to their latency (in milliseconds) from the evoking stimulus. For example, N100 describes a negative wave with a peak after about 100 milliseconds and P300 a positive wave that peaks after about 300 milliseconds.

In this research, behaviors (such as sensory-motor threshold and pain sensitivity) are studied as dependent variables to determine if they change as a function of modification of brain potentials through operant techniques. As pointed out by Lawrence (1984), such central nervous system phenomena could potentially contribute to performance on tasks having low-amplitude signals. Thus, if auditory ERP latencies could be decreased by means of biofeedback techniques, this would be interpreted clinically as reflecting improved hearing.

Operant control of early brain stem potentials (20 to 40 milliseconds), particularly wave V (P8-N1) of the auditory potential and sensory-evoked potentials (N14-P22), has been demonstrated (see Finley, 1984, for a review). In these studies, one group received contingent visual feedback, and their ERPs were compared with those of a yoked, noncontingent control group. Although the contingent feedback did not consistently show significant effects on latency of the ERP components (e.g., Finley, Karimian, and Alberti, 1979), the feedback group achieved significant differences in the amplitude of component V on the second and third days of training. These findings were later replicated. Finley (1984) has also demonstrated an increase in amplitude and a decrease in latency for sensory and motor thresholds (as measured by current intensity necessary to evoke a sensation or thumb twitch) of spine-injured patients showing sensory-motor deficits in the upper extremities.

Similar results have been achieved by other investigators (Roger, 1984; Roger and Garland, 1983) with visually evoked potentials (VEPs). Compared with pseudoconditioned controls, 51 percent of the subjects were given feedback to learn to modify VEPs. As in the above-mentioned studies examining auditory- and sensory-evoked potentials, some subjects who received feedback never learned the task. Roger (1984) found that the personalities of the learners may have been different; they scored higher than nonlearners on restraint, emotional stability, objectivity, and cooperativeness.

Sensitivity to pain has also been modified following operant conditioning of evoked potentials from the orofacial pain path. Rosenfield and co-workers (1984) trained rats to increase or decrease the segments of a potential evoked by electrical shocks to the facial trigeminal nerve (surface P20-70). As a result of this training, the typically observed facial rubbing following shocks to the whiskery area of the face occurred later and less often. Similar results have been found with humans when several feedback-trained subjects decreased both P200 amplitude and pain sensitivity. From their series of studies, Rosenfield et al. (1984) concluded that: (1) the conditioning is localized to that cortical area to which reinforcement contingency is explicitly applied; (2) the correlated perception of pain is localized to the body surface tissue represented in the conditioned cortex; (3) not all body surface areas can be affected by biofeedback of ERPs; and (4) the conditioning of ERPs modified a true pain-evoked component, since its habituation can be blocked by the endorphin-inhibiting drug naloxone.

In summary, several biofeedback studies demonstrate that sensory (auditory, visual), motor, and pain thresholds can be altered by operant feedback techniques. The statistical and methodological rigor demonstrated in most of these studies tends to rule out experimental artifacts as mediators of these behavioral results. It is also quite clear that not all feedback-trained subjects are able to learn control of the ERPs. This naturally limits the widespread applicability of these results to military personnel. For those who can benefit from ERP biofeedback, future research should determine if performance would be improved on operational tasks necessitating decreased auditory, visual, motor, or pain thresholds.

Slow Potentials

Slow potentials refers to the characteristic slow negative potential shifts (DC shifts) recorded from the scalp that are often observed during waiting periods prior to an alerting stimulus (e.g., the preparatory interval in a reaction-time paradigm). This type of potential occurs whenever two stimuli are associated, or contingent, in that the first stimulus (i.e., warning stimulus) signals an upcoming response or information processing required for the second, imperative stimulus. Slow potentials can be positive or negative. The negative slow potential, often referred to as an expectancy wave or contingent negative variation, is considered to be a state of preparation or mobilization of cerebral resources for response anticipation or information processing. By contrast, positive slow wave shifts are believed to reflect a consumption of resources (Birbaumer et al., 1981).

Research has shown that negative slow potentials are associated with better performance than zero or positive shifts. For example, for choice reaction-time (RT) performance, negative shifts in the frontal electrode site were associated with faster and less variable responses (Stamm, 1984). Compared with positive shifts, choice RTs following negative slow potentials were up to 53 milliseconds faster. On the other tasks (e.g., word matching), faster responses were associated with negativity, compared with positive pretask shifts in the parietal location (Stamm, 1984). Furthermore, performance on stimulus-response pairs (number and syllable) was better following negative slow wave shifts (Bauer, 1984). This research demonstrates the effectiveness of negative slow wave shifts on task performance and suggests specificity in the relation between type of task and the location of the negative shift—the cerebral area assumed to contribute to task performance.

Using a paradigm involving feedback generated by movement of a stylized representation of a rocket ship across a television screen (see Elbert et al., 1979, for a detailed description), research has shown that within 80 to 160 trials human subjects can learn to deflect this rocket ship upward or downward by self-regulating their slow wave polarities (Elbert et al., 1980). Subjects were able to learn to control slow potentials without any conscious knowledge about the dependent variable in the biofeedback design (i.e., their own slow cortical potentials). In addition, generalization of control was demonstrated, since subjects were also able to maintain control during trials without continuous feedback. However, slow wave differentiation was reduced when task difficulty was increased.

A comparison of autonomic, muscle tension, and subjective reports indicated that subjects who relied less on somatovisceral maneuvers and more on cognitive strategies (i.e., imagery, thoughts, concentration) were more successful in achieving large differences on tasks requiring negativity than on tasks requiring positivity of the slow wave signal. According to Rockstroh et al. (1984), this latter finding suggests that in these cases the brain regulates itself by brain processes rather than by peripheral mediation.

Considering that negative slow potentials are assumed to indicate preparatory processes to activate brain regions needed for the anticipated task, subjects operantly trained to self-regulate negative potential shifts would be expected to perform better on a variety of tasks. In a series of studies, Lutzenberger and colleagues (Lutzenberger et al., 1979, 1982; Rockstroh et al., 1980, 1982) were able to show that, with feedback to increase rather than decrease slow wave negativity, subjects (1) pressed a button faster (mean RT difference, 13 milliseconds) on transfer trials, (2) checked the solutions of moderately difficult arithmetic problems more quickly (mean latency difference, 6 seconds), and (3) deteriorated less on a 240-trial vigilance task of signal detection performance. It also appeared from the signal detection results that a moderate amount of slow wave change (-5 millivolts) was optimal for best performance, whereas no shifts or shifts greater than -10 millivolts resulted in poorer signal detection.

A recent study (Lutzenberger et al., 1985) found that the preparatory negative slow wave potentials were hemisphere-specific when stimulus input, processing, and motor output were lateralized. It was also shown that this lateralized response could be learned via feedback procedures and that RTs were improved with feedback from the right hemisphere. Rockstroh et al. (1984) suggest that the performance benefits are brought about by the activation of brain regions involved in the task rather than by a modulation of unspecified arousal systems.

The relation between slow wave potentials and performance on a variety of tasks has been observed enough times to promote reasonable confidence in its validity. The effects appear to involve brain regions known to be involved in performance of the task, and the magnitude of the performance differences appears to be impressive enough to warrant further research in operational environments. As pointed out by Lawrence (1984), it is not always clear from these studies "whether the improved performance on any given trial reflects increased slow wave negativity during that trial, or rather ensues from, say, a cumulative effect of previous trials where slow wave negativity has been achieved" (p. 12). In determining its usefulness for relatively simple operational tasks, it would be helpful to know the characteristics of voluntarily regulated slow wave shifts during and immediately preceding performance on a given trial.

Further research is also needed to determine if extended biofeedback or more sophisticated training techniques can overcome the present limitations of relatively poor slow wave differentiation of more complex tasks. Unless this limitation is overcome, self-regulation of slow wave potentials may be incompatible with simultaneous performances which exist in many operational tasks.

HEART RATE

It has been established that individuals can exert control over heart rate (HR). Unlike voluntary control of EEG parameters, nearly all subjects have shown success in controlling HRs by means of cardiac feedback. There is also some evidence (Harris, Stephens, and Brady, 1974; Stephens, Harris, and Brady, 1972) to indicate that voluntary HR increases are easier to achieve than HR decreases.

While extensive research literature exists on exteroceptive feedback effects on HR control, most of this research is directed toward general reduction of arousal rather than enhancement of performance. For review purposes, the performance-based research that is available has been grouped into two areas: (1) HR self-regulation effects on concurrent task performance and (2) HR feedback effects on the economy of effort in performing static and dynamic exercise.

Concurrent Task Performance

In a series of studies, Harris and his colleagues (Harris, Stephens, and Brady, 1974; Stephens, Harris, and Brady, 1972; Stephens et al., 1975) examined whether (1) engaging in concurrent tasks modified voluntary HR control and (2) if this ability to control HR affects concurrent task performance. Harris, Stephens, and Brady (1974) compared subjects trained to raise or lower HR to a rest condition on their ability to perform simple RT tasks, vigilance tasks, and mental arithmetic problems. They found that all subjects could perform the RT and vigilance tasks satisfactorily without interfering with HR self-regulation. For the RT task and for one of the vigilance tasks (i.e., Mackworth Clock Vigilance), there were no discernible effects of HR self-regulation on task performance.

Harris, Stephens, and Brady (1974) also examined vigilance on the Continuous Performance Task. The subject's task was the identification of the letter "x" from among various letters presented every two seconds on a display in front of them. In one part of this study (see Brady et al., 1974), the previous HR control conditions (increase, decrease, and rest) were examined under stressful (i.e., electric shock) and nonstressful conditions. Across all 13 subjects, the accuracy of response (i.e., percentage correctly identified) was not affected by the biofeedback conditions. However, response time to identify the letter "x" was longer when HR was lowered, it was shortest when HR was raised, and it fell between the two when HR was in the rest condition.

Under conditions of stress, subjects could no longer decrease HR, and their ability to increase HR was approximately half that observed under nonstress conditions. As expected, performance accuracy dropped under conditions of stress. Compared with the 73 percent drop in the rest treatment, performance accuracy fell to 60 percent during periods requiring HR decreases. By contrast, under conditions of HR raising, the decrements associated with the stressful electric shocks were virtually eliminated. Harris, Stephens, and Brady (1974) believed that the elimination of the performance decrement as a result of HR raising demonstrated the potential for autonomic self-regulation in reducing performance decrements due to aversive stress. According to Lawrence and Johnson (1977), the relationship of voluntary HR control and task performance under stressful conditions should be studied further.

Economy of Effort in Static and Dynamic Exercise

A recent area of scientific inquiry has been the use of biofeedback to modulate the HR response to exercise. Until now, only therapeutic implications have beeen drawn from this research for the potential benefit of patients with hypertension or angina. However, enough HR biofeedback has been done with healthy human subjects to suggest that physical capacity (both anaerobic and aerobic) might also be enhanced. Although this research has not examined whether subjects trained to control HR can exercise longer, the majority of studies (see Table 4) has shown that subjects trained to self-regulate HR have greater economy of effort in accomplishing the same amount or duration of physical work. This would appear to have potential relevance for many military situations in which sustained physical work may play a significant role in quality of performance.

The effect of HR feedback in attenuating the tachycardia associated with exercise has been consistently demonstrated with dynamic exercise (Fredrikson and Engel, 1985; Goldstein, Ross, and Brady, 1977; Lo and Johnston, 1984; Perski and Engel, 1980; Perski, Tzankoff, and Engel, 1985; Talen and Engel, 1986). In these studies, subjects performed at submaximal levels (75 percent of maximum predicted HR) by either walking or running on a treadmill, pedaling on a bicycle, or performing isotonic weight lifting. Compared with no-feedback control subjects, subjects provided with beat-to-beat information (feedback) about cardiac rate were able to lower HR from 5 to 21 beats per minute while they were engaged in dynamic physical exercise. Where measured, ventilation data suggested improved efficiency, since subjects in the experimental group had a tendency to use less oxygen late in training (Fredrikson and Engel, 1985; Goldstein, Ross, and Brady, 1977; Perski and Engel, 1980; Perski, Tzankoff, and Engel, 1985). These effects were interpreted as learning rather than physical conditioning, since there was no reduction in HR in the control groups exercising without feedback (Fredrikson and

Engel, 1985; Perski and Engel, 1980; Perski, Tzankoff, and Engel, 1985). Furthermore, studies indicate that attention (Perski and Dureman, 1979) and instructions (Lo and Johnston, 1984) can be ruled out as factors mediating the HR training effect.

The evidence for HR attenuation during static muscular work, compared with that during dynamic exercise, is not as consistent. Although subjects trained to increase HR while engaged in varying levels of muscular work have consistently been successful in increasing it above exercise-only levels (Carroll and McGovern, 1983; Clemens and Shattock, 1979; Magnusson, 1976; Moses, Clemens, and Brener, 1986), attempts to train subjects to decrease HR have produced equivocal results. For example, Clemens and Shattock (1979) found that subjects trained in HR biofeedback were also able to decrease HR while engaged in static handgrip exercise at 10, 30, and 50 percent of maximal isometric contraction. Moses, Clemens, and Brener (1986) used the same levels of exercise but did not find that subjects were able to modulate the tachycardia of exercise. In their study, HR control (particularly decreases) was progressively impaired as the exercise demands increased.

A point of current debate concerns whether the above-mentioned static and dynamic exercise findings can be interpreted as evidence for cardiospecific control. With the exception of the Goldstein, Ross, and Brady (1977) study, studies examining dynamic exercise have found that blood pressure does not change; the only apparent training effect appeared to be specific to the target response (HR) of the training (Fredrikson and Engel, 1985). Aside from blood pressure, however, the studies examining ventilation have supported the interpretation that the cardiac changes imposed on exercise were largely nonspecific, involving parallel changes in oxygen consumption and respiratory patterns. Moses et al. (1986) maintain that none of the experiments on static and dynamic exercise supports "the inference that individuals may learn to modify the normal tissue-perfusion functions of the heart" (p. 519). Instead, in most of the studies HR has been closely associated with metabolic rate.

RESPIRATION

As pointed out in the previous section, respiratory factors parallel the HR attenuation that is believed to result from HR feedback during exercise. Although the major research emphasis has been on cardiac feedback, the potential significance of respiration biofeedback for economy of effort in exercise is just beginning to be understood. In fact, it has been suggested by B.D. Hatfield (personal communication, December 16, 1986) that subjects may be able to modulate respiration more easily than HR during exercise.

TABLE 4 Heart Rate Feedback (HR FDBK) Training and Its Effect on Various Measures

Primary Investigator	Subjects	Experimental Conditions	Training Duration	Performance Measure	Results
Fredrikson and Engel (1985)	12 borderline hypertensives	(a) Beat-to-beat FDBK (b) No FDBK	5 days, 25 trials	Cycling HR	FDBK reduced exercise HR 10 beats per minute (bpm)
Talen and Engel (1986)	3 monkeys (*macaca mulatta*)	(a) Exercise only (b) Exercise and FDBK (beat-to-beat)	6–15 weeks, 4 sessions per day	HR while lifting weights	FDBK reduced exercise HR 21 bpm
Lo and Johnston (1984)	36 healthy college students	(a) Verbal instructions to lower HR and blood pressure (b) Interbeat internal FDBK (c) FDBK product of ''b'' and pulse transit time	4 sessions, each with five 6-minute trials	Cycling HR	Product FDBK reduced exercise HR 5 bpm

Study	Subjects	Conditions	Sessions	Task	Results
Perski and Engel (1980)	10 young, untrained subjects	(a) FDBK (b) No FDBK	Five 45-minute sessions	Cycling HR	FDBK reduced exercise HR 15 bpm
Perski et al. (1985)	10 healthy, conditioned men	(a) FDBK (beat-to-beat) (b) No FDBK	4 sessions, each with 5 exercise trials	Cycling HR	FDBK reduced exercise HR 5 bpm
Moses et al. (1986)	20 college men	(a) FDBK (b) No FDBK	Three sessions	Static arm force	No differences between FDBK and control group
Goldstein et al. (1977)	18 adult volunteers	(a) FDBK during exercise (b) No FDBK	10 weekly sessions, five 10-minute trials	Walking on treadmill at 2.5 miles per hour, 6% grade	After 5 weeks, group receiving HR FDBK during exercise had lower HRs (12 bpm) than group with no FDBK
Clemens and Shattock (1979)	8 college men	(a) HR FDBK increase (b) HR FDBK decrease (c) No FDBK	4 consecutive daily sessions, 1-hour duration	Static handgrip of 10%, 30%, & 50%	Subjects demonstrated bidirectional HR control, even with elevated baselines induced by muscular effort

The efficacy of respiration feedback was recently investigated by Hatfield et al. (1986). In this study, 12 aerobically trained athletes were provided with ventilatory feedback on a digital display updated every 15 seconds. With regard to the HR biofeedback studies, the exercise was of greater intensity (i.e., just below calculated ventilatory threshold). A within-subjects design was employed, with subjects receiving, in random order, three conditions (feedback, control, and distraction) during a 36-minute run. The distraction condition consisted of a coincident (antici-pation) timing task with timing feedback given every 3 to 4 seconds. During the control condition, subjects were instructed not to attend to feedback of any kind.

The results revealed that the metabolic cost of the run was undiffer-entiated across conditions. However, minute volume and ventilatory equivalent were significantly reduced with feedback compared with the control and distraction, which were not differentiated. Similar results were found for pressure of end tidal O_2 and CO_2 inhaled by producing relatively more CO_2 with each expiration.

Although this is only a single study, the results are consistent with the running economy results found for HR feedback. Taken together, these results demonstrate that feedback procedures can alter metabolic effi-ciency during intensive activity in trained athletes. These results are particularly impressive considering the near maximal intensity of the work performed. Considering the magnitude of the effects at high levels of exercise intensity, it would be useful in future research to compare HR and respiratory feedback in modulating a number of physiological and biochemical parameters associated with exercise.

THERMAL SELF-REGULATION

Although many clinicians have found thermal training useful as an aid in treating migraine headaches, frostbite or frostnip, and Raynaud's and other vasoconstrictive disorders, thermal self-regulation with biofeedback may have other cold-weather applications as well (Kappes and Mills, 1985; Taub, 1977). For instance, it is known that extrinsic warming of the hands improves manual efficiency and reduces pain in conditions of extreme cold stress (Lockhart, 1968). In order to perform effectively in cold environments, it is necessary to preserve surface finger temperature to prevent a loss of both tactile sensitivity and dexterity. With obvious implications for the military, Kitching, Bentley, and Page (1942) have examined the usefulness of insulation in increasing hand temperature. Unfortunately, such attempts have often been counterproductive for performance, since heavy insulation often obstructs movement and decreases hand efficiency. Thus, it would be advantageous if hand warming in operational environments could be achieved by other means. One alternative that has gained attention recently is the use of biofeedback to increase hand temperature.

Research on the self-regulation of hand temperature in cold environments (see Table 5) has shown, with few exceptions, that feedback training of digital skin temperature can slow a loss of peripheral skin temperature. In the three studies examining performance (Hayduk, 1980, 1982; Kappes, Chapman, and Sullivan, 1986), the ability to maintain hand temperature resulted in increased performance. For example, Hayduk (1980) was able to train six subjects to increase skin temperature by 5.64°F, and this increase was found to be related to decreased pain as well as improved performance on measures of manual and finger dexterity, hand strength, and tactile sensitivity. A one-year follow-up (Hayduk, 1982) confirmed that these same subjects maintained their learned ability to self-regulate hand temperature. Unfortunately, the interpretation of feedback effects in the Hayduk studies is confounded by training consisting of both classical conditioning and biofeedback components. However, other researchers have achieved the same temperature (Kappes and Chapman, 1984; Kappes, Chapman, and Sullivan, 1986) and performance (Kappes, Chapman, and Sullivan, 1986) results as Hayduk, even when training had been restricted to biofeedback practice accompanied by a relaxation audiotape.

With the exception of the Donald and Hovland (1981) study, the studies listed in Table 5 trained and tested subjects' thermoregulatory abilities inside controlled temperature chambers with total body exposure. Training of this type has led to much better transfer of temperature self-regulation to cold environments than studies that have trained subjects in warm environments with only their hands exposed to cold stress (Donald and Hovland, 1981; Simkins and Funk, 1979; Stoffer, Jensen, and Nessett, 1977). Comparisons of indoor and outdoor environments have shown that skin temperatures of subjects trained outdoors increased, while subjects trained indoors could only maintain their temperatures when tested in an outdoor environment (Kappes and Chapman, 1984). By contrast, the temperatures of the control subjects continued to go down in the cold environment. Although the results of this study suggest a thermal specificity of the training environment, subsequent work has failed to confirm this finding (Kappes, Chapman, and Sullivan, 1986).

It has yet to be determined if the impressive performance gains achieved with hand warming can generalize beyond the resting state. Future research needs to determine if self-regulation of hand temperatures can be of operational use in situations in which subjects are more physically active, have greater cognitive load, or are exposed to additional forms of stress (i.e., competition, combat, and so on). It would also appear that

TABLE 5 Thermal Feedback (FDBK) Training and Its Effect on Body Temperatures and Various Performance Measures

Primary Investigator	Subjects	Type of Cold Environment and Temperature	Training Methods and Design	Results		
				Average Temperature Change	Pain Self-Report	Performance
Hayduk (1980)	6	1 experiment in cold chamber; +6.8°F	Classical conditioning (warm water); FDBK = 4.4 hours; imagery/ABA design	+5.64°F	Decreased pain	Increased finger and manual dexterity; greater strength and tactile sensitivity
Zeiner and Pollack (1981)	10	1 experiment in cold chamber; +68°F	FDBK = 3.33 hours; increase versus decrease baseline design	No reliable increase	—	—
Donald and Hovland (1981)	30	Modified refrigerated target limb; +50°F, +75°F, +100.4°F	FDBK = 20 minutes; increase versus decrease design with augmented relaxation	+0.570°F; −0.414°F	—	—

	N					
Hayduk (1982)	6	1 experiment in cold chamber; +6.8°F	1 year follow-up of 1980 study; ABA design	+5.7°F	Same as 1980 study	Same as 1980 study
Kappes and Chapman (1984)	25	Arctic tent in outdoor environment; tent temperature, +52°F; outside temperature, +42°F	FDBK = 4 hours, plus twice daily practice in outdoor versus indoor; tested outdoors pre and post	Outdoor, +3.0°F; indoor, +0.0°F; control, −2.6°F	—	—
Kappes et al. (1986)	48	2 experiments in cold chambers: +37°F and +50°F	FDBK = 4 hours in a 2×2×2 pre- and postdesign; counterbalanced by sex, room temperature and time of day	37°F: FDBK +0.80°F, Cont. −0.60°F; 50°F: FDBK +1.70°F, Cont. −0.20°F	Decreased pain	Increased finger and manual dexterity

biofeedback research on performance in cold environments (mountain-eering and skiing, as well as operational tasks important to the military) should examine subjects' accuracy in recognizing hand temperature. The protocols used in the studies in Table 5 did not call for subjects to be trained in the specific skill of temperature estimation; instead, they were trained to increase temperatures by relaxing. Thus, when asked to estimate their peripheral skin temperature, subjects were uniformly inaccurate (Kappes and Chapman, 1984). Perhaps discrimination could be improved by having subjects, as part of the training protocol, report subjective changes in skin temperature.

MULTIPLE AUTONOMIC RESPONSES

There are a few examples in the research literature of biofeedback for which more than one autonomic response has been given. One study examined the combined effects of feedback and open-focus attention training (a cognitive relaxation procedure) on economy of effort in bicycle ergometer work (Powers, 1980). The four subjects in this study were given 20 sessions of EMG and temperature feedback–open-focus attention training following baseline sessions to determine oxygen consumption, heart rate, and systolic blood pressure. To demonstrate acquisition of skill, subjects had to reduce mean EMG levels as well as finger and toe temperature to preestablished criteria.

The Powers results indicated that all but one subject had significantly improved efficiency of pedaling the bicycle ergometer. For all subjects, the percentage reductions from pretest to posttest were as follows: heart rate, 8.35 percent; oxygen consumption, 11.75 percent; and systolic blood pressure, 9.35 percent. Although the magnitude of these findings is impressive, the failure to employ a placebo control group and the confounding of biofeedback with open-focus training limits a strictly biofeedback interpretation for the findings. Despite these limitations, Powers suggested that the mechanism for the biofeedback self-regulation process

. . . may be an organization by means of attentional cortical open focusing leading to bilateral brain hemisphere synchrony; this, in turn, promotes trophotropic processes of the limbic and midbrain area, normalizing the regulatory centers of the hypothalmus, autonomic nervous system, and reticular activating system. (1980:3928-B)

According to Powers, the end result is a state of homeostasis that facilitates optimal functioning.

In an interesting series of studies by Cowings and associates (Cowings, 1977; Cowings, Billingham, and Toscano, 1977; Cowings and Toscano,

1977, 1982), a training method involving biofeedback, autogenic therapy (Schultz and Luthe, 1969), and distraction from symptoms was employed to deal with problems associated with the onset of motion sickness. Cowings (1977) found that, compared with either biofeedback or autogenic therapy alone, the combination produced larger magnitude, less variable response changes that were more stable over time. The 12-day training method, called "autogenic feedback training" (AFT), also accounts for individual response stereotypy (Lacey et al., 1963) by often presenting up to four simultaneous sources of autonomic feedback (heart rate, respiration rate, blood-volume pulse, galvanic skin response, or intercostal muscle activity). The subjects could choose the feedback (auditory or visual) for the given autonomic variable most relevant to their own autonomic response to the motion sickness experienced before testing. The AFT method is believed to deal directly with the final common path of autonomic manifestations of motion sickness, and thus it should work equally well when the underlying mechanisms are different (e.g., Coriolis acceleration affecting the semicircular canals and linear acceleration affecting the otolith organs).

To create nausegenic stimulation by means of Coriolis acceleration, Cowings employed a rotating chair (6 to 30 revolutions per minute) combined with 45° head movements. Experimental subjects given AFT training were able to withstand the stress of Coriolis acceleration significantly longer than control subjects (Cowings, Billingham, and Toscano, 1977). The findings were the same whether subjects were initially found to be moderately or highly susceptible to Coriolis acceleration (Cowings and Toscano, 1982). Symptoms of motion sickness were alleviated for subjects given AFT training only when compared with subjects performing a distracting task (Black Jack task) or no task at all (Toscano and Cowings, 1982). In this latter study, five of the six subjects undergoing AFT training either significantly reduced or totally suppressed symptoms.

A recent study by Dobie et al. (1986) showed that a treatment combining biofeedback (EMG and temperature) and cognitive-behavioral therapy (confidence building and desensitization) was effective in increasing tolerance to stimulation-eliciting motion sickness. However, when the separate effects due to biofeedback versus cognitive-behavior therapy were examined, only the cognitive-behavior group increased tolerance to stimulation and reported less symptomatology than the biofeedback and control groups. This could suggest that biofeedback may have little to do with Cowings's findings. However, Dobie et al. (1986) interpreted their findings as perhaps due to (1) the minimal stimulation experienced in their study; (2) not basing feedback on the unique type of autonomic distress experienced by subjects during pretest acceleration tests; and (3) not exposing the feedback and control groups to similar adaptive exposures of visually induced motion, as given to the combined and cognitive-behavior groups. Considering these design and procedural variations, it is difficult to conclude much from the Dobie et al. findings. It may be that biofeedback is only efficacious if the symptoms are severe or if the relevant autonomic response system is known and then specifically trained in each individual.

CONCLUSIONS

Two major problems appear repeatedly throughout the research on biofeedback and performance. One problem, which limits any clear interpretation of biofeedback effects, is the use of biofeedback as part of broader therapeutic techniques, for example, biofeedback plus classical conditioning (Hayduk, 1980, 1982) or autogenic therapy (Cowings, Billingham, and Toscano, 1977). The other problem, primarily evident in studies examining training in EMG, EEG (alpha or theta), and HR while subjects are performing tasks, is that no prior knowledge is available concerning what the most desirable levels of EMG, EEG, or HR should be to produce optimal performance on the tasks of interest. In other words, the training criteria were not based on EMG, EEG, or HR levels known to be important for effective task performance.

In the areas in which biofeedback has shown more consistent performance benefits, the relations between, for example, ERP and various thresholds, slow wave potentials and readiness to respond to various tasks, HR or respiration and running economy, and hand warmth and finger dexterity, have been established by previous research. Thus, the direction and magnitude of the physiological parameter to be trained could be more clearly established. Provided subjects could be trained on the particular physiological measure, a performance enhancement was generally found. Until more is learned about the most effective EMG, EEG (alpha or theta), and HR levels for the execution of particular tasks, biofeedback research in these areas should not be pursued.

Although the biofeedback research on event-related and slow wave potentials, HR slowing during exercise, and hand warming has been more consistently related to performance enhancement, specific problems must be addressed before these techniques can be implemented into military training programs. For instance, more research needs to be conducted on the most efficacious training programs for producing a greater percentage of subjects who can be trained. In addition, the generality of the laboratory-generated relations needs to be tested in operational environments important to the military. It needs to be determined if the fairly robust effects found in the laboratory can extend to performance of more complex tasks having greater cognitive load or while physically active subjects are exposed to additional forms of stress (e.g., competition or combat). Further research is also needed to train subjects to determine when EEG, HR, and temperature levels are inappropriate for task performance so the self-regulation process can be initiated.

Finally, the performance effects of biofeedback need to be compared with other performance-enhancing techniques (e.g., autogenic training, relaxation, imagery, knowledge of performance or results). In reviews comparing biofeedback with relaxation training, Silver and Blanchard (1978) concluded that there was no consistent advantage of one form of treatment over the other across all of the psychophysiological disorders examined. Even though certain types of biofeedback have been shown to improve performance, biofeedback has not been shown to work better than some other, less costly techniques. In addition to determining what technique is most efficacious and cost-effective, future research also should consider what technique is most efficient (works faster), durable (beneficial effects hold up longer), generalizable (benefits a larger proportion of people), and convenient (easier to administer and easier to perform) (Silver and Blanchard, 1978).

SOURCES OF INFORMATION

Our conclusions are based on several sources of information that were made available to the subcommittee. The literature on mental practice was reviewed according to meta-analysis procedures in the Feltz, Landers, and Becker paper prepared for the committee. In addition, the subcommittee received briefings from practitioners involved in the development of visual training exercises. Useful information was also conveyed by product developers during site visits. These visits enabled subcommittee members to better understand how training programs are developed from certain assumptions about psychological processes, some of which may have a basis in the research literature.

6

Altering Mental States

The relation between mental states and performance has received considerable attention in scientific and popular writings and therefore came under the committee's scrutiny. There is little doubt that our internal states fluctuate during the course of a day and with different activities. Just how these changes influence performance is less clear. This chapter reveals some shortcomings in the idea of an optimal state for all performances; recent work suggests the existence of more complex processes involving cortical system computations. Further understanding of these processes should have implications for the way in which various techniques for altering states may affect performance.

The idea of brain asymmetry and hemispheric specialization has received considerable attention in recent years by both researchers and practitioners. Despite a history of claims to the contrary, the committee found no evidence that links performance or learning to differences in function between the brain hemispheres. This conclusion is based on the subcommittee's review of literature, which was aided considerably by the availability of an earlier review undertaken by Davidoff and his collaborators (1985). Practical applications have been derived from the assumption of a relation between specialized functions and performance. This assumption is the basis for techniques that claim to enhance different kinds of performances by increasing information-processing functions. The committee evaluates a technique that presents material to the two hemispheres in order to integrate hemispheric activity.

ALTERING MENTAL STATES FOR PEAK PERFORMANCE

There seems to be little doubt that mental state can greatly influence one's ability to perform both physical and mental tasks. The idea that people can achieve an internal state that will be optimal for a broad range of performance has been an appealing one. Typically it has been assumed that there is an optimal level of arousal for performance of a given complexity (Duffy, 1962; Yerkes and Dodson, 1908). Usually the concept of arousal is thought of as an element of stress; there is associated with any level of stress some particular arousal level. According to this view, simple tasks require a high state of arousal in order to maintain alertness; complex tasks require a lower state of arousal in order to reduce reliance on stereotyped or overlearned responses, which tend to dominate when arousal is high (Easterbrook, 1959). This argument has been used to support the idea of an optimal level of arousal that is reduced as task complexity increases.

The optimal arousal concept fits with behavior theories that were popular in the 1950s. These theories required a source of energy or drive to keep the organism active. The discovery of the ascending reticular activating system in the brain (Moruzzi and Magoun, 1949) as a diffuse physiological basis for activating the cortex fostered this conception. As our knowledge of the variety and specificity of neurotransmitter systems has increased (Robbins and Everitt, 1982) and as psychological theories have moved from gross behavior to the study of cognition (Kahneman, 1973), a more complex view of internal states has emerged. We have begun to think of cognition as involving a large number of cortical computations in highly distributed neural systems (Rumelhart and McClelland, 1986). Different transmitter systems serve to modulate these cortical computations in varying ways (Robbins and Everitt, 1982). This underlying complexity makes it much harder to suppose that any training technique will provide optimal conditions for all forms of physical and mental activity. Consider, as an example, the clear changes that seem to take place in one's level of alertness during the course of the day. We often feel at a low level of alertness early in the morning and at a much higher level as the day wears on. Body temperature increases over the course of the day. When alertness is high later in the day, one's speed of responding and sensory thresholds are also improved, but the number of items that can be reported back from memory after a single presentation is reduced (see Posner, 1975, for a review).

Several methods have been designed to alter a person's internal state, either through learned forms of self-control or through the control of others. Collectively these methods are said to produce altered states of consciousness; they include meditation, hypnosis, relaxation, and bio-feedback. At one level these effects should not be surprising. The internal state of the organism is constantly in flux. It changes with time of day, health, interest level, mental activity, and alertness. Since many of these factors are under voluntary control, it is a relatively easy matter to train people to produce different internal states. These altered internal states do affect physiological processes, including the electrical activity recorded from the scalp and autonomic systems (Tart, 1969). Changes in internal state are also frequently accompanied by subjective reports of feelings of well-being, relaxation, increased concentration, and so on (Tart, 1969).

There is also some evidence that differences in internal state may lead to changes in performance. This is particularly true of physical activity. For example, if a person is warned about the occurrence of a signal for which a response is needed, there is a marked change in internal state during the time between the warning and the signal to perform. This change in alertness will lead to more efficient processing than if the person had not been prepared for the signal (Kahneman, 1973). It is also widely believed that the focus of attention during skilled performance is important. During the early phases of skill training, it is useful to concentrate on the skill to be learned, particularly on elements to be imported from already-learned skills (Fitts and Posner, 1967). It is thought that attention serves to aid the transfer of concepts from related skills to the new one. Studies of mental practice confirm the utility of attention to the phases of a skill during learning (see, for example, guided imagery in Chapter 5). There is also evidence that training people to adopt a particular mental state can sometimes produce changes in internal state that, for example, can be measured by EEG and that serve to reduce the usual strong tendency for performance to decline with periods of sustained concentration (Beatty et al., 1974).

These established findings provide little support for the existence of a general state of consciousness that will improve performance over a wide range of skills such as those found in battlefield conditions. Unfortunately, time did not allow the committee to explore the evidence for the wide variety of specific training or induction methods that might provide a basis for technologies for manipulating internal state. The evidence that optimal conditions for rapid responding are different from optimal conditions for the best memory performance raises doubts that there is any generally optimal state. The acts involved in thinking about or attending to information themselves seem to change internal state by producing alterations in blood flow, metabolism, and electrical activity (Hillyard and Kutas, 1983; Roland, 1985) within the neural systems most closely related to the focus of thought. These very specific changes during focal mental activity may serve to counteract any general state induced by training. Nonetheless, it appears to the committee that the Army might undertake careful literature reviews of links between several technologies for altering internal state (e.g., hypnotism, meditation) and change in performance.

There are no theories to date of how modulation of cortical areas by the state of the organism affects the computations performed by these same cortical systems. In the absence of theories that relate computation to state, it is difficult to evaluate claims about how a specific alteration in state will affect performance. The development of knowledge about the relation of changes in state to computation may be the best way to proceed in evaluating claims in this area as well as in fostering future developments in the field. Accordingly, we recommend research support of areas relating changes in state to computation.

One area in which computation studies have been undertaken in relation to neural systems is brain asymmetry and hemispheric specialization. The committee devoted considerable time to a consideration of these findings, which are discussed in the next section.

BRAIN ASYMMETRY

In the last 20 years there has been a dramatic increase in research dealing with the differences in function between the hemispheres of the brain. A substantial body of literature now points to differences in the way the two hemispheres process information, as well as to anatomical, electrophysiological, and metabolic correlates of these functional asymmetries (for reviews, see Bradshaw and Nettleton, 1983; Springer and Deutsch, 1985). Accompanying this research has been much speculation regarding its implications for enhancing human performance. Among the ideas that have been considered as possible ways to enhance performance are (1) increasing the channel capacity of the brain by presenting stimuli to each hemisphere separately, (2) training individuals to utilize hemispheres differentially, (3) selecting individuals for tasks depending on their pattern of hemispheric utilization, and (4) synchronizing the activity of the hemispheres to enable them to work more effectively in concert.

In this section we present briefly what is currently known about hemispheric asymmetry of function and consider each of the strategies for application listed above. In each case we evaluate the link between the state of knowledge in the field of hemispheric asymmetry of function and the rationale for the particular approach, as well as the evidence supporting the value of the technique, that is, the empirical evidence for its usefulness. Both approaches are important in assessing the value of a technique. While a technique may prove to be useful in various applications, it may be only weakly tied to a purported underlying neurological mechanism. Conversely, a technique may follow directly from research findings and be well-founded in theory, yet it may fail for various reasons to be useful in practice.

THE NATURE OF HEMISPHERIC DIFFERENCES

Substantial bodies of research with three types of subjects—unilaterally brain-injured, commissurotomized, and neurologically normal—have converged unequivocally on the basic finding that the hemispheres of the brain are functionally asymmetric. Investigators working with unilaterally brain-injured subjects focus on the defects that follow from damage to one hemisphere. Those working with commissurotomized subjects—split-brain patients who have had fibers connecting the hemispheres cut for medical reasons—compare performance of the two hemispheres by presenting material separately to each one. Testing situations designed to deliver visual, auditory, or tactile material are used for this purpose.

Work with neurologically normal subjects uses many of the same approaches as the work with split-brain subjects, although the presence of fibers connecting the hemispheres leads to the prediction that the differences observed will be considerably smaller in magnitude than those found in commissurotomized patients. In addition, several techniques designed to measure ongoing brain activity have been employed by investigators looking for evidence of asymmetries: electrophysiological recordings, regional cerebral blood flow measurements, and positron emission tomography.

The most robust differences that have been demonstrated between the hemispheres involve the production and perception of speech and language and visual-spatial processing, which are specializations of the left and right hemispheres, respectively. The left hemisphere, in almost all right-handed persons and a majority of left-handed persons, has almost exclusive control over expressive language (i.e., speaking and writing) and appears to be superior to the right hemisphere in most aspects of speech and language *perception* as well (Rasmussen and Milner, 1975; Zaidel, 1978). The right hemisphere, in contrast, is superior to the left in tasks with a visual-spatial component (DeRenzi, Faglioni, and Scotti, 1971; Warrington and Rabin, 1970).

Considerable effort has been expended to extend these findings and develop a catalog of other hemispheric differences and to determine what underlying principles may characterize them. The result has been a shift away from an emphasis on the nature of the stimulus as critical in determining differential hemispheric involvement, to an emphasis on the kind of task a subject must perform with a given stimulus. One widely cited but controversial generalization that accounts for a fair number of findings is the claim that the left hemisphere is specialized for analytic processing, while the right hemisphere is specialized for holistic processing (Bever, 1975).

Following quickly in the wake of research on the nature of hemispheric asymmetry of function has been work dealing with individual differences in the distribution of function between the hemispheres. Handedness and gender, the two variables studied first and most extensively, have both been shown to be related in complex ways to patterns of hemispheric differences (Hardyck and Petrinovich, 1977; McGlone, 1980).

Although few persons would dispute the existence of hemispheric differences, it is important to note that there is considerable controversy in the research on brain asymmetry. A frequently occurring problem is failure to replicate findings. Many factors appear to affect the outcome of studies on brain asymmetry, and until we have a good understanding of their effects, replication of experiments can be problematic. Another concern is the looseness in the basic terminology. *Hemispheric specialization* is sometimes used to refer to an all-or-none difference between the hemispheres, while in other cases it is assumed that both hemispheres possess the ability to perform a given task but do so in ways that differ qualitatively or quantitatively. The extent to which each hemisphere becomes involved in a given task and in what way are questions asked only infrequently. Most investigators are well aware of these difficulties and the limitations they place on interpretation of research findings. The problems tend to be overlooked, however, by more popular extensions of brain asymmetry findings, and the distinction between what can reasonably be taken as fact and what is speculation is too often blurred. In the sections that follow, this distinction is emphasized.

INFORMATION-PROCESSING CAPACITY

Early work with split-brain patients suggested that each hemisphere could function relatively independently. A task such as a simple visual discrimination could be performed by either hemisphere, as long as an opportunity was provided for the right hemisphere to respond nonverbally by pointing. A hypothesis developing from this finding was that the total processing capacity of the brain might be increased by distributing information between the hemispheres so that each side could operate independently; that is, presenting each hemisphere with a different task might double the brain's capacity to deal with information. The greatest support for this hypothesis was predicted to come from patients with surgically separated hemispheres; less dramatic effects were also predicted for neurologically intact subjects.

One experiment required split-brain subjects to pick out target letters from an array of alternatives. In one condition, two letters or digits were flashed in one visual field, hence restricting the input to one hemisphere. In the other condition, stimuli were flashed in each visual field simultaneously, resulting in presentations to both hemispheres. The results did not show an increase in total processing capacity when stimuli were presented to both hemispheres. Performance was generally higher with unilateral presentation; bilateral presentation frequently produced neglect of the stimuli sent to the right hemisphere (Teng and Sperry, 1973, 1974). More promising findings emerged from another study, in which split-brain patients were compared with normal controls on two simultaneous visual discriminations, one to each hemisphere. While control subjects took considerably longer to respond to two discriminations compared with one, the split-brain patients responded as quickly to two as to one; however, their reaction times were considerably longer than those of the control subjects, making simple interpretation of these findings difficult (Gazzaniga and Sperry, 1966).

More recent work has pointed to the level of difficulty of the simultaneous tasks as critical in determining the outcome of such studies. It appears that the two hemispheres of the brain act as independent channels only if the tasks are relatively easy and do not require attention from both hemispheres at once. When processing demands are increased, the apparent independence of the hemispheres breaks down, and the advantage of separate presentation to each hemisphere is lost (Kreuter, Kinsbourne, and Trevarthen, 1972). Effects with neurologically normal subjects would be expected to be even weaker, since the two hemispheres remain in constant communication at the cortical as well as subcortical levels. Thus there is no evidence at the present time that would suggest that presentation of material separately to each hemisphere would be of practical value in enhancing processing capacity.

HEMISPHERICITY

The term *hemisphericity* generally refers to the idea that each person may naturally have a preferred mode of cognitive processing that in turn reflects greater activity of the left or right hemisphere of the brain. Attempts to apply this concept to human performance have involved assessing an individual's particular pattern of hemispheric utilization to permit an appropriate match between the individual's processing style and the tasks that are to be assigned to that person. A related application involves attempts to train hemisphericity, that is, to train an individual to utilize the left or right hemisphere to a greater extent, presumably leading to enhanced performance when an appropriate match between person and task is made.

The first step in any evaluation of the concept of hemisphericity and its application to performance involves a review of the paradigms used to measure it. Davidoff et al. (1985) cite four approaches—lateral eye movements, electrophysiology, cognitive tests, and questionnaires.

Lateral eye movements refer to the shift in gaze that occurs when an individual is engaged in cognitive activity. Depending on the nature of the activity, individuals have characteristic and stable patterns of eye movement that have been claimed to reflect hemispheric utilization. A rightward gaze is presumed to reflect greater activity of the left hemisphere, while a leftward gaze is seen as evidence of right hemisphere involvement. A thorough review of the eye movement literature by Erlichman and Weinberger (1978), however, concluded that the link between eye movements and hemispheric asymmetry is not well established. Later work is consistent with this conclusion as well (Beaumont, Young, and McManus, 1984).

With regard to electrophysiological recordings to assess hemisphericity, Davidoff et al. (1985) note that there are serious methodological difficulties associated with their use to measure hemispheric asymmetry. While aware that there is considerable debate among neuropsychologists regarding the potential of electrophysiological measures of asymmetry, they conclude that no experimental paradigm has yet been established that would permit a reliable index of lateral hemisphere function (of the sort needed to assess hemisphericity) to be derived from EEG or evoked potential recordings.

Questionnaires have been the most popular measure of hemisphericity. Typical of the questionnaires currently in use is *Your Style of Learning and Thinking* (Torrance and Reynolds, 1980), which contains items asking about an individual's preference for different kinds of cognitive activity. Results obtained with this questionnaire correlate with various measures of creativity, reflecting the developers' belief that "there is considerable evidence to suggest that the essence of creativity is a specialized function of the right hemisphere" (Torrance and Reynolds, 1980:2). Evaluations by Beaumont, Young, and McManus (1984) and Fitzgerald and Hattie (1983) conclude that these questionnaires are poorly constructed psychometrically and weak in their theoretical rationale. Beaumont, Young, and McManus (1984) state that at the present time there is no evidence in the neuropsychological literature to support an association between the right hemisphere and creativity, and hence no basis for the assertion that the questionnaires currently in use can assess the differential contribution of the hemispheres to cognitive function. Nevertheless, such questionnaires continue to be very popular measures of hemisphericity, appearing in the media as well as in various seminars and courses for businesses seeking to make the best possible match between employee and position. Their appeal is their simplicity, both in administration and scoring.

Batteries of cognitive tests have also been used to measure hemispher-icity. As Davidoff et al. (1985) note, a major problem with these tests is the need for independent validation of their relationship to patterns of hemispheric activity. It is often the case that a test is included in a battery because it appears to involve left or right hemisphere skills, although there is no direct, independent determination that it does indeed do so. Thus, a test with a large verbal component may be included to assess involvement of the left hemisphere, although no independent evidence is presented to show this association.

A notable exception to this absence of independent validation is the work on the Cognitive Laterality Battery by Gordon (1986). This battery was adapted from tests of brain-damaged patients that were shown to reflect left or right hemisphere abilities. Gordon's initial attempts to use his battery in an applied setting have met with some success (Gordon, Silverberg-Shalev, and Czernilas, 1982). In particular, he found that combat pilot trainees performed better on tests believed to measure right hemisphere function than did helicopter pilots or navigators. Gordon himself states, however, that

. . . while it is true the tests were selected on the basis of hemispheric research . . . the value of the Cognitive Laterality Battery is that it gives information about the relative performance of these specialized hemispheric skills, and does not measure the relative efficiency or activation of the hemispheres themselves. (1986:224)

In summary, it would appear that at the present time we do not have the kind of independently validated measures of hemisphericity that would make it a truly useful concept. Such measures may be forthcoming, but they are not here yet. Without such measures it is impossible to answer the questions of whether hemisphericity has important implications for performance.

With regard to the related question of training hemispheric involvement, we have no direct evidence that differential hemispheric utilization can be trained. Just as we lack validated measures of hemisphericity, we lack any way to measure the changes in brain hemisphere involvement that are presumed to accompany certain training strategies. As Davidoff et al. (1985) note, cognitive style can probably be affected by training. There is no evidence, however, to show that such modification has a neurological substrate that involves differential utilization of the hemispheres. Such a link may exist; at the present time it has not been demonstrated.

SYNCHRONIZING HEMISPHERIC ACTIVITY

The notion of increased channel capacity resulting from presentation of material to separate hemispheres is based on the assumption that each half of the brain functions independently. Similarly, the concept of hemisphericity emphasizes the differences in function between the hemispheres and the value of differential hemispheric involvement. An entirely different approach to brain asymmetry and its relation to human performance stresses the value of having the hemispheres act synchronously. Hemi-Sync℠, short for Hemispheric Synchronization, is a patented technique developed by Robert Monroe of the Monroe Institute of Applied Sciences in Faber, Virginia. The process uses the phenomenon of binaural beats "to help create simultaneously an identical wave form in both brain hemispheres." (All quotations are from "Inquiry, Information, Innovation," a Monroe Institute information brochure.) To produce binaural beats, a tone of one frequency is presented to one ear and a tone of a slightly different frequency is presented to the other. Given the proper circumstances, one hears a warbling sound whose frequency is equal to the difference between the original tones. According to the Monroe Institute's literature, "this third signal is not an actual sound, but an electrical signal that can only be created by both brain hemispheres acting and working together, simultaneously. The unique coherent brain state that results is known as Hemispheric Synchronization, or Hemi-Sync℠." This identical wave form is believed to assist the user in using "more of his brain power" and to facilitate such diverse activities as sleep, concentration, learning, and surgical recovery because "both hemispheres of the brain can be focused on the same state of awareness at the same time."

The evaluation of Hemi-Sync℠ by the committee involved a search and review of the literature relevant to its underlying rationale, a review of the extensive material provided by the Monroe Institute and others relating to the application of Hemi-Sync℠, and a site visit to the Monroe Institute. The subcommittee toured the facilities and met with Robert Monroe, a staff member, and two professional members of the Institute (a speech pathologist and a clinical psychologist) who use the Hemi-Sync℠ tapes in their work.

There are three main principles underlying Hemi-Sync℠. The first is that presenting two tones of slightly different frequency simultaneously, one to each ear, results in the perception of a third tone as the result of some process involving the two hemispheres. The second principle is that the binaural beat phenomenon results in an alteration of the main frequency component of the EEG such that "frequency following" takes place. The third asserts that certain EEG states facilitate particular types of performance.

With regard to the theoretical rationale underlying Hemi-Sync℠, the scientific literature suggests that the binaural beat effect is most likely due to binaural interaction at the level of the superior olivary nucleus (Oster, 1973), which means that binaural beats are not a cortical phenomenon and are not produced by the two hemispheres working in concert. With regard to frequency following, a small literature relevant to this claim was found. Frequency following in the auditory evoked response has been demonstrated with both tone bursts and continuous tones over a range of frequencies from 70 hertz to 1,500 hertz (Glaser et al., 1976). In addition, frequency following responses to 500-hertz tone bursts presented to the left ear and 540-hertz tone bursts presented to the right ear have been obtained by Hink et al. (1980), demonstrating frequency following to binaural beats under certain conditions. With regard to the third principle, no evidence that frequency following the stimuli employed in Hemi-Sync™ exists was provided by the Monroe Institute or obtained through a search of the literature.

At the site visit, Robert Monroe indicated that the Institute has not focused its efforts on generating the kind of research that would satisfy the criteria for publication in refereed scientific journals. Its emphasis has been on the development of techniques that users find to be beneficial by whatever criteria they personally choose to employ. However, in response to the need of the committee for scientific evidence of the utility of Hemi-Sync™, we were referred to a variety of articles published by members of the Monroe Institute in a newsletter and were given the names of 13 individuals who had reported successful uses in a variety of applications and who could be contacted for further information.

Hemi-Sync™ has been claimed to be of value in a wide variety of educational and therapeutic settings. Of greatest interest for purposes of this report are those applications involving human performance. For the sake of completeness we wish to note that material was provided to us documenting its use in pain control in cancer patients and in cases of alcohol abuse, retardation, autism, and seizure disorders. In these instances patients typically listened to Hemi-Sync™ sounds accompanied by music or other stimuli through headphones as part of their therapy. Reports typically took the form of individual case studies or, in some cases, self-reports of beneficial effects.

The committee found what came closest to formal research designs in three studies of educational applications. In the first study, Hemi-Sync™ was employed with students in the basic broadcasting course at the Defense Information School to determine its effects in enhancing performance and inducing relaxation. The study employed a variety of tapes using Hemi-Sync™ sounds listened to individually through headphones during a ten-week course by 22 subjects whose performance was compared with that of a previous class not using the tapes. Self-reports of stress level and motivation throughout the study, as well as the students' assessment of the tapes' usefulness, were obtained. Although no statistical analyses were reported, the subjective measures produced evidence supporting the value of the tapes. Motivation was reported as higher and stress as generally lower in the tape group, and the group reported that they perceived the tapes as useful. Comparing the test class with the previous class on performance, however, produced mixed results. Although a slightly higher percentage of the test class eventually graduated (50 versus 45.8 percent), more of them required special tutoring than was the case in the control class (66.7 versus 53.7 percent). Thus, the value of the tapes in improving performance was not demonstrated, although some effect in motivation and stress reduction was observed. It is important to note, however, that all participants were fully aware of the purpose of the tapes from the outset, making it possible that expectancy effects or Hawthorne effects were responsible for the results. In addition, in the absence of evidence showing the equivalence of the test group and control group on relevant dimensions, any comparison of the two is open to multiple interpretations, especially in light of the absences and dropouts that occurred in the course of data collection with a small sample.

Another study, conducted by a professor of music who is a member of the Monroe Institute, examined the effect of Hemi-Sync™ on the performance of students required to identify melodic and harmonic intervals as part of an ear training course. Forty-five students participated, with assignment to Hemi-Sync™ and control groups done on a random basis. The series of six taped lectures, each with a pretest and posttest, was identical for both groups, except for the presence of Hemi-Sync™ stimuli in the experimental condition. Students were not informed of the nature of the study, nor were personnel involved in distributing the tapes aware of the assignment of individuals to conditions. A 5.5 percent advantage for the experimental group (averaged across sessions) was found, although the difference was not statistically significant. The investigator notes that the Hemi-Sync™ sounds themselves may have interfered with the sounds the students were asked to judge, resulting in lower performance than might otherwise have been expected.

The third study involved the random assignment of half of a class of 48 community college students enrolled in introductory psychology to a Hemi-Sync™ condition. All students attended the same lectures and used the same text, but the Hemi-Sync™ students supplemented these with a series of tapes consisting of Hemi-Sync™ sounds mixed with sentences, up to four seconds long, defining terms and key concepts in psychology. On five of six tests, the experimental group performed significantly higher, averaging 10.19 percent better performance. The investigator noted the problem of confounding the effects of Hemi-Sync™ with exposure to material on key concepts and reports that, to control for this, the lecturer presented the same statements through headphones to all students in the classroom. The investigator did not, however, acknowledge the advantage that the Hemi-Sync™ group would have as a result of its additional exposure to these concepts on their tapes.

Other references are made in the material that was received by the committee to the use of Hemi-Sync™ in educational settings involving the presentation of stimuli through speakers placed on either side of the classroom. No data were provided from studies using this procedure in a formal classroom setting. Although the presentation of Hemi-Sync™ sounds in free field does not preserve the conditions necessary for binaural beats, the Monroe Institute reports that adequate separation of speakers produces comparable results in terms of frequency following.

The review of Hemi-Sync™ in educational settings presented above illustrates the problem with the evidence that has been presented to support it. Most findings are either anecdotal in nature or weak, with multiple potential confoundings such as failure to ensure equivalence of groups or to obtain pretest data, Hawthorne or expectancy effects, and other problems in interpretation. An additional difficulty in evaluating the use of Hemi-Sync™ in educational settings results from its use in conjunction with other procedures and stimuli such as guided imagery and music. For example, a typical Hemi-Sync™ tape involves the binaural beat stimuli presented at near-threshold levels, embedded in a background of the sounds of ocean surf or music of various types. Hemi-Sync™ as such is rarely studied in isolation; thus its effects, if any, become confounded with the other stimuli and procedures that accompany its presentation.

CONCLUSIONS

A review of the literature on brain asymmetry reveals a variety of interesting differences in function between the hemispheres. The current state of knowledge suggests, however, that attempts to apply what is known about hemispheric differences to the enhancement of learning and performance are premature.

Valid and reliable measures of hemispheric activity in individuals will be necessary before claims linking the performance of an individual to his or her particular pattern of differential hemispheric involvement can be evaluated scientifically. Attempts to increase information-processing capacity by presenting material separately to the two hemispheres do not appear to be useful. Current support for the value of techniques to integrate hemisperic activity to enhance performance (such as Hemi-Sync™) does not meet generally accepted criteria for scientific evidence. Such techniques should be considered further by the Army only if such evidence is provided to and evaluated by the Army Research Institute.

7

Stress Management

None of the topics treated in this volume has received more attention than the management of stress. Its popularity is due at least in part to the more general environment in which we live, referred to by some as the Age of Anxiety. Its importance is due to observed effects on performance. The costs of stress have been widely documented in terms of losses in work time and efficiency. Clearly, techniques that effectively reduce stress are likely also to improve performance. One purpose of this chapter is to review programs and approaches to stress reduction. The review has been aided by a thorough survey of stress reduction programs in the military prepared for the committee by Raymond Novaco (Appendix B). The discussion of techniques is preceded by a more general treatment of the nature of stress. Drawing on a large literature, this section summarizes what we have come to understand as the stress response. Seymour Levine's background paper (Appendix B) provided the committee with a comprehensive review of literature in several disciplines on the relations among stress, arousal, and performance.

Research on stress has resulted in a number of compelling insights. Most notable perhaps is the finding that different techniques for reducing stress are likely to succeed to the extent that they focus on the reduction of uncertainty about, and an increase in control over, important events in a person's environment. To the extent that any technique reduces stress, it will help a person think more clearly, increasing his or her chances of coping with challenging situations. However, the implications of these findings must be developed in the context of institutional constraints. Most efforts to reduce stress in nonmilitary settings are based on the presumption that it is functional to be relieved of stress. This may not be as clearly the case in the military. A soldier's stress may be seen as legitimate and even valuable. Reducing it to very low levels may reduce combat effectiveness. This suggests the larger issue of distinguishing between what one can do and what one ought to do, a dilemma that is discussed in the chapter.

STRESS IN THE MILITARY

That stress management should be of concern to the military is no surprise; in many ways the experiences of a soldier are a paradigm for what behavioral scientists know about stress in both human beings and animals. For a soldier, there is little control over and much uncertainty about events; life is sometimes threatened or, when not actually threatened, endangered in analogous ways; tolerance for error is minimal; and mistakes are generally followed by harsh reprimands and other punishments.

Although stress is generally equated with fear or anxiety, it is useful to remember that other affects are probably part of the stress response in human beings, for example, anger, guilt, shame, and depression or sadness. Boredom might also be mentioned, in light of the fact that considerable amounts of military time, even during war, are spent idly.

Our focus in this chapter is on the deleterious effects of stress. We are mindful of the need for soldiers at work to be motivated and aroused and of the need to introduce stressful conditions during training in order to acclimate the novice to the demands of a new life. Thus, basic training will necessarily have elements that mimic battle and other working military conditions. Soldiers have to get used to arduous, stressful situations. But stress has its costs. We discuss these costs as well as means that have been employed to assist people in coping with stress, even if some of the research and methods may not be readily implemented in military settings.

It is generally believed by the military—and rightly so—that the learning and performance capabilities of soldiers who are under stress are less than they could be if they were not under stress. Moreover, since Selye's (1936) classic work on stress and the more recent acceptance by both the psychological and medical communities of the role of stress in physical illness (e.g., Rahe and Lind, 1971), the military has good reason to be concerned about the losses in work time and efficiency of task performance that arise from ongoing stress, medical leaves, and sick call.

A notable feature of the stressfulness of Army life is the so-called zero defect rule: a single mistake can have lasting negative consequences on a career, both for noncommissioned and for comissioned officers. The anxiety that must be generated by this widely known management principle would seem neither to reduce stress nor to encourage the kind of independent problem solving and risk taking that are part of enhanced performance.

Given this context, the Army is faced with a dilemma: the ultimate work of soldiers and officers is to inflict injury on the enemy or to be prepared to do so, as well as to ward off the enemy's efforts to do the same. The target situation, in other words, is an inherently stressful one. And to prepare young men and women for these unpleasant tasks, the Army intentionally creates conditions during training to get them used to noxious or at least noisome living and working conditions. The basic training that all members of the Army must experience, as well as the highly regimented and frequently uncomfortable living and working conditions, are often experienced as negative, if not actually stressful, by many soldiers.

Recognizing, then, that the business of the armed forces is ultimately (if not always directly) to harm an enemy and that such preparation and readiness are not positive activities, how can one reasonably design interventions of a preventive, remedial, and quasi-therapeutic nature that stand some realistic chance of reducing stress reactions to a moderate level while allowing for effective and efficient learning and performance?

We turn first to a consideration of the nature of stress, drawing on research on both animals and people. We then discuss stress management procedures in general, followed by stress management in military settings. We conclude with a note on ethical issues.

THE NATURE OF STRESS

Our focus is on stress as a psychobiological phenomenon that can and does impair performance, particularly in critical situations such as combat. In broad terms, some small degree of stress may well be a good thing. The time-honored inverted-U relation between arousal level and performance indicates that some intermediate degree of arousal is optimal for performance, the degree dependent on the task and many other factors. Indeed, too little arousal (boredom) may well be an issue of concern for a peacetime army.

Arousal and stress are to some degree related notions; *arousal* is a broad and ill-defined term, whereas *stress* at least has specific biological indicators (e.g., concentrations of cortisol in the blood, catecholamines; secretion of endorphins). In this chapter we use *stress* to refer to the right side of the inverted-U, that is, the degree of arousal that impairs performance. Using such a definition has made possible a much clearer characterization of the nature of stress. In the discussion that follows, selected examples are given; extensive documentation is provided in the papers prepared for the committee by Levine and Novaco (see Appendix B).

Stress and anxiety are core concepts in the field of psychopathology and are implicated in the full range of disorders, from psychophysiological disorders such as essential hypertension and asthma, to the several anxiety disorders, to the affective disorders and schizophrenia. Indeed, a prevalent general model, or paradigm, is termed *diathesis-stress*; it assumes that most disorders arise from a complex interaction between environmental stressors and (usually) biological predispositions that make a given individual more prone to break down under a given stressor.

There is a good deal of evidence that stress and physical illness are related, in both animals and human beings. Considerable correlational research has been and is being done on measuring stress in people (since one is constrained ethically from employing true experimental designs). One example is the Social Readjustment Rating Scale of Holmes and Rahe (1967). Subjects are given a list of life events (e.g., death of spouse, being fired from a job, changes in responsibilities at work, vacation, Christmas) and are asked to indicate those that have occurred recently. High scores have been related to heart attacks (Rahe and Lind, 1971), onset of leukemia (Wold, 1968), and colds and fevers (Holmes and Holmes, 1970). With due caution given to the correlational nature of the findings—being sick could lead to dismissal from a job, for example—the relations are striking enough to encourage similar research, some with improved instruments. Indeed, a succession of small stressors can also lead to disruption and breakdown.

How might stress of a psychological nature negatively affect the physical (in addition to the psychological) health of a person? The immune system has been implicated; Jammot et al. (1983) have shown lower levels of immunoglobin (lg A) in people after great stress than under little stress. Since lower levels of lg A are associated with certain infections, an explanatory link may emerge.

A moderating factor that is being researched is hardiness, a constellation of behaviors and attitudes that Kobasa, Maddi, and Kahn (1982) find to be associated with resistance to the deleterious effects of stress. People high in commitment (rather than being alienated), control (rather than feeling helpless), and challenge (rather than viewing challenges as a threat) get sick less often. Hardiness may thus moderate the relation between stress and illness.

There is a growing consensus in the vast animal and human research literatures. Earlier, in the classic studies of Selye (1936), stress was seen primarily as physical trauma—tissue damage, blood loss, shock, exposure to cold. Selye identified major categories of response to stress: activation of the autonomic nervous system and pituitary-adrenal axis, impairment of the immune system, gastrointestinal disturbances, and impairment of behavioral performance (Levine; Novaco). All these aspects (and more) of the stress response have been studied at length in the animal and human literature, with an initial focus on the adrenal gland and behavior; the immune system has only recently become a focus, engendering the new field of psychoneuroimmunology (Levine paper).

It is now clear that stress cannot be identified simply with physical trauma: stress is in the eye of the beholder. The extent to which situations are stressful is determined by appraisal—how the individual understands, interprets, sees, and feels about a situation (Lazarus, 1966; Baum, Singer, and Baum, 1981). It is fundamentally a cognitive phenomenon, depending more on how the individual construes the situation than on the nature of the situation itself. The key aspects are uncertainty and control—the less knowledge the individual has about a potentially harmful situation, the less control he or she feels can be exerted, and the more stressful the situation is. Conversely, the more understanding and certainty the individual has about a situation, the more he or she feels in control, and the less stressful it becomes. Another way to put this is that stress arises ". . . in the face of *demands that tax or exceed the resources of the system* or . . . demands to which there are no readily available or automatic adaptive responses" (Lazarus and Cohen, 1977:109).

We and other mammals appear to be driven by nature toward certainty. This may in fact be the basis for the existence of various belief systems. A person firmly committed to such a belief system does in fact "understand" the world and the nature of the controls that operate, even though this understanding may be fallacious. The anthropologist Malinowski (1948) made a similar point years ago in his classic book on magic, science, and religion.

There are many examples from both the human and the animal literatures. The first time a person donates blood, for example, the concentration of cortisol in the blood (a measure of the adrenocortical response to stress) skyrockets. The second time, there may be no elevation, yet the physical trauma is the same (blood loss—hemorrhaging—is a traditional physical stressor) (Levine). In an early study of the Harvard boat race (Renold et al., 1951), a decline in eosinophil count was marked in the crew four hours after the race. This decline could have been due entirely to the physical stress of the race, but the coxswains and coaches had similar eosinophil drops, even though their stress was purely psychological.

A classic study was conducted on human beings in parachute training (Ursin, Baade, and Levine, 1978). In that study, the hormonal and behavioral responses of a group of Norwegian paratroop trainees were examined after repeated jumps off a 10-meter tower on a guide wire. After the first jump there was a dramatic elevation of cortisol in the blood, but as soon as the second jump there was a significant drop to basal levels; basal levels persisted on subsequent jumps. It is also important to note that the fear ratings changed dramatically following the first and second jumps: there was very little fear expressed after the second jump, even though there had been a very high rating of fear prior to the first jump.

To take a simple example from the animal literature (Dess et al., 1983), dogs were subjected to a series of electric shocks that were either unpredictable or predictable. The predictable condition involved presenting the animal with a tone prior to the onset of shock. In the unpredictable condition, no such tone was presented. The adrenocortical response observed on subsequent testing of these animals clearly indicated the importance of reducing uncertainty by predictability. Animals that did not have the signal preceding the shock showed an adrenocortical response that was two to three times that observed in animals with previous predictable shock experiences.

It should be noted that the procedures used in this experiment are typical of those used in experiments examining learned helplessness (Seligman, 1975). Learned helplessness refers to the protracted effects of prolonged exposure to unpredictable and uncontrollable stimuli of an aversive nature. It has been observed that organisms exposed to this type of experimental regimen show long-term deficits in their ability to perform appropriately under subsequent testing conditions. Furthermore, these animals show a much greater increase in adrenocortical activity when exposed to novel stimuli (Levine et al., 1973) than do control animals. Thus, an organism exposed to an uncontrollable and unpredictable set of aversive stimuli shows not only a dramatic increase in adrenocortical activity while exposed to these conditions but also long-term deficits in other, unrelated test conditions.

The key element in these examples and in virtually all recent work on stress is uncertainty (Mason, 1968; Levine). This applies also to positive or rewarding events. In animal studies, frustration, with the attendant elevation of serum corticosterone (an animal hormone comparable to human cortisol), can be induced by changing the conditions of reward so that previously learned expectancies no longer hold.

The key is that the uncertainty exists in the organism. Situations are stressful if the organism views them as being unpredictable and uncontrollable. Studies of troops in Vietnam seem consistent with this view (Bourne, 1970, 1971; Levine). Members of an experienced combat unit of Special Forces enlisted personnel, upon being informed of an impending attack, were enthusiastic and spent much time in task-oriented activities such as fortifying defenses. The concentration of a cortisol metabolite, 17 OHCS, in their urine did not rise on the day of the expected attack. Although they could not directly control the behavior of the enemy, they felt in control of the situation. Their young captain, by contrast, was in a state of uncertainty about whether the orders he would receive would be considered inappropriate by his experienced soldiers. Concentrations of 17 OHCS in his urine were markedly higher on the day of the expected attack.

This research on stress implies that successful strategies for coping involve increased predictability, understanding, knowledge, and a sense of control. It may even be helpful sometimes to simply be able to do something, even if that something does not really control the situation. Rats allowed to fight after receiving strong, unpredictable shock showed far less elevation of serum corticosterone than rats given the same shocks but not allowed to fight (Levine).

STRESS REDUCTION:
GENERAL APPROACHES AND CONSIDERATIONS

A useful way to organize our discussion of stress management is to distinguish between techniques that focus on intrapsychic and individual change versus those that aim to change the environment. For example, if a person feels too warm, he or she can either attempt to cool off (by drinking cool liquids, removing clothing, and so on) or attempt to alter the environment (turning on the air conditioner, and so on). Since environmental change is often very difficult to achieve, behavioral scientists have devoted most of their energies to devising procedures for reducing individuals' stress reactions to negative events.

INDIVIDUAL AND INTRAPSYCHIC APPROACHES

Intrapsychic approaches can be discussed under the following rubrics: arousal reduction, cognitive restructuring and problem solving, and behavioral skills training.

Arousal Reduction

Relaxation Training. Given the fact that stress reactions are frequently marked by elevations in such physiological indexes as heart rate, muscle tension, and blood pressure, training in relaxation has prima facie relevance. There is in fact an extensive literature on teaching people to quiet themselves when physiologically aroused. These techniques have in common a reduction in external stimulation, a focus on internal stimuli (such as the state of one's muscles or a mental image), slowed and regular breathing, and a letting go of one's muscles. In general, the instructor speaks in a reassuring, soothing, sometimes soporific voice. Best known are the procedures of and variations on the work of Edmund Jacobson (1938), a physician who believed that emotional states could not exist in the absence of muscle tension. For years he conducted workshops for teaching health professionals his very detailed, painstaking techniques for relaxing the striate musculature. Abbreviations of Jacobson's procedures were developed by Joseph Wolpe in the 1950s (Wolpe, 1958) as part of his systematic desensitization, fear-reduction technique; they were modified still further by Lazarus (Wolpe and Lazarus, 1966) and Paul (1966). Some persons have gone even further by putting the instructions on audiotapes for practice at home (Goldfried and Davison, 1976). Independently developed was autogenic training (Schultz and Luthe, 1969), procedures that rely on passive concentration and suggestions of looseness and warmth in the muscles.

These approaches are in many ways similar to Eastern practices of meditation. Of considerable interest in the 1970s was the work of Benson (1975), a Harvard professor of medicine who developed what he called "the relaxation response," which was really a westernized version of transcendental meditation.

Biofeedback. It is important to distinguish between feedback in general (knowledge about outcomes) and biofeedback as a specific technology. The former is an integral part of the general proposition that increased understanding, including feedback about a situation (i.e., reduced uncertainty) reduces stress. Classic animal studies illustrate this point (Weiss, 1971a, 1971b, 1971c). Rats given inescapable and unpredictable shocks followed immediately by a sound developed fewer stomach ulcers than animals not given the sound but treated identically otherwise. Levine interprets the Norwegian paratrooper study in part in this context: "Although the situation (second 10-meter jump) was potentially dangerous and threatening, the trainees had gone through the experience and suffered no bad consequences. Thus, a maximum amount of feedback about the absence of danger in a potentially threatening situation became quickly obvious" (Levine paper: 19–20).

Although we discussed biofeedback in Chapter 5 in terms of motor skills, here we discuss it as a technique that has been applied to stress reduction. While the most common paradigm uses EMG recordings, EEG recordings are also used to determine the percentage of time EEG alpha occurred, providing subjects with visual or auditory cues (see Chapter 5 for definitions). The subject's goal is to reduce EMG or increase the proportion of EEG alpha waves. This literature has been reviewed in several volumes (Beatty and Legewie, 1977; Schwartz and Beatty, 1977) and more recently by Lawrence (1984). The work raises several issues relating to the ubiquitous questions of reliability and validity:

1. Are subjects able to decrease the amplitude of recorded EMG (or increase EEG alpha)?
2. If so, does this mean they are learning to become more relaxed?
3. If so, does this have any significant effect on stress reduction and on performance?

The answer to question 1 is mixed; some studies report significant change in the actual physiological measure used (EMG reduction, increased percentage EEG alpha), others do not. Similarly, the answer to question 2 is mixed. EMG is often recorded from the frontalis muscle, but EMG reduction in this muscle does not always correlate with EMG changes in other muscles (Arnarson and Sheffield, 1980; Suarez, Kohlenberg, and Pagano, 1979). Perhaps most critical, the answer to question 3 is generally no. There is no evidence to indicate that biofeedback training—induced reduction of EMG activity or increased percentage of EEG alpha—has any effect on stress or on performance under conditions of stress (Lawrence, 1984). The strongest conclusion that can be drawn in a positive vein is that some studies do report decreased EMG activity in the muscle or muscles being recorded from as a result of biofeedback training, so under some conditions biofeedback training may be a useful adjunct to relaxation training. To the extent that learning to relax can in fact enhance performance under stress, then biofeedback training may be of some limited use; but given the time and instrumentation required, and its relatively low reliability and validity, biofeedback would seem far less useful than the more general cognitive approaches to stress management, to which we now turn.

Cognitive Restructuring

We all accept that the way we look at things, including ourselves, matters. If one mistakes a person standing some distance away for a long-lost friend, one's emotions and behavior will be different than they would have been had that person not reminded one of a friend. Beyond such commonplace understanding is the assumption of Ellis (1962) and Beck (1976) that severe emotional and behavioral disorders can be favorably affected by altering a person's perception or conception of the situation. Great faith is placed, then, on intellectual capacities to influence one's affect and actions. (Not all clinicians have such faith in our intellectual capacities. Clinicians as different from one another as Freud and Wolpe, for example, place little reliance on the power of the conscious mind to change the way one feels and behaves when in bad psychological shape.)

Ellis's "rational emotive therapy" (RET) holds that people are unhappy and worse because they "catastrophize" about what is merely annoying or inconvenient, blow it out of proportion, and respond to their exaggerated conception of the situation (Ellis, 1962). Thus, to fail an examination is, in Ellis's words, "a pain in the ass," but it does not have to be construed as a catastrophe, for it is irrational to demand that one succeed in everything one attempts or that one never incur the disapproval of others. There is a growing body of reasonably controlled research confirming the usefulness of this general therapeutic approach in alleviating a wide range of anxiety-based disorders (see Haaga and Davison, in press).

Beck's "cognitive therapy" (1976) focuses more on the data of experience and one's inferences therefrom. Thus, for example, I conclude that, because Dorothy has rejected me, no one likes me. Beck involves the patient in a collaborative empirical testing of the generalization that no one likes me based solely on the experience of one rejection. Beck has worked primarily with depressives, although in recent years his efforts have been directed toward the anxiety disorders as well (Beck and Emery, 1985). There is considerable and very strong evidence that Beck's general approach (which is considerably more complicated than just summarized) is effective with even severe and long-standing depression (e.g., Rush et al., 1977; Blackburn et al., 1981).

A third approach is exemplified by the early work of Meichenbaum (1977), who advocated an emphasis on self-instructions to guide overt behavior. Meichenbaum and his co-workers have been successful in helping impulsive children control their behavior and thereby improve their problem-solving abilities and in helping college students who are anxious about taking tests improve their performance by talking themselves through their activities (e.g., "OK, take it slow. Let's see, what's the formula for figuring time and distance in travel? I won't worry if I don't get it right the first time").

A fourth cognitive approach is social problem solving, a way to approach the inevitable difficulties in life and overcome them. The core of this approach, as presented by D'Zurilla and Goldfried (1971), is the conceptualization of human distress as problems to be solved. Several stages are posited, consisting of (1) a general orientation or set (that, indeed, my distress arises from specific, solvable conundrums); (2) problem definition (translation of what may appear to be a hopeless mess into a problem that is conceivably amenable to a solution); (3) generation of alternatives (sometimes referred to as brainstorming, the free and easy production of possible solutions but without evaluation just yet as to their utility or practicality); (4) decision making (deciding on a solution to explore first); and (5) verification (attempting the solution or at least developing it abstractly to check out whether the benefits and costs are what one finds acceptable at a given time and in a given place).

Evidence is beginning to accumulate confirming the usefulness of this approach. For example, depressed older adults in a nursing home were relieved of much of their depression after they were trained in this fashion (Hussian and Lawrence, 1980), and other adult problems can be ameliorated with such an approach (D'Zurilla and Nezu, 1982).

Though not formally recognized as a cognitive change method, the simple *provision of information* is a rational way to reduce uncertainty and increase a person's sense of control over an upcoming challenge. Early work was conducted by Janis (1951), who found a beneficial effect on the emotional impact of an impending stressor (air attacks) when information about it was provided in advance. This work had previously been reported in the *American Soldier* project (Stouffer, 1949). Similar results come from work with surgery patients (Janis, 1971). A risk to be considered and avoided in this approach is the possibility of overloading a person on the aversiveness of an upcoming situation, lest he or she become traumatized by the information. By the same token, however, if advance information on a stressor is going to be traumatic, chances are the actual stressor will be also. This provision of realistic information was subsequently incorporated into a "stress inoculation training" package (Meichenbaum and Cameron, 1983) and is described below in connection with the Novaco-Sarason project with Marine drill instructors.

The implication of this approach for the military is that individuals should be given maximum knowledge and understanding of potentially harmful situations and as much control over them as possible. This conclusion seems just the opposite of the accepted military philosophy of giving the individual the least amount of information necessary for a given task or situation. In a combat situation it would seem that each soldier should be given as much information as possible about his situation and that of the enemy to help him manage stress levels and maintain arousal at a useful motivational level.

Behavioral Skills Training

Chapter 5 of this report discusses the learning of motor skills. It is important to allude to this in the context of stress, because people's stress levels will be high if they correctly perceive themselves to be deficient in the behavioral skills necessary to accomplish a task. To find it stressful, for example, to be in the driver's seat of a Bradley tank is not unreasonable and is, one hopes, impossible to become acclimated to unless one has the skills to operate it safely and effectively. In our focus in most of this chapter on the reduction of arousal and the acquisition of adaptive cognitive strategies, one should not lose sight of the importance of having in one's behavioral repertoire the skills it takes to do the job.

One example of a useful behavioral skill commonly employed in the corporate sphere is time management. Especially for high achievers, learning to avoid excessive obligations can be difficult. Lakein (1973) outlines a systematic approach to time management that entails a goals statement, a priority list of tasks, and a schedule. He distinguishes between tasks that require concentration and tasks that involve dealing with people and suggests that, for the former, one needs "internal prime time" and for the latter "external prime time." Interruptions should be avoided during internal prime time so that the mind can concentrate on a particular task that does not require the involvement of other people. Anyone who has worked as a secretary or who has one working for him or her can appreciate the stress created by the need to monitor the phone and greet visitors to the office while having as an important task the typing of a complex manuscript.

The secretarial example brings us to the next major section, environmental change as an approach to stress reduction, for what comes to mind is the difficulty a secretary usually has in shutting out external distractions in order to create internal prime time for working on the manuscript. The work environment itself may proscribe or at least make extraordinarily difficult the structuring of the context that would be most conducive to the reduction of stress and thereby the enhancement of performance. In psychology, the focus on environmental change for the betterment of the human condition is generally the bailiwick of community psychologists, who, it has been pointed out (Davison and Neale, 1986), are inherently political and therefore sometimes revolutionary in their perspective. What follows is doubtless problematic in as complex and tradition-rich an environment as the military, but it is important to present the issues at least briefly.

STRATEGIES FOR CHANGING THE ENVIRONMENT

Earlier we mentioned that for a person who is uncomfortably warm the options include environmental change, such as leaving the hot area for a cooler one or cooling the hot area with air conditioning. The discussion of the nature of stress at the beginning of this chapter suggests that greater levels of certainty (or predictability) and of control reduce stress on both the psychological and physiological levels in human beings and animals. While reduction of uncertainty and increase in control can be achieved by working intrapsychically, a community psychology or environmental orientation would look to contextual change as a powerful avenue to stress management.

Some examples of behavioral research already exist or are under way in the armed forces, and we discuss them below in connection with the Novaco-Sarason work with drill instructors in Marine boot camp. Such research, aimed at teaching anger control and other strategies to drill instructors, is intrapsychic in nature vis à vis the drill instructors being trained, but it is effectively environmental change as far as the "grunts" are concerned, for as a result they are confronted with a training environment that is likely to be different from the typically more aggressive atmosphere prevalent in Marine boot camps.

Desired changes produced in an individual are successful insofar as they enhance his or her skill in dealing with environmental demands. If stress is reduced by the acquisition of a relaxation skill or of a less catastrophic way to construe one's behaviors, then one's interaction with the environment is likely to change in a positive way. A soldier who is less anxious can concentrate better on M-1 training exercises. A drill instructor who is not depressed can meet his leadership obligations better and continue career-long learning. These overt behaviors, whether already in the person's repertoire or yet to be acquired, will have a favorable impact on the environment. In a constantly reciprocal fashion, the improved environment will present a picture to the person that is different from that which would have been presented had he or she continued to be stressed and less functional. Success builds on success; evaluating one's efforts and building a sense of self-efficacy (Bandura, 1977) emboldens one to forge ahead, doing so with less and less stress, even though the tasks undertaken are likely to be increasingly complex and challenging.

Though the foregoing approaches have attracted a great deal of research attention, there is a paucity of published research on stress management in military settings; the few examples are discussed in the next section. This is not to say that military people have not from time to time attempted to relax soldiers, encourage positive outlooks, or suggest problem solving—rather that systematic inquiry, which would be persuasive to most social scientists, is lacking.

STRESS REDUCTION IN MILITARY SETTINGS

There are basically two points at which one can intervene in matters of stress: before (much) damage has been done and afterward. We are concerned in this chapter primarily with the former, but any discussion of stress in military settings must also include the nature and treatment of posttraumatic stress disorder.

POSTTRAUMATIC STRESS DISORDER*

Symptoms and Diagnosis

In posttraumatic stress disorder (PTSD) a traumatic event or catastrophe of the worst order, such as rape, combat, or a natural disaster, brings in its aftermath difficulties with concentration and memory, an inability to relax, impulsiveness, a tendency to be easily startled, disturbed sleep, anxiety, depression, and above all a psychic numbing. Activities previously enjoyed lose their appeal. There is a feeling of estrangement from others and from "the passing parade" and, if the trauma was shared and took the lives of companions, a deadening sense of guilt for having survived. As for the experience itself, the person has great difficulty keeping it out of mind. Flashbacks—vivid and intrusive recollections of the painful event—and recurring nightmares and dreams of it are common. Posttraumatic stress disorder may be acute, chronic, or delayed. It is believed to be more severe and longer-lasting after a trauma caused by human beings, as in war, physical assaults, or torture, than after a catastrophe of nature, such as a flood or an earthquake. Symptoms often worsen when the individual is exposed to situations that resemble the original trauma: a thunderstorm may remind a soldier of the firings and rumbles of battle.

People diagnosed as having posttraumatic stress disorder, although surely different from one another in countless ways before trauma, do have in common in their lives a major, salient, and powerful happening—in the words of the third edition of the *Diagnostic and Statistical Manual* of the American Psychiatric Association (1980:236), "a psychologically traumatic event that is generally outside the range of usual human experience." The manual goes on to state, as the literature on trauma has for years, that "the stressor producing this syndrome would evoke significant symptoms of distress in most people" (p. 236). Current thinking is that PTSD symptoms can also arise from a series of subtraumatic events. Although clinicians had written about a disorder that they called traumatic neurosis, the previous edition of the manual lacked a specific category for stress disorders of some duration. That posttraumatic stress disorder is

---

*Most of the discussion of PTSD is taken from Davison and Neale (1986:138–143).

listed in the third edition represents no small change in overall point of view, for it constitutes a formal recognition that, regardless of premorbid history, many people may be adversely affected by overwhelming catastrophic stress and that their reaction should be distinguished from other disorders. The newly listed disorder can be seen, then, as shifting the "blame" for the problem from the survivor to the event. Instead of implicitly concluding that a person would be all right were he or she made of sterner stuff, the third edition of the manual acknowledges the onerousness of the traumatizing circumstances (Haley, 1978).

Treatment of PTSD

There is very little controlled research on the treatment of PTSD in the military, although there are many case reports of therapeutic interventions with personnel suffering from the disorder (formerly called shell shock or battle fatigue). The classic book by Grinker and Spiegel (1945) described the treatment of PTSD in World War II personnel, and this and related work have more recently been discussed by Lifton (1976). In general, the treatment of combat-related stress is guided by three principles: immediacy, proximity, and expectancy. Treat the soldier as soon as possible when signs of breakdown (e.g., sleeplessness and great anxiety) are detected; do so as close to the battle situation as possible; and do so while conveying the expectation that he will soon return to his unit.

Treatment has generally involved a review with the affected person of the traumatizing situation. The assumption has been that the person needs to face up to the frightening situation and work through his anxiety about it. Sometimes hypnosis or drugs are used to facilitate the emotional recall.

The aftermath of the Vietnam War has been different from the periods following the two world wars and the Korean War, primarily because of society's rejection of Vietnam veterans for some years after their discharge from the military. It was not until 1982 that the now highly regarded and much-visited Vietnam War Memorial was established and both official and nonofficial welcomes were accorded the veterans of this conflict. It took several years for the Veterans Administration (VA) to gear itself up for the postwar trauma problems of many of the Vietnam veterans.

Indeed, prior to large-scale governmental efforts in the late 1970s to bring more Vietnam veterans into the VA system, veterans themselves, with the assistance of Robert Jay Lifton, an academic psychiatrist at Yale, established self-help "rap groups" that had a twofold purpose: a therapeutic one of healing, by talking through their concerns with strong mutual group support; and a political one of forcing the American public to understand the human costs of this exceedingly unpopular war.

The focus of the rap groups has been the residual guilt and rage felt by the veterans: guilt over what their status as soldiers required them to do in fighting a guerilla war in which enemy and ally were often impossible to distinguish; and rage at being forced to risk their lives in a cause to which their country was not fully committed. Group discussions have also encouraged traumatized veterans to confront in vivid recollections their negative wartime experiences.

Whether the treatment be psychoanalytic, behavioral, or human-istic-existential, exposure to the trauma is deemed to be the most powerful curative factor, bringing to mind an ancient Chinese proverb, "Go straight to the heart of danger, for there you will find safety."

PREVENTIVE PROGRAMS

Dealing responsibly with PTSD is generally regarded as therapy, even when conducted by the participants themselves, and it is remedial in nature; that is, it attempts to fix something that has been broken. The Army is concerned, however, with preventing breakdown and reducing stress in soldiers at large so that they can learn and perform at optimal levels. Especially in peacetime, the challenge with regard to stress is not to heal the scarred veteran, but to maintain the soldier's arousal level at the middle of the inverted-U function, where it is known that the best learning and performance take place.

The earliest and perhaps most crucial period for the soldier is basic training, or boot camp, that unique period of four to ten weeks when a young civilian is turned into a military person through a carefully planned and closely supervised regimen of highly demanding physical and psy-chological challenges. Beds are to be made only one way, answers to questions delivered in just a certain way, posture maintained in a certain way, and many complex skills acquired, from shooting a rifle to pitching a tent. It is appropriate, then, that the few stress management programs whose procedures and results have been published concern primarily this first stage of a military person's development, when important learning must take place.

Studies by Beach, Prince, and Klugman (1977) at Fort Dix, by Datel and Lifrak (1969) at Fort Ord, and by Horner, Meglino, and Mobley (1979) are difficult to interpret because of sampling and other methodo-logical problems, but they do have in common attempts to provide realistic information to recruits of what lies in store for them. A more recent study by Novaco, Cook, and Sarason (1983) with Marine recruits in San Diego is more comprehensive than the earlier work. It entailed a 35-minute videotape called "Making It," which depicted skills necessary for coping with the rigors of boot camp. The tape contained positive expectancies of success while at the same time informing recruits of the difficulties of the training and their likely distress, worry, and confusion. Details of the ingredients of successful performance were also provided. Results suggested that recruits viewing this film manifested higher expectations of personal control and efficacy than did recruits seeing a control film.

It is worth commenting that this tape may have reduced uncertainty and enhanced a sense of personal control by providing factual information while at the same time explicitly telling recruits what it takes to make it. The extreme physical stressor that is boot camp, therefore, came to be viewed and reacted to as less of a stressor, consistent with our earlier observations about the cognitive core of stress.

A study being done by Novaco and Sarason at both Parris Island and San Diego endeavors to impart to drill instructors coping information and encouragement regarding anger control, evaluation anxiety, the virtues of patience, and the utility of supportive social relationships. Model coping strategies are presented in conjunction with typical problem situations. It is hoped that the findings will provide clues to how stress can be reduced in drill instructors and how their performance can be enhanced, as indexed by, among other things, lower recruit attrition.

CONCLUSION AND AN ETHICAL NOTE

We can relate all these stress management procedures to each other and to our earlier discussion of the nature of stress by focusing on the reduction of uncertainty and the increase in control that would seem to follow from any of them. The amelioration of stress by any means is going to help people think more clearly and thereby increase the chances that they can cope with a challenging situation. Stress reduction will also improve learning capacities and thereby add to their ability to acquire new adaptive skills (which, in turn, will increase control and lessen uncertainty about a situation).

Since the abuses of the Nazi doctors in World War II and the establishment of human subjects committees in research settings in the United States, scientists have become more sensitive to the moral dimensions of their work. When it comes to matters of stress in an organization whose mission is inextricably bound up with destruction, it is only at our risk that we ignore the ethics of stress reduction. A clinician consents to help a patient reduce stress caused by a set of circumstances only if that stress is jointly agreed to be inappropriate. In other words, one has to believe that it is morally right not to be stressed (so much) by those circumstances.

At what point should one view a soldier's stress reaction as legitimate and even valuable? Should we be concerned with the long-term effects of any interventions that permit us to teach more efficiently and more effectively the various arts of war? What role should civilian oversight play, if any at all, in the determination by the military of what the goals of training should be? These and related questions should be raised in any effort to change people's behavior. We do not mean to single out the military for exclusive attention and implied criticism. At the same time, however, the moral dimensions of stress reduction should be mentioned in order to sensitize social scientists, policymakers, and the military to the distinction between what one can do and what one ought to do.

8

Social Processes

The chapters to this point have focused largely on individual performance. Little attention has been given to the social contexts for performance or for the performance of groups and organizations. Our concern with performance in large organizations like the Army makes it imperative that we examine these topics in some detail. Social processes are treated at both the interpersonal and intergroup levels of analysis: the first section focuses on influence strategies, with an emphasis on a particular technique referred to as neurolinguistic programming (NLP). The second section discusses the cohesion of groups within organizations. Implications from research are drawn for one particular application of cohesion concepts, the Army's COHORT system.

The social psychological literature on influence provides many insights that can be used to improve communication and persuasion. The academic community has not, for the most part, packaged these insights for consumption in the marketplace or for specific use by military and other organizations. One consequence has been to concede the market to entrepreneurs not trained in academic social science traditions. Neurolinguistic Programming is a well-known package offered to a variety of consumers and professionals. Studies to date indicate that its effects on perceptions do not translate into enhanced performance; however, another use of NLP may provide an approach to modeling expert performances that can be adapted to specific training programs, and as such merits further consideration.

Of the topics considered by the committee, none shows a larger discrepancy between what we think we know and the existing evidence than that of cohesion. It is common for both academics and practitioners to assume that cohesive organizations perform better than those that are not cohesive or divided. However, the size of the gains may be smaller than anticipated, and there may be unintended consequences that are harmful to an organization. Available research provides few insights into the particular conditions that produce either positive or negative outcomes. The studies on the COHORT system suggest positive effects of cohesion (in COHORT units versus non-COHORT units) on attitudes and such behaviors as attrition and reenlistment. Next steps should include a focus on other group characteristics that may increase team performance and morale, as well as the observed reciprocal relationship between performance and cohesion. They should also consider the way in which cohesive units perform on tasks that require intergroup coordination.

STRATEGIES FOR INTERPERSONAL INFLUENCE

There are many ways in which training can be accomplished, from passive instruction to motor skills training to vicarious performance. One aspect of training that is often suggested is the use of interpersonal influence. In this section, we briefly examine the general nature of interpersonal influence and discuss techniques that might be applied to training. Organizational development is a widely used procedure in organizational and industrial settings; we examine its potential as a training procedure for influencing groups. Other techniques seek to modify individual performance through either influence or expert modeling; we focus in detail on one such popular technique, neurolinguistic programming, and the evidence for its assumptions and effectiveness. We also assess the use of neurolinguistic programming as a system for modeling behaviors of experts to use as training regimens for neophytes. Finally, we discuss the more general issues of evaluation and transfer of social psychological knowledge into practical applications and propose recommendations on these issues.

There is a large and varied literature in social psychology and sociology on the ways in which small groups or organizations are able to influence others or persuade them to accept the influencer's point of view. These issues appear in the literature under such topics as pressures to uniformity, conformity, social influence, obedience, deviation, autonomy, resistance to persuasion, and others. Most of the research on these topics has centered on the role of influence in modifying opinions and attitudes; considerably fewer studies have focused on the modifications of behaviors or performances. Basic researchers in social psychology have shown a concern for the process by which influence-produced change becomes internalized so that the influenced individual maintains the altered beliefs after the attempt to influence has passed. In contrast, few studies of influence have been carried out with the longitudinal time frame necessary to evaluate its success or to guide one toward practical applications, such as military training.

There are no simple rules for constructing a successful attempt to influence. The number of variables to be considered is very large, and the evidence suggests that the combinatorial rules for aggregating them are complex: many of them serve as moderators for other relationships. Experimental studies of influence often succeed in establishing effective influence regimens by restricting the range and the scope of variables to be studied. For example, studies of the effectiveness of an influence group as a function of its size often ignore the factor of stratification within the group, and studies of the role of a dissenting partner in resisting influence often ignore the nature of the future interaction of the group's members.

Much of the discussion of influence attempts in actual situations has taken an analytic tack. That is, it has examined an actual influence procedure or situation and broken it down into its constituent social psychological elements. Two recent reviews that provide good expositions and extensive references are Cialdini (1985) and Moscovici (1985). These describe influence attempts in actual situations as well as the theoretical underpinnings of a science of influence. They are not particularly helpful, however, in designing influence procedures or in choosing between two or more proposed procedures.

ATTITUDE CHANGE THROUGH PERSUASIVE COMMUNICATIONS

Attitude formation, maintenance, and change have been widely studied in contemporary social psychology. A major reason for this interest was the series of research efforts conducted during World War II and collectively published as a four-volume work, *The American Soldier* (Stouffer, 1949). This work was continued in the succeeding decades primarily by Hovland and his colleagues at Yale.

The earlier studies investigated specifics of effective communication, for example, one-sided versus two-sided messages or the relative effectiveness of primacy and recency. Despite initial success in establishing some general principles, it was soon discovered that each of these findings was applicable only to a particular set of circumstances (audience, communicator, type of message, social context, and a host of other factors). Research has since shifted to questions of how attitudes are formed and more recently to the cognitive steps that underlie an attitude—

how new information is processed, stored, recalled, and reconciled with existing cognitions and beliefs. The models that have been developed have been useful in a variety of situations, including political campaigns, advertising, and birth control advocacy.

These models have not been intensively studied as a means of increasing motivation or as methods for improving training or performance. This lack of application restricts their usefulness to a study of performance enhancement techniques. To the extent that the models apply to elements of a composite enhancement program, however, they may prove to be useful analytic tools. A recent comprehensive review of attitude models is found in McGuire (1985).

ORGANIZATIONAL DEVELOPMENT PROGRAMS

One of the developments of the social psychological group that coalesced around Kurt Lewin was the application of the principles of group dynamics to organizational and industrial contexts. The applications that came from this effort were based on a belief in the effectiveness of induced motivation and an effort to bring the group's or the organization's goals into correspondence with those of the individual.

The most widely disseminated of the organizational development programs were the *T-groups,* or *sensitivity training,* of the late 1960s and early 1970s. When applied to training in organizations, these programs were based on the explicit assumption that, by increasing members' or workers' satisfaction, one would also increase their performance and productivity. Many critics who regard that assumption as questionable have rejected organizational development (OD) programs out of hand.

Many OD programs, however, do not rest on that belief. Rather, they focus on improving performance and satisfying the organization's goals. Porras and Berg, in their 1978 review of the effectiveness of organizational development programs, list five distinct types of programs:

1. *Laboratory training with a process emphasis.* This is the classic T-group, or sensitivity training, the explicit goal of which is to improve the individual, with organizational productivity to follow as a consequence.

2. *Laboratory training with a task emphasis.* Groups in a laboratory are given guided experience with a set of structured problems. The development of individual potential is ancillary to the group's learning to accomplish its tasks efficiently.

3. *Managerial grid organizational development.* This involves a group training task that consists of a set of six structured exercises aimed at teaching managers in the organization specific problem-solving skills.

4. *Survey feedback.* This technique teaches managers how to acquire

data from the organization's members in order to identify, isolate, and construct solutions to task-related problems.

5. *Residual sets of programs.* These consist of a mixture of techniques and elements from the other forms of organizational development.

T-groups, or sensitivity training groups, were the most common of the programs until the late 1970s, and they were the least effective. Recently, several of the other procedures have been employed. While such techniques are run as group sessions, their goal is often to change individual behaviors. Their success can be evaluated on two levels: the extent to which individual attitudes and behaviors are modified and the extent to which group or team performance is improved. Overall, the techniques have been more effective in changing performance variables than in changing individual satisfaction. The most effective interventions—the non T-group types—seemed to have a greater effect on individual performance than on group structure.

Various time factors appear to have influenced effectiveness. The longer the program, up to about 21 days, the better the resulting performance. Increasing the length of time the program consultants were involved beyond 21 days did not further improve performance, although it increased participants' satisfaction. Finally, more effective programs used a greater number of techniques or were more eclectic in their approach.

Although there are various descriptions of organizational development programs, there are fewer overall evaluations. Two of the descriptive sources are Beckhard (1969) and Hornstein et al. (1971). For a review and evaluation, there are several cogent articles, such as Friedlander and Brown (1974) and Porras and Berg (1978).

There have been numerous attempts to apply the demonstrated principles of persuasion to influence both attitudes and behavior. Advertising and political campaign strategies draw heavily on rules of thumb and loosely formulated principles that are based on social psychological studies. From the committee's perspective, these activities have several important shortcomings. First, they are not often explicitly stated in a way that leads from one situation to another. An effective TV campaign for a new cereal may not be applicable to the indoctrination of Army recruits. Second, they are not often evaluated in a way that provides cumulative evidence in support of the general principles rather than the specific intervention. Third, while these practical attempts at influence address behavior, they seek to persuade someone to buy a product or to vote in a certain way. They do not have a training component; they do not seek to impart a new skill or to improve a way of doing things.

Formal patterns of change induced by influence procedures have been studied in several traditional academic research traditions. Some researchers attempt to formulate theories about changes that occur in group settings, such as organizational development; others concentrate on the mechanisms by which individuals are induced to modify their beliefs and behaviors. Other procedures, developed independently of these academic traditions, offer a set of rules and practices for influencing others. These are not devised as preludes to validating research and are often sold as proprietary products in the marketplace. In addition to claims of general success in interpersonal influence, these programs also stress their divorce from academic theory with claims of novelty and revolutionary approaches. Many of them are successfully merchandised, and persons who have bought them often become staunch advocates of their virtues. Because these programs are proprietary, complete descriptions may not be available, and assessment studies, if conducted, are not published in a form amenable to scientific scrutiny.

One type of program that has achieved a measure of success is called neurolinguistic programming. Various purveyors of this system offer training seminars in many cities on a regular basis. Respected and responsible people who have been trained in the system report positively on their perception of improved performance attributable to the system; some branches of academic disciplines, such as counseling psychology, have given serious theoretical and research scrutiny to the system.

NEUROLINGUISTIC PROGRAMMING

Neurolinguistic programming is a system of procedures and models that purports to enable people to increase their communicative and influence effectiveness. It was developed by Bandler and Grinder in the early 1970s and was described in a series of books written for a broad, nontechnical audience. The background, method, and implementation of NLP are disseminated primarily through proprietary workshops and training courses.

The system was developed in answer to the question of why three particular psychotherapists were so effective with their patients. Rather than explore this question in terms of psychotherapeutic theory and practice, Bandler and Grinder sought to analyze what the therapists were doing at an observational level, categorize it, and apply the categories as a general model of interpersonal influence. NLP seeks to instruct people to observe, make inferences, and respond to others, as did the three original, very effective therapists.

Basic Features of NLP

At the core of NLP is the belief that, when people are engaged in activities, they are also making use of a representational system; that is, they are using some internal representation of the materials they are involved with, such as a conversation, a rifle shot, a spelling task. These representations can be visual, auditory, kinesthetic, or involve the other senses. In addition, a person may be creating a representation or recalling one. For example, a person asked to spell a word may visualize that word printed on a piece of paper, may hear it being sounded out, or may construct the spelling from the application of a series of logical rules. The basic NLP assumption is that a person will be most influenced by messages involving whatever representational system he or she is employing at the moment.

NLP postulates six representational systems: constructing of visual images, remembering of visual images, constructing of auditory images, remembering of auditory images, attending to kinesthetic sensations, and holding internal dialogues. NLP maintains that, as a person uses each of these subjective representational systems, his or her eyes and posture conform to each system's requirements. Over the course of time, the NLP system has become more detailed in characterizing the outward manifestations of these representational systems. Figure 1 shows the relation of eye movements to the representational system; NLP specifies the exact relation among eye position, posture, and representational system. In addition, NLP postulates that a person's language, in particular the choice of predicates, will also reflect the representational system used. Thus, a person using a stored visual image will employ phrases such as "I *see* a way to . . ."; one in an auditory mode, "that *sounds* right to me . . ."; in a kinesthetic system, "I *feel* we should . . ."; and so on. Finally, people can be asked which system they are using.

NLP descriptions suggest that each person can be characterized by the system he or she is most likely to use, called a Preferred Representational System (PRS). The PRS is an individual difference variable and

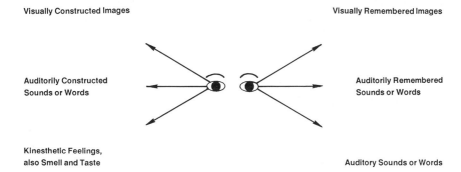

Visually Constructed Images

Visually Remembered Images

Auditorily Constructed Sounds or Words

Auditorily Remembered Sounds or Words

Kinesthetic Feelings, also Smell and Taste

Auditory Sounds or Words

FIGURE 1 Neurolinguistic programming scheme (adapted from Stevens, 1979).

provides the NLP practitioner with a simple key to an influence strategy for that person. NLP theory does not indicate whether the PRS is like a trait, difficult to modify, or whether it is a learned pattern, capable of change and modification.

There is no definitive NLP system. Although the basic features have remained stable from exposition to exposition, the emphasis or importance of particular aspects varies from description to description, sometimes in a contradictory manner. For example, PRS is prominently placed in *Frogs into Princes* (Stevens, 1979) and *Structure of Magic* (Bandler and Grinder, 1975), two early NLP descriptions. At a meeting with Richard Bandler in Santa Cruz, California, on July 9, 1986, the influence subcommittee (see Appendix C) was informed that PRS was no longer considered an important component. He said that NLP had been revised, and he provided the committee with two books, *Neuro-Linguistic Programming*, volume 1, *The Study of the Structure of Subjective Experience* (Dilts et al., 1980) and *Roots of Neuro-Linguistic Programming* (Dilts, 1983).

These two volumes reduce the emphasis on PRS in describing NLP yet offer new suggestions that PRS is correlated both with Sheldon's (1942) somatotype-personality hypotheses and with habitual EEG patterns. These volumes also expand on the identification of a person's currently active representational system by stating that patterns of posture, voice tone, and breathing accompany the use of each system. The basis for the relation of eye movements to representational systems rests on assumptions about laterality of brain function and use of language, in particular, the postulate that the speech center for right-handed people is located in the left cerebral hemisphere. This rationale is present in all of the NLP source books. The implication is that standard NLP analysis applies primarily or exclusively to right-handed people. This presumption was deemphasized by Bandler, who told the subcommittee that the handedness requirement was no longer considered a restriction on the generality of the NLP model. The basis for the shift in reliance on hemispheric specificity was not theoretical, but pragmatic. Bandler stated that NLP was a system based on modeling, not theory. Any aspects that worked were retained; those that seemed incorrect, such as the limitation to right-handed individuals, were dropped.

NLP is a system for modeling a person's behavior and thought processes in relation to a specific topic or behavior. As such it has two main focuses, one more highly developed than the other. The focus receiving most attention has been the marketing of NLP as a set of techniques for interpersonal competence, with respect to influence, and as a psychotherapeutic system or adjunct. This use of NLP requires that the practitioner do a very restricted and limited sort of modeling: the tracking of a target individual's representational systems on a continuing basis and the use of controlled language and cues to modify and shape the target's thoughts, feelings, and opinions. Within the NLP system, this function can be carried out by persons who have passed the two lower levels of certified NLP training, Practitioner and Master Practitioner.

NLP can also be used as a modeling system for the development of training protocols, although it is neither marketed nor frequently used in this manner. Presumably, persons trained at the highest NLP level, Trainers, would be able to analyze in NLP terms an expert performing a task, such as shooting a rifle, in terms of the sequence of representational systems and anchors used by the expert (see Appendix D for terms). The NLP sequence description could then be used as a template for instruction of beginners.

Internal Consistency of NLP

The proponents of NLP do not put forward their procedures as scientific theory, nor do they regard their models of processing systems as a variety of cognitive psychology. Rather, they claim they have developed an empirical working model of the behaviors that accompany subjective experiences. They do present both scientific support for the bases of their assertions and some quasi-experimental evidence for some of the stated relationships. The scientific underpinnings are presented in most detailed fashion in the *Roots of Neuro-Linguistic Programming* (Dilts, 1983). A careful reading of these materials reveals the following:

1. Many of the theories cited as congruent with NLP are metaphors that have little impact or acceptance in the scientific literature. Pribram's theory of the holographic brain and John's description of the statistical brain (Dilts, 1983:42, 48) have not been the basis for modern neuroscientific theorizing.

2. There is *no* direct support cited for the NLP-postulated relation between eye gaze direction and representational system.

3. The experiments presented in support of NLP, presuming to demonstrate a relation between NLP and EEG, are at best case studies and demonstrations. Even a controlled experiment that showed consistent EEG patterns related to specific eye movements or instructions to visualize would reveal nothing about representational patterns or the structure of subjective experiences. It would merely demonstrate that certain instructions or volitional patterns of action produce consistent brain waves.

4. The underpinnings of NLP are not a set of findings and propositions arranged so that they imply the NLP statements of structure; instead, they are a series of concatenated anecdotes and facts that lead to no

particular conclusion. The fact that there are different types of neurons or that the brain is organized hierarchically in no way implies that one who is right-handed looks up and to the left when recalling visual images.

5. The descriptions of basic biological processes are filled with minor but significant errors. For example, a synapse is defined as a dendrite-dendrite connection rather than as a dendrite-axon connection (Dilts, 1983:7).

6. The biological and psychological references are dated. There is no mention of neurotransmission in describing brain organization, and the cognitive psychology cited omits the last 20 years of work in this area.

In brief, the NLP system of eye, posture, tone, and language patterns as indexing representational patterns is not derived or derivable from known scientific work. Furthermore, there is no internal evidence or documentation to support the system. If one were to randomly match the six labels and six patterns described in Figure 1, the internal evidence would be as applicable to the 719 possible other patterns as it is to the NLP alternative.

Research on NLP

Most of the studies testing one or another aspect of NLP have been concerned with the accuracy of the concept of representational systems, particularly the adequacy of the behaviors postulated to accompany each type. There are approximately 20 such studies, reviewed both in the published literature (Sharpley, 1984) and in papers prepared for the committee by Harris and Rosenthal and by Dean G. Pruitt, Jennifer Crocker, and Deborah Hanes (Appendix B).

Individually and as a group these studies fail to provide an empirical base of support for NLP assumptions for several reasons:

1. Many of the studies are concerned with testing whether influence attempts that match the PRS are more effective than those that do not match. Sharpley's (1984) meta-analysis of these studies and Harris and Rosenthal's discussion of this meta-analysis conclude that there is no effect. Since the emphasis on the Preferred Representational System (as distinguished from the representational system currently in use) has been reduced in importance in recent NLP literature and explicitly disavowed in informal communication, the relevance of this negative finding is diminished.

2. There is no support for the claim that the indexes of representational systems are mutually consistent. Studies have failed to find significant correlations between eye movements, choice of predicates, and self-reports, all of which are postulated to be keyed to the representational systems (e.g., Gumm, Walker, and Day, 1982). Some studies have used

predicate matching as an influence technique (thereby selecting it as the primary index of representational system). None has been found that matches predicates to eye positions. Existing predicate-matching studies do not support the hypothesis that predicate matching increases influence (Sharpley, 1984).

3. The general effectiveness of matching strategies discussed by Pruitt, Crocker, and Hanes refers to matches of rewards and punishments between two bargainers. Rewards in this context are reciprocal concessions; punishments refer to a failure to reciprocate another's concessions or a retraction of concessions made earlier. The matching discussed in NLP refers to the sensory modalities used in predicates in conversations between people not necessarily engaged in bargaining—a different domain of concern (see, for example, Mercier and Johnson, 1984). They may not be interpreted as either rewards or punishments.

4. Studies of the effectiveness of NLP are limited in a number of ways. The dependent measure used in most studies is client-counselor empathy, as measured on a paper-and-pencil scale (e.g., Hammer, 1983). This is not a satisfactory index of the therapeutic effectiveness of the counselor. One can find a counselor very empathetic but nonetheless ineffective in modifying behaviors or feelings. There are no studies comparing the effectiveness of NLP as an influence technique with other interpersonal influence techniques. None of the studies testing aspects of NLP has used NLP-certified Trainers as counselors, therapists, or eye movement monitors; thus studies that fail to support NLP are subject to the criticism that, if properly trained people had been used, the results would have been more positive. Ignoring where the burden of proof lies, the fact remains that the experimental evidence fails to provide support for NLP.

5. There are no studies in the scientific literature on NLP as a way of modeling experts for training purposes. NLP could be used as a technique for systematically coding expert behavior as a sequence of processing steps, such as "recalls visual image, expresses emotion, constructs audio image," and so on. Two informal studies have attempted to use the NLP coding of expert marksmen in order to construct a template, or training procedure to instruct beginners. One modeled experts shooting .45 caliber pistols and compared an NLP-derived motor learning sequence with conventional instruction. The design of the study was experimentally flawed, and no valid conclusions can be drawn from it. The other study derived a model of rifle shooting from an NLP analysis of expert shooters and created a training program for Army recruits based on it. A comparison of the NLP-derived regimen with a traditional training regimen yielded no differences.

Overall, there is little or no empirical evidence to date to support either NLP assumptions or NLP effectiveness. Different critics may attach different values to the quality of these studies, but the fact remains that none supports the effectiveness of NLP in improving influence or skilled motor performance.

Current Status of NLP

NLP is a widely known technique that is marketed by a number of individuals and firms. Other programs of communication improvement, advertised to organizations and corporations, state that they are based on NLP or draw from NLP principles. Although no figures are available on the number of seminars, workshops, and training institutes offering instruction in NLP, there is anecdotal evidence through advertisements and brochures that many such sessions are offered each year.

The committee was unable to discover the formal proprietary status of NLP. This status is not discussed in the NLP materials available to us. The information we have was given to us by NLP practitioners employed by the Army.

Although it exists in many variations and forms, NLP has been referred to as a single system. Our reference is to the common elements of the training, whether or not these elements are part of a legally protected system. Different people who have received NLP training will probably have been exposed to different variants of the system: we assume that within broad limits their training has been comparable. Because many of the NLP materials are proprietary, they are not available in the scientific literature or on the open market. As a consequence, changes or revisions in the system or its procedures are not part of the public record.

We have received subjective, informal reports from people who have received NLP training. Some reports are negative with respect to the efficacy and usefulness of NLP, but the majority are from satisfied trainees who believe that NLP has improved their communication skills and made them more effective in exercising interpersonal influence. While subjective feelings of change are not necessarily a reliable guide to program efficacy, they do suggest that the NLP system may be effective in increasing self-confidence in its trainees. This gain in self-confidence is characteristic of many training programs and is not a reliable guide to increased performance.

The committee has not located acceptable studies evaluating the ability of NLP to achieve either of its two major objectives. The closest we have found to a study of its primary objective, improving interpersonal influence (Hammer, 1983), uses client ratings of therapist empathy as a dependent variable. Such judgments may or may not be indicative of therapists' effectiveness, but they constitute at best a rather indirect approach to evaluation of NLP as an influence technique. For the secondary objective, using NLP as an expert modeling system, only two studies have been located, both unpublished, one so far unwritten. Even if the NLP model were consistent with other motor performance knowledge, many general questions would remain. How many experts should be sampled to construct a model? How can an NLP-constructed model be validated? Under what circumstances is the use of the model disruptive and distracting?

The lack of evaluation is not apt to be easily remedied. For one thing, the proprietors, purveyors, and practitioners of NLP are not experimentalists and are not interested in conducting such studies. More important, at least for the influence or therapeutic aspect of NLP, a successful evaluation is a major enterprise. It can be equivalent to a clinical trial, in which an extended time frame is required before a judgment on effectiveness can be reached—how long a time is an unsettled question. For example, descriptions of NLP (*Structure of Magic*) claim that it is an effective technique for the treatment of phobias, bringing about change in as little as 20 minutes. There are no studies testing this claim, but any evaluation of it would be faced with many difficult choices regarding criteria for success and testing for relapse. There are not enough examples of motor performance models constructed through the use of NLP techniques to provide a phenomenon to be evaluated. In any case, if such an evaluation produces a negative outcome, the evaluator would have to distinguish between failure of the NLP technique to produce an adequate model and a situation in which the use of an expert model, however accurate, is inappropriate for the task and training conditions.

Unintended Consequences of NLP

To recapitulate, the evidence for a scientific basis of NLP or of validation for its construct is generally weak and negative. There is the logical possibility that NLP may be effective for reasons other than those proffered by its developers; no studies that test this possibility exist. If NLP were effective as an influence and communication protocol, it would be for reasons other than those advanced by its proponents. For example, someone trained in NLP who conscientiously practices it in interaction with another person is engaging in a series of behaviors with the following characteristics. The NLP practitioner is maintaining eye contact and is giving complete attention to the other person; is coding the verbal output of the other person in an overt, analytic manner; is monitoring his or her own verbal output (censoring it and recoding it as a prelude to an attempted predicate, or representational system, match); and is letting the other person's choice of topics and metaphors structure the conversation, reacting to them rather than initiating new directions in the interchange.

It is not known whether the NLP practitioner's monitoring of his or her own behaviors is itself disruptive. Some people trained to maintain eye contact as a communication skill can appear to be manipulative; others, attending to the system's procedures during ordinary conversation, may seem to be distracted. In brief, it is not known whether attending to a set of procedures such as NLP while engaged in conversation enhances or detracts from the ostensible influence goals of the conversation.

The attentional, coding, and organizing behaviors described above are a plausible alternative to the NLP model of representational systems and matching. A course in NLP may well train people to be better communicators and influencers than they were before the course, but people trained in the basic principles of attention and organization might do even better than those with NLP. A proper study of this issue would require at least three groups: a group with NLP training, a group with training in its effective components (listening, attending, self-monitoring), and a control group without either the NLP regimen or its components. Before such a study could be designed, a number of subsidiary questions would have to be answered. Is the size of the effect of practical significance? Which variant of NLP is to be employed? Does the choice make any difference? Are there any structured communication training programs that can be used in contrast to NLP? What is the effectiveness of NLP relative to these other programs? What standards should be used for assessing communicator effectiveness?

NLP as a Modeling System

The use of NLP as a modeling tool raises another set of issues. One important issue is the delineation of the conditions under which it is desirable and useful to use a model of expert behavior to instruct beginners. Many skills are built from the ground up, with early training concentrated on simple units that are later combined into more complex behaviors. Even an accurate model of an expert's behavior might be of no use, or perhaps disruptive or discouraging to a trainee. A person learning to play the violin may reach an intermediate or advanced level and still not benefit from a model of the playing of a virtuoso. Similarly, a beginner may be disrupted by modeling a nonvirtuosic expert's playing. Questions regarding the circumstances in which an expert's performance will be beneficial for training and what level of expertise to match to the trainee's level of proficiency have not been thoroughly explored.

Given that there are circumstances under which such a training procedure is appropriate, how are the expert's behaviors to be decoded, and how is the training template to be constructed? NLP provides a set of algorithms for both tasks. Without evaluations we do not know if the products obtained are optimal or even accurate, but at least they are obtainable. NLP practitioners have not raised the issue or explored the question of whether its expert models are valid. They have not addressed the need for model validation at all.

The process of using NLP to construct models is described in general terms in some of the training materials. For example, if the goal is to teach someone to pilot an airplane, experienced aviators could be placed in a simulator and asked to perform a task, such as flying the plane to a simulated target. The NLP practitioner could encode the pilots' performance, that is, what representational systems were used at what point in the procedures, when anchoring occurred, and so on. The encoding of this information in NLP terms and symbols could provide the protocol for instructing fledgling pilots in the simulator, providing directions on when to visualize the target, when to concentrate on muscular feel, when to listen for engine sound changes, and so on. There are, however, several obstacles to this process. First, there is no guarantee that such a model will accurately describe the salient features of what the expert is doing. Second, even if it is an accurate description, there is no guarantee that the model is optimal: a similar but different model may do a better job of describing the expert's behavior. Third, even if the model works, there is no guarantee that the training template generated from the expert protocol is useful or optimal.

NLP is a protocol for modeling certain types of behaviors. There may be other ways to describe these behaviors, but the committee has no knowledge of any system for deprogramming experts that can be taught as an algorithm. The strengths and weaknesses of NLP as a method of constructing expert systems for teaching are unique; they cannot be judged in relative terms because there are no other methods with which they can be compared. At best, one could compare the full set of NLP procedures with partial sets containing only those aspects that prior knowledge would suggest make a difference. To the extent that NLP may eventually prove to be successful as an expert modeling system, the possibility exists that it may be cost-effective to employ.

Consider the analogy to a software package for a microcomputer. If someone wants a particular filing system, he or she may find that none of the readily available commercial alternatives is exactly what is needed. Each of the packages is missing some of the features that would be desirable, yet each may be a better choice than programming, or paying to have programmed, a custom-designed filing system. The difficulties, expense, and time spent in developing a custom program may make it a less useful option than working with the incomplete, or partially flawed, product that is ready and available on the shelf. When there is time for development and enough potential use for the completed product, the custom product may justify its higher cost in greater effectiveness and utility. In similar fashion, although there may be potential for custom-designed expert modeling systems, NLP provides a convenient, existing way of modeling. It could be argued that the convenience of a more or less codified system, combined with the absence of competitors, makes NLP a more attractive option than it might otherwise be. Given the lack of basic research support and the absence of evaluative studies, even this possibility does not seem likely.

In sum, then, the absence of any evaluation of the effectiveness of NLP and the lack of any scientific basis for it constitute serious reservations against using it for expert modeling purposes, despite its uniqueness. The committee cannot recommend the employment of such an unvalidated technique. If NLP is used for the limited task of constructing expert modeling systems for specific training programs, this should be done only if a program evaluation is incorporated into the implementation.

Transfer of Technology

Applying the findings of social influence to training raises the general question of converting basic science to technology. This has been an undeveloped area of social psychology. Models for the transfer of basic findings into applied programs for specific problems do exist. For example, the work of Varela (1971) on the application of social psychology to industrial consulting provides an interesting set of examples. Research to learn more about a process can always be recommended. The major question is one of priorities: What is the best area in which to invest scarce research funds? The committee suggests that research funds are better spent on testing the effectiveness of combinations of known components and the issues of technology transfer in social science than on evaluation of techniques not substantiated by research.

CONCLUSIONS

We have examined some of the issues regarding the potential for using influence techniques as training procedures and as adjuncts to training, including the nature of formal attitude change programs in social psychology, and we have noted their relative lack of direct applicability to training. We scanned one particular set of procedures, organizational development, which is widely used in industrial and organizational settings, for its applicability to training. (These procedures are also discussed later in the section on group cohesion.) We noted that some nonacademic systems that have been privately developed and commercially marketed claim to use aspects of interpersonal influence as training procedures. One widely known technique, neurolinguistic programming, was examined in some detail. Two general questions were asked. First, does NLP work? There is insufficient information to provide a definitive answer to this question; all the evidence that does exist is either neutral or negative. Second, if aspects of NLP have potential merit, by what means do they achieve their results? The committee concluded that the potentially positive aspects are not unique to NLP and are not related to what is offered as a theoretical underpinning to an empirically developed set of procedures.

Our examination of NLP did bring a number of issues to light and provides the basis for a set of recommendations:

1. There is a need for better ways of transferring social science research findings (in this instance, findings in social psychology) to applied programs. The work of Varela in constructing interventions from social psychological findings is a good model for the type of general research that would be more beneficial than repeated assessment of the possible effectiveness of procedures not substantiated by research.

2. When techniques are to be evaluated, pilot tests should be conducted to assess specific effectiveness in a training setting.

3. When new techniques are to be evaluated, the evaluations should be complemented by periodic reevaluations of existing and currently employed techniques. The same criteria of effectiveness should be used for both current and proposed techniques.

4. There should be a standard format through which vendors or proponents of new techniques provide whatever evidence there is for the efficacy or basis of their techniques. It could be similar to the U.S. Public Health Service's form for research grant proposals or a specified form for contract proposals in response to a federal request for proposals. Besides putting information on new techniques into comparable formats, it would ensure that the questions relevant to a fair and accurate evaluation are addressed and places the burden of proof for evidence of effectiveness on the proposers of the techniques.

GROUP COHESION AND ORGANIZATIONAL EFFECTS

In this section we focus on a property of social units that social scientists label *group cohesion*; it refers to the effects of cohesion on larger social groupings, such as organizations. We consider this topic from both a micro (small group) and a macro (organization) perspective. In effect, the overriding issue is: How does what happens at the micro level affect what happens at the macro level? This general issue leads in turn to the two specific questions that receive primary attention in this section:

1. How is group cohesion developed?
2. What are the consequences for an organization if group cohesion is developed?

The concept of group cohesion was developed in the 1940s at the Research Center for Group Dynamics at the Massachusetts Institute of Technology and later transferred to the University of Michigan (Zander, 1979). With respect to the definition of cohesion, one team of social scientists notes that it "has been defined variously as referring to morale, 'sticking together,' productivity, power, task involvement, feelings of belongingness, shared understanding of roles and good teamwork" (Schachter et al., 1951:192). Nevertheless, a definition cited by Zander (1979) seems to be commonly, though not universally, accepted: "the desire of members to remain as members of a group." Zander goes on to point out, however, that (p. 433):

. . . current [social science] researchers accept this definition, but in the absence [as of 1979] of a reliable method for measuring cohesiveness in a natural setting, or a reliable procedure for creating it in the laboratory, one cannot be sure to what phenomena investigators are attending when they examine its origins or effects.

This is an extremely important and pertinent observation for us.

In this vein, it is important to stress that some people have broadened the concept by removing the restrictive term *group* and simply referring to cohesion. In such cases, presumably, the intention is to employ the essence of the concept without the implied requirement that it be limited to small groups. Thus, for example, Henderson, in his book on cohesion, cites the following definition, which he uses in considering the concept in the context of Army organizations (1985:4): ". . . the bonding together of members of an organization/unit in such a way as to sustain their will and commitment to each other, their unit, and the mission." This use of cohesion, it should be noted, allows the term to be applied to units of any size (the total organization or some unit within the organization, or both). Furthermore, it can encompass both lateral (member to peer group) and vertical (member to member above or member below) cohesion (or, in Army terminology, *bonding*). This concept of cohesion is broader than that used by social psychologists, but it is probably more relevant to organizations comprising a number of different groups within an overall structure.

It should be noted that in the military context this broadened use of the term cohesion is sometimes called *military cohesion* (Henderson, 1985:9). Military cohesion is typically defined to include acceptance of the organization's goals. When cohesion is defined in this manner, there can be no argument about its benefits, and it is easy to see why military cohesion is so universally accepted as a positive concept. This definition is, however, essentially circular and therefore not very useful—it does not help us to understand how people come to accept the organization's goals in the first place.

One other term used somewhat similarly in organizational contexts is *organizational commitment*. While it is a close relative, so to speak, of cohesion, it is not identical, because it has been used to refer explicitly to a member's relation to the encompassing social unit, namely, the organization.

The relations among the three terms—*group cohesion, organizational commitment*, and *cohesion* (bonding)—might be summarized as follows:

• *Group cohesion* refers to the member's relation to his or her immediate (small) unit.

• *Organizational commitment* refers to the member's relation to the larger organization, which includes his or her own as well as other units.

• *Cohesion* refers to the member's relation to both the immediate unit (peers and leaders) and the larger organization of which the immediate unit is a part.

In this chapter, we employ all three terms but with a preference for the more restricted term *group cohesion*, because we believe that term, with its associated definition, is of most use for the analytical objectives of this project.

Clearly, cohesion is a property of social units that has a great deal of relevance for any large organization, such as a corporation, a government agency, or a military organization. On the surface, at least, it is a property that would seem to have many advantages: lower member turnover, higher concern of individual members for the common good, greater willingness to pursue organizational goals, increased resistance to external attacks (of any type) on the organization, and the like. Many of these positive features of cohesion as they relate to the Army are extensively discussed in the book by Henderson (1985). Likewise, books in the popular press relating to business firms (e.g., Peters and Waterman's *In Search of Excellence*) cite these and other advantages of efforts to generate high commitment to organizations. Such approaches to the topic tend to assume that cohesion or organizational commitment is good, and that more of it is even better.

There are also potential negative consequences of group cohesion, and these should be taken into account by any organization that contemplates promoting it. We reserve consideration of such consequences for a later section; for the moment it is important only to point out that not all effects are necessarily positive.

In the sections that follow, we briefly review the scientific research literature as it relates to cohesion, especially group cohesion. We consider what steps organizations can take to develop cohesion and then analyze the potential consequences—both positive and negative—of cohesion if it is developed. We conclude with a discussion of application issues and several recommendations.

EVIDENCE FROM BASIC RESEARCH

Cohesion in Small Groups

The literature pertaining to cohesion in small, face-to-face groups can be partitioned into two categories: the causes of cohesion and the consequences of cohesion.

Causes of Group Cohesion. The available research literature points to three factors that have the potential for generating increased group cohesion: (1) strong interpersonal attraction among group members; (2) high performance of the group; and (3) high level of conflict with other groups.

Although the evidence for the first factor is fairly consistent (for example, see the studies by Stokes, 1983; Terborg, Castore, and DeNinno, 1976), empirical support for the latter two factors is not clear-cut. For example, recent work by Landers et al. (1982) raises issues about the adequacy of the research designs of earlier studies purporting to show strong evidence of good group performance leading to increasing cohesion, even though this result seems to be widely accepted. With respect to whether conflict with "out" groups increases cohesion within a given group, Stein (1976) reviewed work from a number of social science disciplines and concluded that "there is a clear convergence in the literature . . . that suggests that external (to the group) conflict does increase internal cohesion *under certain conditions.*" We have italicized these three words to emphasize the fact that such conditions—for example, the ability of the group to cope effectively with the threat, consensus about the importance of the threat—may be crucial in many real-world situations. Indeed, the extent to which this particular conclusion (external conflict leads to greater internal cohesion) needs to be qualified by the consideration of various conditions has led a major researcher in this field to state:

These are perennial questions [regarding the possible effects of modifying conditions] and it is not surprising that recent social psychological research [has] continued to find no more than piecemeal answers to them. . . . A good deal of useful data have been collected without achieving what would amount to a major theoretical breakthrough providing a new perspective on the old established functional relationship. (Tajfel, 1982:16)

Consequences of Group Cohesion. Research on the consequences of group cohesion has focused primarily on two areas: (1) conformity of individual members' beliefs to group norms; and (2) performance of the group.

With regard to the first of these consequences, both laboratory and field studies tend to show that groups with higher levels of cohesion (as measured by some instrument that purports to measure it) tend to have greater conformity to some set of norms and are willing to take greater risks.

With regard to group performance as a consequence, however, the findings are much less clear-cut and are particularly sensitive to the criterion problem, that is, the necessity to select, on an arbitrary basis, a measure or measures that constitute good performance. As a loose generalization, the research evidence appears to show that high group cohesion can be linked to either high or low group performance, depending on what the group norms are (Berkowitz, 1954; Schachter et al., 1951; Seashore, 1954). (The issue of causality is clearly relevant here: Does high group cohesion coupled with positive performance norms lead to increased group performance, or are the two variables merely correlated? Strong evidence for causality appears not to have been established to date.) Thus, the widely held, commonsense assumption that more cohesion inevitably results in better performance is not uniformly supported by the available data. For example, one realm in which one might expect such a relationship to hold with great regularity is competitive sports. As Landers et al. (1982:170) have stated: "The relationship between social cohesion and sport participation has had an enduring fascination among coaches and researchers alike. They have often assumed that when players on a team display unity and 'stick together,' they will have a greater chance of team success." They go on to note: "Unfortunately, this intuitively appealing assumption is not as straightforward as it might appear. Although some evidence supports it, there is also research which fails to provide support.''

In summary, then, research findings on the consequences of high cohesion in small groups fail to provide unequivocal evidence regarding causality, or even evidence that high cohesion is always associated with better group performance. Such findings do, however, indicate that the issue of performance norms (and how to affect them) is critical in determining the direction (positive or negative) of any association between the two variables.

Cohesion in Organizations

For our purposes, the literature based on studies carried out within organizational contexts can be categorized into three areas: organizational development, organizational commitment, and organizational culture.

Organizational Development Studies. For the past decade or so, many persons in the field of organizational development have talked about the concept of team building, usually referring to attempts to make intact work groups in organizations more effective at their particular tasks. Unfortunately, there have not been many solid, well-controlled research studies (as opposed to case studies of single organizational situations) dealing with the particular organizational intervention of team building. The conclusions that Friedlander and Brown came to about 15 years ago still appear to be valid (1974:328–329):

The literature contains a number of case studies of group development activities from the vantage point of the consultant. But these case studies offer little more than the flavor of the experience. . . . The critical elements of the team-building process remain only partially explored. . . . It remains unclear . . . what mechanisms operate in successful team development activities, or what critical conditions must be satisfied for successful generalization of learnings outside the team, or what effects group development has on actual task performance.

Organizational Commitment Studies. The field of organizational psychology (organizational behavior) has produced a large number of studies in recent years on issues concerning how individuals relate to the larger organization, not just their immediate work group. Some of this research has focused on individuals' commitment to the larger organization. The concept of organizational commitment is closely akin to group cohesion (Zander, for example, sees it as the same), but the research has not had the small group focus of the typical social psychology study of cohesion. At the risk of over-generalizing, it can be stated that research to date appears to associate organizational commitment clearly with lower rates of member (usually employee) turnover but much less clearly with other measures of organizational performance. Furthermore, partly because most studies in this area have been of a correlational nature, there is little or no solid scientific evidence that attempts to increase organizational commitment have resulted in increased performance (Mowday, Porter, and Steers, 1982).

Organizational Culture Studies. The cultural dimension of organizations has received attention recently. Schein (1985), for example, provides a framework for understanding the role played by culture in organizational settings. He conceptualizes it at progressively deeper levels, referred to as artifacts (e.g., technology, art), values (i.e., a sense of what ought to be), and basic assumptions (e.g., the nature of human relations). The deepest level, basic assumptions, is the foundation for a wide variety of group decisions. It can be understood only by probing the thinking and behavior of members within the organizational setting. Schein's analysis leads to insights about the functions of culture in organizations, how culture develops, and how it changes. These insights in turn could provide the basis for intervention strategies, that is structured attempts to shape a "desired environment."

Schein's approach is rooted in the proposition that culture is pervasive and therefore cannot be ignored. He and other organizational scientists believe that the elusiveness of the concept is not a reason for ignoring its consequences. Culture is basic: it makes possible changes in policy and organizational design, which are (according to this view) only superficial aspects of culture. It affects a group's strategy, its structure, and the ways in which members relate to each other. A strong culture is purported to allow for organizational change without itself being changed. Elton's (1984) description of the traditions of the Army's project COHORT illustrates the contention that strong cultures are more likely to be found in highly cohesive units. Whether culture can be manipulated effectively to produce cohesion or, more important, to enhance performance is an issue we consider below.

Conclusions

Strong empirical associations between cohesion (however defined in particular studies) and other relevant variables have not been well established on a consistent basis. The many potential third variables that could modify such relations appear to militate against the operation of reliable associations and make them highly contingent on other, uncontrolled factors. Thus, if associations or correlations between cohesion and other key variables have not been produced on a regular basis, then generalized cause-effect relations obviously also have not been demonstrated. Taken together, the pattern of available evidence is not encouraging for organizations that might want to promote and develop cohesion in order to improve desirable organizational outcomes.

We cannot rule out the possibility that strong positive evidence regarding cohesion (especially its effects) could be developed in the future. Therefore, organizations that believe that efforts to increase cohesion will ultimately be found to be effective must proceed largely on faith. In doing so, they should be aware of both the potential negative consequences as well as the hoped-for positive consequences.

POTENTIAL APPROACHES TO DEVELOPING COHESION IN LARGE ORGANIZATIONS

Before the consequences of cohesion can be considered, it is necessary to consider how this property of groups and organizations might be developed. In social science terms, we must first consider cohesion as a dependent variable: What variables, if changed, will result in greater cohesion?

Implications from Research on Cohesion

As noted earlier, social psychological research on small groups has focused on three factors that have the potential for increasing group cohesion. Such factors might be considered at least as starting points for thinking about how organizations could develop or build cohesion. Translated from the research sphere, the corresponding guidelines would be stated as follows: (1) increase members' attraction for each other; (2) increase the performance of the group, unit, or organization; and (3) heighten the salience of conflict or competition with other groups. Two questions immediately emerge in connection with such guidelines: (1) How feasible would they be to implement? (2) How effective would they be if implemented? We consider each of these in turn.

Feasibility. The first guideline—increasing members' attraction for each other—is a possibility, but one that would not be particularly easy to achieve. One approach might be to group together individuals with similar values or other relevant characteristics. Another avenue might be for organizations to provide members with various types of information about each other in an effort to increase attraction or liking. The success of either of these two approaches would depend on a number of other factors that might not be easily controlled, such as the prior strength of attitudes of each member about other members (or categories of members) of the group.

The second guideline, increasing the performance of the group in order to increase its cohesiveness, involves a clear paradox: if increased performance is the ultimate criterion, then increased cohesion could only come about as a result of performance rather than as a cause. Actually, of course, it is easier—and perhaps more appropriate—to think of a recurring reciprocal relation: that is, increased performance leads to increased cohesiveness, which in turn leads to increased performance. From a practical standpoint, the initial problem in implementing this guideline would be to decide where to enter this cycle. Which variable should be worked on first if both are low? By implication, increased cohesion, which will lead to increased performance, should be easier to generate if a social unit is already performing reasonably well.

The third guideline, involving competition or conflict with external groups, might be implemented relatively easily in situations in which there is an easily identified other group. An obvious example is team sports: the criterion of performance is clear, the membership of one's own team is clear, and the identity of the competing group is clear. For many other types of organizational situations, however, it is much more difficult to identify the competitor. While a total organization (e.g., an automobile company, the army of a particular country, a university) may find it easy to identify external competitors, it is not so easy for particular units within an organization to identify their competitors. Often it is similar units within competing external organizations, but in many cases it is other units within their own organizations (e.g., another group of similar size, a larger unit, or even the total organization itself). The latter circumstances could occur, for example, where there is competition for scarce organizational resources. Thus, in any contexts other than the one of a single group against one or more clearly specified other groups, the use of this method to increase internal cohesion would involve a great deal of complexity, which could substantially increase costs. To put this another way, a given group often has multiple agendas, and it is not a simple matter to restrict their competitive energies to a single target.

Effectiveness. The other critical issue for evaluating the potential usefulness of guidelines suggested by social psychological research on small groups is their effectiveness in producing the intended results (i.e., increased cohesion). Earlier in this chapter we reviewed the available literature, which showed that the first guideline, increasing members' interpersonal attraction, would be effective if it could be implemented. The literature was not consistent regarding the other two guidelines, namely, increasing group performance and emphasizing conflict with "out" groups, indicating that those guidelines could not be counted on to produce reliable effects across a variety of situations. In other words, the effort expended to implement the approaches might not produce proportionate benefits. At the least, these research findings argue for modest expectations on the part of anyone attempting to develop more cohesion with either of these methods.

To this point we have been discussing the utility of several guidelines emerging from small group social psychological research. However, this does not exhaust all possible approaches an organization might take to increase its cohesion and the cohesion of the units within it. One potentially powerful approach is to pay attention to the culture (shared ways of viewing the world) of the organization and its constituent parts. As discussed earlier, there has been considerable recent scholarly work in this area, and it is to this literature that we turn for other possible guidelines that organizations might follow to increase overall cohesion.

Implications from Research on Organizational Culture

Organizational culture views cohesion as a result of both structural and cultural factors. Its primary contribution is to add cultural variables as mediators between group structures and attitudes or performances. The same group structures may produce different outcomes, depending on cultural processes. These processes have implications for levels of cohesion and for the success of the Army's project COHORT. Some of these implications are developed in the paper prepared for the committee by Boaz Tamir and Gideon Kunda (Appendix B) and are summarized briefly below.

Horizontal Cohesion. Structural integrity (no rotation of members) is a necessary but not sufficient condition for achieving horizontal cohesion (bonding between members at the same level in an organization). Differences among members in basic assumptions would reduce group cohesion. A case in point is the often-cited racial tension among peers in the U.S. Army in Vietnam (see Moskos, 1975).

Vertical Cohesion. Structural integrity of units can be dysfunctional for vertical cohesion (bonding between members and leaders). Cohorts can develop a subculture that rejects standard operating procedures, which call for management from the top down. This phenomenon is illustrated by Van Maanen's comparison (1983) of the Harvard and MIT graduate programs: the former program's cohort structure produces strong horizontal cohesion among students but weak vertical bonding between students and professors; the latter program emphasizes individual training and leads to strong vertical bonding but weak friendships among peers. Further implications can be drawn for promotion. It can be argued that strong internal cultures suppress initiative, encouraging loyalty to the unit rather than identification with, and aspiration to, the officer corps.

Cultural Conflict. Demands for loyalty to the cohort unit can conflict with civilian values. Earlier socialization produces values that may not coincide with the unit's assumptions: examples are civilian legal principles of military subordination to the civil government, the larger ethical and moral foundations of the society, and identity as an individual and private citizen. The challenges of resocialization are considerable and may be made even more difficult by certain demographic elements. One of these elements is the large number of enlisted soldiers without alternative economic choices: the elite spirit fostered by the cohort system conflicts with a possible second-class spirit resulting from disappointment in the civilian marketplace.

Each of these implications calls attention to the importance of cultural dimensions. Analyses of cohesion that concentrate only on structural factors are limited. So, too, are policies based on structural arrangements that overlook the development of subcultures. Those subcultures can serve to either increase or decrease a unit's overall cohesion, and the consequences may differ for horizontal and vertical bonding.

POTENTIAL CONSEQUENCES OF COHESION

As we have mentioned several times above, cohesion can create either positive or negative consequences, or both.

Positive Consequences

The prevailing opinion of military decision makers and analysts, as well as many managers from industry, is that cohesion is highly functional for group and organizational performance. Elton (1984) makes this argument in support of the Army's project COHORT. He implies that those structural and cultural factors that enhance unit cohesion also enhance unit performance. (By cohesion he means primarily the bonding that occurs among members of the unit, i.e., horizontal bonding.)

Henderson (1985) elaborates this argument in several directions. He claims that the heightened nationalism and self-worth that develop in cohesive units contribute to a better fighting unit. (His definition of cohesion emphasizes the bonding that occurs between group members and the leader, i.e., vertical bonding). Drawing on a sociological perspective, he imputes certain consequences to cohesion, for example, low member turnover and more effort on behalf of the group.

Perhaps the strongest recent statement of Army belief in the positive consequences of cohesion is contained in Technical Report No. 3 on "The New Manning System Field Evaluation" by the Walter Reed Army Institute for Research (1986). This report states (p. 9 of the overview) that a panel of "distinguished military officers" and several "civilian scholars"

. . . felt very strongly that the value of military cohesion for effective combat operations rests on historical experience, and need not be correlated with measures of garrison performance to command attention at the highest levels of the Army. The panel accepted as fact that military cohesion is an important inhibitor of psychological breakdown in battle. They emphasized the importance of this relationship above and beyond the research community's ability to demonstrate relationships between cohesion and unit training performance.

The research community is supportive to some degree regarding the potential of cohesiveness for generating positive impact. For example, the research discusses such consequences as willingness to perform tasks not required by a member's role, higher conformity to the organization's norms and rules, and a propensity for taking risks, including altruistic behavior on behalf of the group (e.g., Katz and Kahn, 1966; Campbell, 1975). These consequences are assumed to be—and may well be—functional in the context of competitive intergroup or interorganizational relations.

Most of the above arguments are considerably more speculative than conclusive. Several reasons can be given for treating them as hypotheses rather than proven conclusions. First, most treatments of the issue are not sufficiently analytic to separate consequences from indicators of cohesion. For example, are nationalistic attitudes (or commitment to the group) a consequence or a defining feature of cohesion? Second, the hypothesized relation between improved cohesion and better unit performance is assumed rather than tested. A distinction should be made between the use of case histories as sources of insight and the use of real or simulated exercises as a setting for testing hypotheses about the cohesion-performance relation. Third, there is a tendency to rely on single-factor explanations for group performance. An alternative approach would consider cohesion one of several factors influencing a variety of performances. Other group properties might include authority structures,

concentration of members, and the nature of standard operating procedures. Effectiveness might be divided into parts such as efficiency,
mobilization for action, and agreement on group goals. Fourth, the
cohesion-performance relation is likely to be more complex than the
simple assertion of positive effects would suggest (see, for example, the
previously cited study by Landers et al., 1982, which highlights the
possibility of reciprocal effects between these two variables).

Despite the general lack of empirical support for arguments that
increased cohesion results in positive consequences, some progress is
being made. One important source of such factual evidence is the
previously mentioned study of the Army's project COHORT being
conducted by the Walter Reed Army Institute for Research. At the time
this chapter was drafted, three technical reports on the COHORT project
had been issued; these present the results of soldier surveys conducted
as part of the New Manning System (NMS) field evaluation. Of particular
interest are the COHORT–non-COHORT comparisons, which to date
have been made on a series of questions pertaining to "soldier will,"
including confidence in the senior command, concerned leadership, sense
of pride, unit social climate, and unit teamwork. The total scale used in
the study has discriminated between COHORT and non-COHORT units
"with some degree of confidence." This evidence suggested to the
reports' authors that COHORT units have been successful in building
cohesive and confident fighting units. Missing from the study, however,
is a link to performance.

Future research on project COHORT may provide evidence for the
cohesion-performance relation. Such measures as proficiency in combat
skills or crew performance would be appropriate, particularly if the
analysis is focused on the level of groups. However, there are some
unresolved problems to be addressed. One of these, for example, is
practical: How does the Army view the relative importance of different
training outcomes? Another is conceptual: Is there a theory about how
COHORT units are supposed to affect soldier morale and group cohesion,
which in turn affect training results and performance? Put differently,
how are attitudes that distinguish between COHORT and non-COHORT
units reflected in relevant performance variables? And, more generally,
is group cohesion a useful concept for understanding this type of relation?
There are some reasons to suggest that, in some circumstances, group
cohesion may be dysfunctional for performance, and we now turn to
those issues.

Negative Consequences

Although cohesion as a property of social units has the potential for
creating a number of positive (i.e., organizationally valued) effects, it

also has the potential for producing negative effects. We draw on an overview of the relevant literature by Porter, Lawler, and Hackman (1975) to summarize some of the possible dysfunctional consequences of attempts to increase cohesion.

Ineffective Handling of Deviance.   In highly cohesive groups there is always the danger that someone expressing opinions or exhibiting behavior that differs from the group's accepted wisdom will not be heard by the group. That poses no problem, of course, if the deviant opinion or action is without merit and would, if attended to, cause the group to misuse its available resources or otherwise engage in ineffective activity. However, if what is considered deviance actually represents a type of creativity that could be used by the group, early rejection would prevent this contribution from being used (Torrance, 1954). The issue here is that both "good" and "bad" deviance may be more easily and firmly rejected by highly cohesive groups than by groups whose members have less fierce adherence to group norms.

Groupthink.   Somewhat related to the above is the danger that groups will fail to examine objectively any negative information (i.e., information the group would prefer not to hear), whether from inside or outside the group. The focus here is not on the source (whether a respected group member, a deviant, another group) but on the content of the information. Groupthink is a phenomenon (Janis, 1972) that has been sufficiently well described in a variety of scholarly and popular publications, so it is not necessary to examine it in detail here. The critical issue is that groupthink is more likely to develop in highly cohesive, closely knit groups or units than in those with lower cohesion, whose members are not as sensitive to the opinions of their fellows.

Increased Impact of any Existing Negative Norms.   Highly cohesive groups are no more likely than less cohesive groups to have negative norms (i.e., performance norms that run counter to those of the organization of which they are a part); however, such research evidence as there is tends to conclude that *if* a group is cohesive and *if* it has such norms, then its performance will be even lower than that of less cohesive groups with similar negative norms. In other words, there is a greater probability of a reverberation effect that could work counter to the interests of the larger organization if the cohesive group is headed in the wrong (so to speak) direction. Thus, in instances of extreme stress, such as wartime fighting conditions, this kind of effect might be especially exaggerated in such groups.

Increased Intergroup Conflict. A potential, but certainly not an inevitable, consequence of high intragroup cohesion is increased conflict with other groups. At the current stage of development of organizational science, it is not possible to predict with any degree of certainty the direction of impact (if any) of high intragroup cohesion on intergroup cohesion within the organization. Thus, there is little available evidence to support the notion that increases in cohesion within groups of an organization will automatically result in increased cohesion between groups in that organization. To our knowledge, there also appears to be little evidence that would definitely indicate the opposite. The point we make here is simply that such consequences have not been studied extensively, and it is possible that, under some circumstances, more small group cohesion might result in greater fragmentation of the larger organization. Such a possibility would suggest that organizations (as opposed to single groups operating relatively independently) might want to be alert to this potential danger in pursuing the development of high cohesion within groups or units.

APPLICATION ISSUES

In this section we briefly discuss three issues relating to the application of cohesion concepts in organizations: the knowledge base available to organizations to apply cohesion as a "technology"; the feasibility and costs of application; and the potential gains and losses from developing increased cohesion.

Knowledge Base

The first important issue regarding the possibilities of applying a cohesion approach to organizations concerns the degree to which we have an available knowledge base for such applications. Such a base would consist of two parts: what is known about cohesion itself and what is known about how to apply it.

Over the past 40 years social scientists have developed a certain amount of basic information about the properties of cohesion that can be moderately useful to organizations. This information appears to be more adequate in understanding the causes of cohesion than it does in helping to predict the consequences. Research evidence on the latter is mixed in terms of the directions of the findings; it is also not substantial in terms of the number of well-controlled studies carried out in organizational settings.

The available evidence concerning how to apply cohesion in organizations is also limited. There are very few studies in the scientific literature of interventions to increase cohesion followed by careful measurement of the consequences (e.g., Tyerman and Spencer, 1983). It can be presumed that some approaches would be much more effective than others—indeed, some approaches might even turn out to be counter-productive for the organization—but to date there is scant evidence concerning the comparative efficacy of different methods of building cohesion in organizations. Thus, there is very little in the way of a knowledge base to guide organizations in how to go about creating cohesion that will have positive consequences.

Feasibility and Costs

A second major, indeed crucial, application issue concerns the feasibility and costs of attempting to build cohesion within organizations. At least four such implementation issues should be considered.

At What Organizational Level Should Efforts Begin?   The degree of cohesion perceived to exist at the top of the organization can have a powerful cascading effect on cohesion at lower levels. Thus, it might seem most effective to begin cohesion efforts in organizations at the topmost levels. However, by starting there, the process of developing cohesion throughout the organization might take so long that it would never reach the lower levels, which contain the bulk of the organization's members. A more direct approach to those members would be to start at the lower levels and work upward, to the extent that there are sufficient time and other resources. If initial efforts to build cohesion begin with the lowest (or at least lower) units in an organization, however, a question can be raised as to whether this will be effective if prior attention has not been given to cohesion in upper levels, the location of role models.

Where Should the Bonding Be Focused?   If cohesion is promoted as a group or unit attribute, this has considerable potential for creating greater bonding among members within the group as well as to the group's immediate leader. That is, concern about the group and the group's fate would be expected to increase. As we have previously stressed, however, greater bonding to the group or unit does not necessarily guarantee more commitment to the larger organization. But if commitment to the larger organization is stressed and unit cohesion is ignored or bypassed, any effects may be greatly attenuated, because so much organizational performance occurs at the group or unit level.

How Much Time and Cost Are Required?   Seldom discussed in the social science literature on cohesion is a consideration of the costs involved in building it. While there appear to be some potential positive consequences of cohesion, these could be outweighed by the costs required to produce them. In particular, the most critical costs may be what economists call opportunity costs; that is, if efforts are directed toward building group or organizational cohesion, other organizational activities would receive less attention. To gauge whether it is worthwhile to try to develop cohesion, an organization must also consider the comparative cost-benefit ratios for other types of desired outcomes. Increased cohesion may or may not fare well in such a comparison, depending on the needs of the organization and the particular circumstances in which it finds itself.

What Are the Most Cost-Effective Methods of Building Cohesion? As stated above, there is almost no scientifically reliable and valid evidence to guide organizations in building cohesion. At the present time, organizations either have to carry out their own experiments or simply use their best judgment.

Potential Gains and Losses

To summarize our discussion, many people believe that developing cohesion in organizations will produce favorable results, but evidence supporting this contention is weak at present. Persons advocating more cohesion in organizations believe it is intrinsically good. They also point to a number of benefits that would accrue if greater cohesion could be achieved. Such potential gains, in principle at least, appear to be attainable if an organization is willing to make the necessary investments of scarce resources (time, money, effort diverted from other activities). The size of such gains, however, is unknown and possibly could be smaller than anticipated. Furthermore, there are some potential unintended consequences that could turn out to be deleterious for the organization. Again, available research is virtually silent as to whether such negative outcomes would in fact occur. All of this suggests that the amount still to be learned about the development and consequences of cohesion in organizations far exceeds what is currently known. Additional rigorous and well-controlled research could prove to be useful in assessing the potential gains and losses from attempts by organizations to increase cohesion within them.

SOURCES OF INFORMATION

In addition to their own reviews of literature, the subcommittees on social processes received briefings on relevant projects and requested the preparation of papers that treated a related subject in depth. The influence subcommittee learned about the practice of neurolinguistic programming by participating in a workshop and interviewing its developer. It was also informed of the large literature on influence strategies, including both verbal and nonverbal communication, through a paper prepared by Pruitt, Crocker, and Hanes. The cohesion subcommittee members were briefed by the Army on projects designed to evaluate the COHORT system and benefited from a paper on the transmission of values in organizations prepared by Tamir and Kunda. The growing literature on organizational cultures proved to be particularly relevant to issues of group processes and performance.

PART III

Parapsychological Techniques

O F ALL THE SUBJECTS TREATED in this volume, none is more controversial than parapsychology. While the flavor of the debates is captured to some extent in this chapter, the subject is treated in the same manner as the other techniques reviewed: we address the question of whether the evidence warrants further consideration of parapsychological techniques for research or application or both.

Emphasized here is information gathering by remote viewing and mindover-matter effects in controlling machine behavior, particularly machines that generate series of random numbers, which are often used in parapsychology experiments. Although scattered results are said to be statistically significant, an evaluation of a large body of the best available evidence does not support the contention that these phenomena exist. If, however, future experiments, conducted according to the best possible methodological standards, are more generally viewed as producing significant results, it would be appropriate to consider a systematic program of research. Such a program should include a concern for the need to proceed from small effects to practical applications.

9

Paranormal Phenomena

BACKGROUND

The primary purpose of this chapter is to evaluate the scientific evidence on parapsychological techniques in selected areas. A more complete understanding of the topic, however, requires that we provide background on the military's interest in these phenomena and treat the conceptual issue of how people come to believe as they do. This background section includes a discussion of the phenomena and the military's interest in them as well as an overview of the committee's focus. A brief examination of the different kinds of justifications for the claims is followed by a more detailed treatment of the evidence in areas that have produced large literatures: remote viewing, random number generators, and what are called Ganzfeld (whole visual field) experiments. In addition, we describe experimental work that the committee actually witnessed by visiting a parapsychological laboratory. Despite the growing scientific tradition in some of these areas, many people continue to rely on qualitative or experiential evidence to support their beliefs; we discuss the problems associated with qualitative evidence in conjunction with the research on cognitive and emotional biases, which is reviewed in the paper by Dale Griffin (Appendix B). Finally, the chapter summarizes the committee's major conclusions.

THE NATURE OF THE PHENOMENA

Parapsychologists divide *psi*—the term applied to all psychic phenomena—into two broad categories: *extrasensory perception* (ESP) and *psychokinesis* (PK). Included in ESP are telepathy, precognition, and clairvoyance, all of which refer to methods of gathering information about objects or thoughts without the intervention of known sensory mechanisms. Popularly called mind over matter, PK refers to the influence of thoughts upon objects without the intervention of known physical processes.

A presentation to the committee by several military officers described in some detail the results of experiments in remote viewing carried out at both SRI International and the Engineering Anomalies Research Laboratory at Princeton University. In these experiments subjects are said to have more or less accurately described a geographical location being visited by a target team. Although the human subjects have no way of normally knowing the target location, the examples recounted appear to indicate, at first glance, some striking correspondences between their descriptions and the actual sites. These studies have been related by some persons to reported out-of-body experiences.

The presentation included discussion of psychic mind-altering techniques, the levitation claims of transcendental meditation groups, psychotronic weapons, psychic metal bending, dowsing, thought photography, and bioenergy transfer. It was indicated that the Soviet Union is far ahead of the United States in developing potential applications of such paranormal phenomena, in particular psychically controlling and influencing minds at a distance. At the presentation, personal accounts were given of spoon-bending parties, in which participants believe they have caused cutlery to bend with the power of their minds, as well as instances of self-hypnosis to control pain and cure illness, walking barefoot on fire and handling hot coals without being burned, leaving one's body at will, and bursting clouds by psychic means.

The media and popular publications, especially in recent years, have discussed various aspects of psychic warfare. Three recent books, by Ebon (1983), McRae (1984), and Targ and Harary (1984), have attempted to document Soviet and American efforts to develop military and intelligence applications of alleged paranormal phenomena. These accounts have been augmented by newspaper stories, magazine articles, and television programs. Many of these sources acknowledge the speculative nature of the proposed applications, but others report that some of the techniques already exist and work.

The claimed phenomena and applications range from the incredible to the outrageously incredible. The "antimissile time warp," for example, is supposed to somehow deflect attack by nuclear warheads so that they will transcend time and explode among the ancient dinosaurs, thereby leaving us unharmed but destroying many dinosaurs (and, presumably, some of our evolutionary ancestors). Other psychotronic weapons, such as the "hyperspatial nuclear howitzer," are claimed to have equally bizarre capabilities. Many of the sources cite the claim that Soviet psychotronic weapons were responsible for the 1976 outbreak of Legionnaires' disease, as well as the 1963 sinking of the nuclear submarine *Thresher*.

POTENTIAL MILITARY APPLICATIONS

Some people, including some military decision makers, can imagine potential military applications of the two broad categories of psychic phenomena. In their view, ESP, if real and controllable, could be used for intelligence gathering and, because it includes "precognition," ESP could also be used to anticipate the actions of an enemy. It is believed that PK, if realizable, might be used to jam enemy computers, prematurely trigger nuclear weapons, and incapacitate weapons and vehicles. More specific applications envisioned involve behavior modification; inducing sickness, disorientation, or even death in a distant enemy; communicating with submarines; planting thoughts in individuals without their knowledge; hypnotizing individuals at a distance; psychotronic weapons of various kinds; psychic shields to protect sensitive information or military installations; and the like. One suggested application is a conception of the "First Earth Battalion," made up of "warrior monks," who will have mastered almost all the techniques under consideration by the committee, including the use of ESP, leaving their bodies at will, levitating, psychic healing, and walking through walls.

THE COMMITTEE'S FOCUS

Although such colorful examples provide the context for our agenda, the cumulative body of data in the discipline of parapsychology enables us to judge the degree to which paranormal claims should be taken seriously. Since 1882 reports of both naturally occurring incidents and phenomena in laboratory settings have been accumulated in journals, monographs, and books. Just to survey the reports in the refereed journals of parapsychology would be an enormous undertaking. As scientists, our inclination is, of course, to restrict ourselves to the evidence that purports to be scientific. But the alleged phenomena that have apparently gained most attention and that have apparently convinced many proponents do not come from the parapsychological laboratory. Nothing approaching a scientific literature supports the claims for psychotronic weaponry, psychic metal bending, out-of-body experiences, and other potential applications supported by many proponents.

The phenomena are real and important in the minds of proponents, so we attempt to evaluate them fairly. Although we cannot rely solely on a scientific data base to evaluate the claims, their credibility ultimately must stand or fall on the basis of data from scientific research that is subject to adequate control and is potentially replicable.

We divided the task into two parts. First, we looked at the best scientific arguments for the reality of psychic phenomena. Our sponsors, as well as our own appraisal of the current status of parapsychology, indicated that the two most influential scientific programs were the experiments on remote viewing and the experiments on psychokinesis using random event generators. In addition, we looked at the research on the Ganzfeld (whole visual field) because this, in the opinion of many parapsychologists, is the most likely candidate for a replicable experiment. We also report on a parapsychological experiment that the committee itself witnessed.

Second, we considered the arguments of proponents who rely on what they call qualitative as opposed to quantitative evidence for the paranormal. Such evidence depends on personal experience or the testimony of others who have had such experience. Most, if not all, of this evidence cannot be evaluated by scientific standards, yet it has created compelling beliefs among many who have encountered it. Witnessing or having an anomalous experience can be more powerful than large accumulations of quantitative, scientific data as a method of creating and reinforcing beliefs. Because personal experience rather than scientific data has been the source of most beliefs in the paranormal, we have devoted some of our resources to considering this sort of cognitive method as a tool for achieving knowledge.

STANDARDS OF EVIDENCE

Diverse justifications have been offered for pursuing paranormal claims. One argument asserts that paranormal phenomena may no longer be anomalous, given the implications of contemporary quantum mechanics. Indeed, a few physicists have supported some parapsychologists in maintaining that certain forms of precognition and psychokinesis are consistent with some interpretations of quantum theory. The other major argument is that we have no choice but to get involved because the Soviet Union already has a program to develop military applications of psychic phenomena.

Several proponents, including some scientists, firmly believe that paranormal phenomena have been scientifically demonstrated several times over. At the same time, most scientists do not believe that psi exists. Many persons on both sides believe this paradox to be the result of irrational and dogmatic belief systems. The proponents accuse the critics of being closed-minded and bigoted. The critics imply that the proponents have allowed wishful thinking to bias their judgment and that they are incompetent scientists and are self-deceived. Both sides can point to examples to back their positions.

One essential question confronts the committee: What does an impartial examination of the scientific evidence reveal about the existence of psi? Such an examination assumes that clear standards exist for judging the adequacy of the evidence, which, in turn, raises the issue of what constitutes sufficient evidence. That issue involves many difficult philosophical, theoretical, and methodological matters. For example, Palmer, in his "An Evaluative Report on the Current Status of Parapsychology" (1985), denies that current parapsychological experiments can provide any evidence for the existence of psi. This is because psi implies paranormality and, according to Palmer, we cannot argue that a given effect has a paranormal cause until we have an adequate theory of paranormality. He further argues, however, that parapsychological experiments can and do provide evidence for the existence of anomalies. By an anomaly, Palmer means a statistically significant deviation from chance expectation that cannot readily be explained by existing scientific theories. The burden of Palmer's paper is that just such anomalies have been demonstrated.

Because parapsychologists other than Palmer do not make this distinction between demonstrating an anomaly and testing a theory of paranormality, we do not carry on this distinction in our own assessment of the evidence. We tend to agree with Palmer on this matter, however. When we talk about evidence for psi in the remainder of this chapter, we are using psi in the neutral sense of an apparent anomaly rather than in the stronger sense of a paranormal phenomenon.

Minimal Criteria

Fortunately, critics and parapsychologists appear to agree on the general requirements necessary to demonstrate psi in a parapsychological experiment. Both Palmer (1985) and James E. Alcock (Appendix B) discuss such criteria in their respective papers. As Palmer points out, psi is defined negatively as a statistical departure from a chance baseline that cannot be accounted for by chance, sensory cues, or known artifacts. Such a negative definition implies the minimal criteria required to justify a conclusion that psi has been demonstrated.

Given the statistical aspect, it is imperative that the data be collected in such a way that the underlying probability model and assumptions of the statistical test are fulfilled. This means that targets must be adequately randomized and that each trial in the experiment must be independent of the preceding ones—and, of course, the statistical procedures must be applied and interpreted correctly. Given that all ordinary explanations must be ruled out, the experimenter must take special precautions to ensure that sensory cues, recording errors, subject fraud, and other alternatives have been prevented. Although it is impossible to rule out completely every possible contaminant or to anticipate every alternative, there are reasonable standards that most parapsychologists would agree should be followed.

Because different research paradigms have their own special requirements, no single set of standards can be specified in advance for all parapsychological experiments. Experiments with electronic number generators, for example, rarely have problems with data recording, but they do require special methods such as tests of randomness and attention to the immediate physical environment that are unnecessary with more traditional parapsychological experiments. One requirement for assessing the adequacy of a given experiment is that its procedures and methods of analysis be adequately documented. Unless we know how the targets were selected, how the results were analyzed, how the possibility of sensory leakage was prevented, and how other such aspects of the study were carried out, we have no basis for evaluating the quality of the information provided by the experiment.

GLOBAL CRITERIA

The criteria mentioned in the preceding paragraphs apply to the individual experiment. More global criteria come into play when one wants to evaluate an entire research program or set of experiments. Here we look for such things as replicability, robustness, lawfulness, manipulability, and coherent theory. These criteria deal with the coherence and intelligibility of the alleged phenomena. It is in terms of such global criteria that parapsychological research has been especially vulnerable.

Much of the objectivity involved in assessing the adequacy of research applies to judging individual experiments. But science is cumulative and depends not so much on the outcome of a single experiment as on consistent and lawful patterns of results across many experiments carried out in a variety of independent settings. Lawful consistency in this sense, according to both parapsychologists and their critics, has never been found in parapsychological investigations in the history of psychic research. Recently a few parapsychologists have expressed the hope that the experiments on remote viewing, random number generators, and the Ganzfeld (the very ones we have chosen to examine in detail in this report) may actually yield the long-sought replicability. The type of replicability that has been claimed so far is the possibility of obtaining significant departures from the chance baseline in only a proportion of the experiments, which is a kind of replicability quite different from the consistent and lawful patterns of covariation found in other areas of inquiry.

Despite the fact that scientific progress in a given area depends on the accumulation of lawful and consistent patterns across many experiments, the methods for deciding that such consistency exists are still quite primitive in comparison with the standards for judging the adequacy of a single experiment. Indeed, it is only within the past few years that serious attention has been devoted to developing objective and standardized procedures for evaluating the consistencies across a body of independent studies. For the most part, judgment about what a body of investigations demonstrates is still a surprisingly intuitive and haphazard process. This probably has not been a serious drawback in those areas of inquiry in which the basic phenomena are robust and experiments can be conducted with high confidence that the predicted relations will be obtained; but such impressionistic means for aggregating the outcomes of several experiments in the domain of parapsychology open the door to all the motivational and cognitive biases discussed in the paper prepared for the committee by Griffin. Not only are the data and alleged correlations erratic and elusive in this field, but their very existence is open to question.

EVALUATION OF THE SCIENTIFIC EVIDENCE

To evaluate the best scientific evidence on the existence of psi, and with the advice of proponents and our sponsors, we conducted site visits to some of the most notable parapsychological laboratories. The parapsychology subcommittee (see Appendix C) visited Robert Jahn's Engineering Anomalies Research Laboratory at Princeton University, where it witnessed presentations and demonstrations regarding psychokinetic experiments on random number generators. Jahn and his associates also briefed the subcommittee on the current status of their work in remote viewing.

The subcommittee also visited Helmut Schmidt's laboratory at the Mind Science Foundation, San Antonio, Texas. Schmidt pioneered the use of random number generators in parapsychology experiments in 1969. His is considered one of the two major research programs on psychokinesis (the second is Jahn's).

As an additional posssible input, the committee agreed to participate in a psychokinetic experiment of new design with Helmut Schmidt. Specifically, Schmidt accepted the suggestion that the committee's consultant, Paul Horwitz, be included in the conduct of the experiment. The work has not yet begun, however, and it now appears that we will not have any results to report before our terms expire.

The chair of the parapsychology subcommittee also visited SRI International, another major laboratory studying psychic effects on random number generators. (This latter research group argues that the observed effects are not due to psychokinesis but rather represent a special form of precognition.) The subcommittee chair also attended the meetings of the Parapsychological Association held at Sonoma State College in California. The entire committee made a site visit to Cleve Backster's laboratory in San Diego (arranged to coincide with the committee's meeting in La Jolla, California).

These site visits enabled the committee to observe firsthand the experimental arrangements and equipment used by some of the major contributors to parapsychological research. They also provided us an opportunity to discuss results, interpretations, and problems with a few important investigators. We were impressed with the sincerity and dedication of these investigators and believe that they are trying to conduct their research in the best scientific tradition. We also got the impression that this type of research involves many unresolved problems and still has a long way to go before it develops standardized, easily replicable procedures. The information obtained from these site visits does not provide an adequate basis for making scientific judgments. For this we rely, as we would in other fields of science, on a careful survey of the literature.

RESEARCH ON REMOTE VIEWING

The SRI Remote Viewing Program

Since the early 1970s, probably the best known research program in parapsychology has been the experiments in remote viewing initiated by physicists Harold Puthoff and Russell Targ when they were at SRI International. In a typical remote viewing experiment a subject, or percipient, remains in a room or laboratory with an experimenter, while a target team visits a randomly selected geographical site (e.g., a shopping mall, an outdoor arena, the Palo Alto airport, the Hoover tower). Neither the experimenter nor the subject has been given any information about the target. Once the experimenter and the subject are closeted in the laboratory, they wait for 30 minutes before the subject begins to describe his or her impressions of the target site.

Meanwhile the target team, consisting of two to four members of the SRI staff, obtains instructions for going to a randomly chosen target site from another SRI staff member. They then drive to the designated target site and remain there for an agreed-on 15-minute period (after allowing approximately 30 minutes to reach the site). During the time that the target team remains at the target site, the subject describes his or her impressions into a tape recorder and also makes any drawings that would help to clarify those impressions. When the target team returns to the laboratory, all the participants listen to the tape recording of the subject's impressions. Then all the participants go to the target site, where the subject is allowed to see how closely his or her impressions agreed with the actual target.

The first subject to participate in such a formal series of trials was the late Pat Price. In the first series, consisting of nine sessions, the duration of each session was 30 minutes. The transcript for each session is rich in detail; the one published transcript in Targ and Puthoff's first book runs to almost six printed pages (Targ and Puthoff, 1977).

Given such data, how does one decide if the experiment was a success? Did Price's descriptions, for example, convey correct knowledge of the different target sites? In fact, two methods have been used to demonstrate the effectiveness of remote viewing. One method is simply to compare the description with the target and make a judgment as to whether the correspondence is sufficient to claim a "hit." The second method uses an independent judge to rank the degree to which each description matches each site and then applies statistical tests to decide if the association is greater than chance.

Unprecedented success was claimed for the early remote viewing experiments in terms of both methods (Targ and Puthoff, 1974, 1977; Puthoff and Targ, 1976). Many examples were supplied of dramatic correspondences between impressions of the percipient and the physical details of the actual target. Such correspondences, no matter how dramatic and compelling, do not carry scientific weight, because it is impossible to assess their probabilities. In addition, much psychological research indicates how such subjective validation can create strong, but false, illusions of matching (see below).

The more formal evidence from the rankings of independent judges was also impressive. The first formal series of nine trials resulted in seven of the transcripts being ranked 1 against their intended target sites by the independent judge. Only one such ranking would be expected by chance. Puthoff and Targ reported the probability of such an outcome being due to chance as only 0.0000029. The second formal series, using Hella Hammid, was equally impressive, producing five first places and four second places in the rankings of transcripts against target sites.

Although subsequent series by Targ and Puthoff, as well as by other investigators, have not always yielded such overwhelmingly impressive results, most of them have continued to display highly significant outcomes (Targ and Harary, 1984). On the surface, at least, this is a reliable, simple, and highly effective recipe for producing paranormal communication. Especially appealing is the claim that remote viewing works with just about everyone. Targ and Harary, for example, provide exercises for anyone who wants to develop and improve his or her ability to pick up information at remote sites. Neither space nor time, its proponents assert, is a barrier. The percipient can pick up information from the surface of Jupiter as well as from target sites that can be visited at some future time.

Scientific Assessment of Remote Viewing

After the first remote viewing experiments were conducted in the early 1970s, many investigators throughout the world tried to follow suit. Most of them believed that their findings supported the claims of the SRI International researchers. The majority of these experiments, however, consisted of informal demonstrations rather than formal scientific experiments and relied solely on subjective matching. In the past 15 years, the number of formal experimental replications of the SRI remote viewing experiments has been surprisingly few.

Targ and Harary (1984) include as an appendix in their book a report by Hansen, Schlitz, and Tart that evaluates all the known remote viewing experiments conducted from 1973 through 1982. "In an examination of the twenty-eight formal published reports of attempted replications of remote viewing," write Targ and Harary, "Hansen, Schlitz, and Tart at the Institute for Parapsychology found that more than half of the papers reported successful outcomes." They concluded: "We have found that more than half (fifteen out of twenty-eight) of the published formal experiments have been successful, where only one in twenty would be expected by chance."

Two comments may be in order with respect to the foregoing conclusion. First, given the enormous publicity and the unusually strong claims, 28 formal experiments in 10 years seems surprisingly few. In comparison, the Ganzfeld psi experiments produced approximately twice as many formal experiments during the same interval. Second, 13 of the 28 formal experiments, or 46 percent, failed to claim successful outcomes. This rate of failure is much higher than what might have been expected on the basis of the earlier claims by Targ and Puthoff (1977), namely, that they had succeeded with every subject they had tried.

Even 15 successful outcomes out of 28 tries is impressive, especially by parapsychological standards. An inspection of the listed studies, however, suggests that the 28 formal experiments vary considerably in their importance. Some of these "published formal experiments" appeared as brief reports or abstracts of papers delivered at meetings of the Parapsychological Association or similar organizations. Others appeared in print only as brief or informal reports in book chapters or letters to the editor. Altogether, 15 of the 28 were published under conditions that fall short of scientific acceptability. Only 13, or 46 percent, of the experiments were published under refereed auspices. As in other sciences, only published reports that have undergone peer review and are adequately documented can be considered seriously as part of the scientific data base.

Of the 13 scientifically reported experiments, 9 are classified as successful in their outcomes by Hansen et al. (Targ and Harary, 1984). Seven of these nine experiments were conducted by Targ and Puthoff at SRI International, the remaining two at other laboratories. This relatively small harvest of nine "successful" experiments suffers from the fact that each is seriously flawed. A variety of problems afflicts the published reports on remote viewing. The documentation, even according to many parapsychologists, is seriously inadequate. Attempts by both neutral and skeptical investigators to gain access to the raw data have typically been thwarted or strongly resisted. Because the essence of scientific justification is public accessibility to the data, this relative inaccessibility suggests that much of the remote viewing data base is not part of science.

Most of the reasons for questioning the acceptability of the evidence for remote viewing lie in a methodological flaw that characterizes all but one of the experiments deemed successful: the successive trials are not independent of one another. This lack of independence has unfortunate consequences for any attempt to draw conclusions about ESP based on the outcomes of such experiments. The concept of independence is technical and somewhat difficult to explain simply, but, since it is critical to understanding why the remote viewing experiments fail to make their case, we supply an intuitive explanation.

Assume that we are considering a remote viewing experiment in which the subject participates in only two trials. In other words, we deal with two randomly chosen target sites. For the first trial, the target team goes to the first target site and remains there while the subject produces his or her first description. Immediately after this trial, the target team returns to the laboratory and takes the subject to the actual target site so that he or she and the others can gain a subjective impression of how closely the description corresponds with the target. For the second trial, the target team visits a second randomly chosen site. While they are visiting this site, the subject produces a second description.

When the experiment is over, the list of target sites (in random order) and the transcripts of the subject's descriptions are given to a judge, who also visits each site. While at a given site, the judge reads the two transcripts and ranks them in terms of how well each one corresponds with the particular site. In our example, one of the transcripts will be ranked 1 and the other will be ranked 2 (with 1 indicating the better correspondence between that target and the transcript). After visiting one site and doing this ranking, the judge then visits the second site and repeats the ranking procedure. The raw data can be set out in a matrix with the target sites as the columns and the transcripts as the rows.

A perfect outcome would be indicated if the transcript produced at the time the team was visiting site A was ranked 1 against that site, and the transcript produced when the team was visiting site B was ranked 1 for that site. (Of course, two trials would be too few to make an adequate statistical assessment of the success of the matching—successful matching would occur too frequently just by chance. The principles we want to illustrate, however, remain the same for two as for many trials.)

If the successive trials in the experiment were independent of one another, and we were interested only in direct hits (that is, outcomes for which the intended transcript was rated 1 against the target site), then we could expect the subject to make between zero and two direct hits. Indeed, if chance alone were operating, there would be four, equally likely, possibilities: (1) no hits, (2) a hit on the first trial and a miss on the second, (3) a miss on the first trial and a hit on the second, and (4) two hits. By this reckoning, the subject could be expected to get two direct hits just by chance in one of every four experiments.

But, as we indicated, the successive trials are not independent. This is because the judge is almost certainly not going to rank a transcript as 1 for more than one target site. This means, in our example, that if he or she ranks the first transcript 1 for target A, then he or she will probably rank the second transcript 1 for target B. In effect, this lack of independence between trials means that, instead of four equally likely possible outcomes there are only two: no hits or two hits. The dependence between trials has created a situation in which the chance probability of two hits is now 50 percent rather than 25 percent.

In this situation, if an experimenter uses a statistical test that assumes independence, he or she will come out with the wrong probabilities. In fact, the statistical test will exaggerate the significance of many outcomes. The failure of the experimenters to realize this problem resulted in exaggerated levels of significance for the early remote viewing experiments. Kennedy (1979), who originally pointed to this problem, recalculated the probabilities for some of these experiments. Puthoff and Targ (1976) reported that five of their first six remote viewing experiments were significant at the .05 level. With Kennedy's corrections for lack of independence, only two remained significant. According to Kennedy, only one of the two successful replications by Bisaha and Dunne (1979) remained significant with the more appropriate test.

One reason for the optimistic initial beliefs in the scientific reality of remote viewing was the fact that the lack of independence between trials produced exaggerated odds against chance results. But even with conservative corrections for lack of independence, approximately one-third of the early experiments still yielded successful outcomes.

One easy way to avoid this problem of dependence is to use a separate target pool of possible sites for each trial. For example, for the first trial one could designate a pool of four possible sites, one of which is randomly chosen to be the actual target site. A second pool of four different possible sites would be used for the second trial. When the trials are completed, the judge is given the list of the four sites for the first trial along with the subject's description for that trial. The judge then ranks each site in terms of its correspondence to the description. The four possible sites for the second trial are then ranked in terms of their correspondence to the subject's description for the second trial. In this illustration, the subject has a probability of 1 in 4 of having the actual target site ranked 1 on each trial, or a probability of 1 in 16 of being correct on both trials.

This second procedure, which is typically used in most free-response parapsychological experiments (such as the Ganzfeld experiments discussed below), not only guarantees independence between successive trials, but also avoids other serious problems, which we discuss next. The fact that the subject is given feedback by being taken to the target site immediately after each trial creates an additional form of dependence between trials. For this reason, other possibilities exist for obtaining "successful" results artifactually. The transcripts can contain clues that provide nonparanormal reasons for judges to associate descriptions with targets correctly. Some of these clues can be quite overt, such as when a subject mentions in the description how the current target apparently differs from a previous target site. When such a clue appears in the description, it provides the judge with information that the current description does not belong with the previous site. This increases the probability that the description will be matched with its appropriate target.

Marks and Kammann (1978) initiated a controversy, still not fully resolved, by claiming that such overt clues were sufficient to account for the striking results of the very first SRI remote viewing with Pat Price. Targ and Puthoff did not deny the existence of such clues in the Price series but argued that they were not sufficient to have accounted for the results. This dispute still has not been settled (Tart, Puthoff, and Targ, 1980; Scott, 1982; Marks and Scott, 1986).

Possibly this controversy over the role of the more overt clues has deflected attention from a much more fundamental and fatally damaging criticism first made by Hyman (1979) and independently by Kennedy (1979). Hyman and Kennedy pointed out that the combination of immediate feedback and lack of independence between successive trials makes it virtually impossible to prevent sensory cueing in the transcripts. As long as both the subject and the experimenter who is closeted with the subject are not blind to the preceding target sites, there is no way to prevent the transcript from being affected in a variety of possible and perhaps subtle ways by the knowledge of the preceding targets.

Hyman (1984–1985) provides an illustration of how such implicit sensory cueing might occur (pp. 131–132):

Say that the target for the first session was the Hoover Tower at Stanford. This will almost certainly influence what both the viewer and the interviewer say during the second and subsequent sessions in the same series. Almost certainly the viewer, during the second session, will not supply an exact description of the Hoover Tower. So, whatever the viewer says during the second session, a judge should find it to be a closer match to the second target site than to the first one. Now, assume that the second target site happened to be the Palo Alto train station. The viewer's descriptions during the third session will avoid describing either the Hoover Tower or the Palo Alto train station. We do not need to hypothesize something as mysterious as psi to predict that a judge should find this third description a better match to the third target site than either of the first two. As we add sessions, this effect of immediate feedback should continue to make the correlation between the viewer's descriptions and the target sites better and better.

No amount of editing for overt clues can overcome this defect of remote viewing experiments that follow the SRI pattern of dependent trials and immediate feedback. The mechanism described by Hyman should result in some dramatic correspondences. These dramatic correspondences, in conjunction with subjective validation, are a highly potent recipe for creating the illusion (for both experimenters and subjects) that ESP has occurred.

Palmer (1985), a major parapsychologist who otherwise carefully considers the criticisms of parapsychology, misses the seriousness of this flaw. In mentioning Hyman's criticism, he writes (p. 50):

It has been suggested by Hyman (1979) that since the subjects in most cases received feedback of the correct target after each trial, the subject could have gained some advantage by avoiding to mention characteristics of targets in earlier trials in their responses in later trials. As noted by Targ, Puthoff, and May (1979), the target pool for the geographical-site experiments was sufficiently large and contained sufficient redundancy that this is unlikely to be a significant biasing factor.

Perhaps such complacency has enabled experimenters to continue conducting remote viewing experiments with this fatal flaw. In fact, the size of the target pool, no matter how large, does not affect the validity of Hyman and Kennedy's criticism. Nor does the claim that the pool contained sufficient redundancy make much difference. Each geographical site is unique and contains a combination of specific characteristics that distinguishes it from the other sites in a given series. Indeed, as the parapsychologists themselves have asserted, unless this were so, there would be no possibility of the transcripts' being uniquely associated with a given target site. In every one of the remote viewing experiments that allows the possibility of subtle cueing, the possibility of the judges' being able to make completely successful matchings because of this artifact is highly plausible; and as long as a highly plausible, normal alternative to ESP can account for the apparent success of the outcomes the parapsychologists, by their own standards, cannot claim evidence for paranormal transmission of information.

As it turns out, all but one of the nine scientifically reported studies of remote viewing (at the time of the Targ and Harary survey) suffer from the flaw of sensory cueing. The one experiment that cannot be faulted for this reason is the long-distance remote viewing experiment of Schlitz and Gruber (1980). However, as Hyman (1984–1985) has pointed out, this experiment suffers from another very serious flaw. Gruber, who was a member of the target team and thus was familiar with the targets, translated the subject's target descriptions into Italian for the judging process. Why the experimenters allowed such potential sources of biased experimental procedures is not known, but the violation obviously negates the results as evidence for psi.

Since the Targ and Harary survey, we have learned of two attempts to replicate the Schlitz and Gruber experiment without the flaw mentioned. One, still unpublished, produced negative results. The second, by Schlitz and Haight (1984), produced marginally significant results. Indeed, if the more acceptable two-tailed test of significance had been used, the results would not have been considered significant by customary standards. Although the report of this study lacks sufficient documentation with respect to certain aspects of procedure, both Palmer (1985) and Alcock agree that this is the best controlled and most methodologically sound of all the remote viewing experiments so far.

In summary, after approximately 15 years of claims and sometimes bitter controversy, the literature on remote viewing has managed to produce only one possibly successful experiment that is not seriously flawed in its methodology—and that one experiment provides only marginal evidence for the existence of ESP. By both scientific and parapsychological standards, then, the case for remote viewing is not just very weak, but virtually nonexistent. It seems that the preeminent position that remote viewing occupies in the minds of many proponents results from the highly exaggerated claims made for the early experiments, as well as the subjectively compelling, but illusory, correspondences that experimenters and participants find between components of the descriptions and the target sites.

Research on Random Number Generators

The Basic Paradigm

The use of random number (or random event) generators for parapsychological research began in the 1960s and became relatively standard during the 1970s as the technology became widely available. A random number generator (RNG) is simply an electronic device that uses either radioactive decay or electronic noise to generate a sequence of random symbols. Originally such devices were used to test ESP, usually clairvoyance or precognition, but the most widespread and widely known work focuses on what is called micropsychokinesis, or micro-PK. In such research a subject, or operator, attempts to mentally bias the output of the random number generator, so that it produces a nonrandom sequence.

Most of the work with RNGs has used binary generators, or what Schmidt calls "electronic coin flippers." The output on each trial is either 0 or 1, that is, heads or tails. If the RNG is unbiased and truly random, then it should produce, on control runs, sequences of 0s and 1s that are independent of each other and that, in the long run, will yield 1s 50 percent of the time.

In a typical experiment, a subject (either a person who claims to be a psychic or a person chosen for availability who does not make such claims) is placed in the vicinity of the RNG and attempts to bias the output either toward more or fewer 1s. When an animal is used as the subject, the RNG output is usually coupled to an outcome whose frequency the animal presumably would like to either increase or decrease. In an experiment carried out with cockroaches, for example, one outcome was electric shock. If, during the time the output of the RNG was coupled with the shock apparatus, the proportion of shocks decreased below 50 percent, this would be taken as evidence of a psychokinetic effect of the cockroach on the output of the RNG.

The RNG experiments have been of interest to some military and governmental personnel because of the possibility, if such micro-PK is demonstrable, of psychically affecting equipment and computers that depend on the output of electronic symbols.

Results of the Experiments

In a recent survey 56 reports published between 1969 and 1984 and dealing with research on possible psychokinetic perturbations of binary RNGs (Radin, May, and Thomson, 1985), the reviewers counted 332 separate experiments. Of the 332 experiments, 188 were reported in refereed journals or conference proceedings, and of these 188 experiments with some claim to scientific status, 58 reported statistically significant results (compared with the 9 or 10 experiments that would be expected by chance). The other 144 experiments were produced by the Engineering Anomalies Research Laboratory at Princeton University; none of them had been published in a refereed journal at the time of the survey. Of these 144 experiments, 13 were classified as yielding statistically significant results. So, in the total sample of 332 experiments, 71 yielded ostensibly significant results at the traditional .05 level. This amounts to a success rate of approximately 21 percent, compared with the rate of 5 percent that would be expected by chance.

Palmer (1985) and Alcock agree that such results cannot be accounted for by chance. In other words, both the parapsychologist and the skeptic, in their respective reviews of the RNG research, agree that something other than accidental fluctuation is producing these results. Palmer calls this something an anomaly, which, while it may or may not be paranormal, cannot be explained by current scientific theories. Alcock points to various defects in the experimental protocols and concludes that no conclusions about the origins of these departures from randomness are justified until successful outcomes can be more or less consistently produced with adequately designed and executed experiments.

Both Palmer and Alcock focus their reviews on the two most influential research programs on RNGs. One is the program of Helmut Schmidt, a quantum physicist who began working on psi and RNGs in 1969. The other is the program begun by Robert Jahn in the late 1970s, when he was dean of the School of Engineering and Applied Science at Princeton University (see Jahn, 1982). These two programs have accounted for almost 60 percent of all known experiments on RNGs. They have also been the most consistently successful in achieving statistically significant outcomes.

Although the results suggest that on each experimental group of trials the number of 1s is greater or less than the 50 percent baseline (depending on the intended direction), the actual degree of deviation from chance is quite small. As Palmer (1985) indicates, Schmidt's subjects have averaged approximately 50.5 percent hits over the years, compared with the expected baseline of 50 percent. This amounts to producing one extra 1 every 100 trials. The reason such a small departure from chance is statistically significant is that an enormous number of trials is conducted with each subject.

Jahn and his colleagues at Princeton have, in a much shorter time, produced on the order of 200 times the number of trials that Schmidt did in 17 years. The Princeton researchers have also produced a significantly lower success rate than Schmidt. In their formal series of 78 million trials, the percentage of hits in the intended direction was only 50.02 percent, or an average of 2 extra hits every 2,500 trials. Again, such an extremely weak effect is statistically significant only when one is dealing with very large numbers of trials.

Scientific Assessment of the RNG Experiments

Palmer (1985) carefully reviews the major criticisms of the work of Schmidt and Jahn. He addresses questions about security, because subjects often are left alone with the apparatus during the data collection. In the Princeton experiments, the data are always collected when the subject is alone with the apparatus. Although the Princeton experiments now contain a number of features that would make it extremely difficult for a naive subject to bias the results, it is not clear that this has always been so. It would make good scientific sense to conduct some trials during which the subject is carefully monitored to see if successful outcomes are still obtained.

The major reservations about the RNG experiments concern the adequacy of the randomization of the outputs. Schmidt applied only limited tests for the randomness of his machines, and most of the control trials were gathered by allowing the machine to run for long periods, usually overnight. Although these controls usually produced results in line with the chance baseline, critics have pointed out that the controls are unsatisfactory because they were not conducted for shorter runs and at the same time as the data from the experimental sessions.

Palmer grants that the critics are correct in pointing out some of the shortcomings in Schmidt's methods for testing and controlling for the randomization of his machines. Palmer also correctly points out that such criticism is somewhat blunted by the fact that the critics have not specified any plausible mechanisms that would account for the obtained differences between the experimental and control trials. He is correct in pointing out that the Princeton experiments provide more adequate controls; however, he has probably assumed that the baseline controls in the Princeton experiments were run at the same time as the two experimental conditions of hitting and missing. It is easy to interpret the somewhat ambiguous description of the procedure in this manner. The relevant part of the authors' methodological description is as follows (Nelson, Dunne, and Jahn, 1984:9):

The primary variable in these experiments is the operator's pre-recorded intention to shift the trial counts to higher or lower numbers. This directional intention may be the operator's choice—the so-called "volitional" mode—or it may be assigned by a specified random process—the "instructed" mode. In either mode, data are collected in a "tri-polar" protocol, wherein trials taken under an intention to achieve high numbers (PK +), trials taken under an intention to achieve low numbers (PK −), and trials taken as baseline, i.e. under null intention (BL), are interspersed in some reasonable fashion, with all other operating conditions held identical. For all three streams of data, effect size is measured relative to the theoretical chance mean. This tri-polar protocol is the ultimate safeguard in precluding any artifacts such as residual electronic biases or transient environmental influences from systematically distorting the data.

At first glance it might appear as if the tripolar protocol requires that the two types of experimental groups of trials and the baseline group of trials always be taken at the same session. This would be consistent with the claim that "any artifacts such as residual electronic biases or transient environmental influences" were thereby precluded "from systematically distorting the data." Such a claim would be justified if, in fact, at each session one group of trials of each of the three types was obtained, provided that each group of trials was of the same length and that the order of the three types of trials was independently randomized for each session.

The description provided by Nelson and his colleagues says nothing at all about the order in which the three conditions were conducted, and a careful reading indicates that the baseline data may not always have been obtained at the same sessions and under the same conditions as the experimental groups of trials. It is not clear what the authors mean by stating that the three trials "are interspersed in some reasonable fashion." In fact, an examination of the data reported for each subject makes it clear that the strict tripolar protocol could not possibly have been followed with much of the data collection, because in many cases the baseline data are entirely absent or occur with many fewer trials than the experimental data. Indeed, it is not even clear that PK+ and PK− trials were always obtained at the same sessions, because for some subjects the total numbers of these trials are not equal.

We suspect that, over the six years or so during which the Princeton group was accumulating its data base, it made many changes in both the hardware and the experimental protocol. The sophisticated procedures currently in use and the requirement that the three types of trials be of equal length and that one of each be conducted at each session are the most recent variations in the paradigm. Unfortunately, the data are not presented in such a way that it is possible to determine whether the successful results are due to the earlier or the later experiments.

Such issues become especially important when we consider the extremely small size of the effect being claimed and when we further realize, as Palmer has pointed out, that the bulk of the significance in the formal series was due to just one subject, who contributed 23 percent of the total data. This one subject achieved a hit rate of 50.05 percent. When her data are eliminated, the remaining data yield a hit rate of 50.01 percent, which is no longer significantly different from chance.

In other words, it looks as if almost all the success of Jahn's huge data base can be attributed to the results from one individual, who, over the years, produced almost 25 percent of the data. This one individual was not only the most experienced subject, but also, presumably, familiar with the equipment. When combined with the fact, as Palmer points out, that the Princeton experiments provide inadequate documentation on precautions to prevent tampering by subjects, it becomes even more important to see if the same degree of success can be achieved when the sessions are adequately monitored.

Alcock, in his review of the same RNG studies surveyed by Palmer, points to a number of weaknesses in both the Schmidt and the Princeton experiments. For example, he faults Schmidt's experiments for such things as inadequate controls, failure to examine the target sequences, overcomplicated experimental setups, inadequate tests of randomness, and lack of methodological rigor. Alcock faults the Princeton experiments for such things as failing to randomize the sequence of groups of trials at each session, inadequate documentation on precautions against data tampering, and possibilities of data selection.

Palmer and Alcock do not really differ in their assessments of the shortcomings of the Schmidt and Princeton RNG experiments. They do differ, however, on what conclusions can be drawn from such imperfect experiments. Palmer emphasizes the fact that the critics have not provided plausible explanations as to how the admitted flaws could have caused the observed results. His position seems to be that, unless the critics can provide such plausible alternatives, the results should be accepted as demonstrating an anomaly. Alcock focuses on the fact that the successful results have been obtained under conditions that fall short of the experimental ideals that parapsychologists themselves profess. He emphasizes that the parapsychologists have no right to claim to have demonstrated psi from experiments that have been conducted with "dirty test tubes." Such a revolutionary conclusion as the existence of psi demands justification from experiments that have clearly used "clean test tubes."

What would it take to conduct an adequate RNG experiment? May, Humphrey, and Hubbard (1980) set out to do just that. After reviewing all available RNG experiments from 1970 through 1979 and taking into account the various deficiencies in these experiments, they gathered together and meticulously tested the components necessary to provide adequately randomized trials. They also devised a careful experimental protocol and set out in advance the precise criteria that would have to be fulfilled before they could call their results successful. Going further, after they completed the experiment with results that met their criteria for success, they subjected their equipment to all sorts of physical extremes to see if they could obtain such a degree of success by a possible artifact.

They report that this singularly well controlled RNG experiment in fact met their criteria for success. It is unfortunate, therefore, that this carefully thought-out experiment was conducted only once. After the one successful series, using seven subjects, the equipment was dismantled, and the authors have no intention of trying to replicate it (personal communication, August 1986). It is unfortunate because this appears to be the only near-flawless RNG experiment known to us, and the results were just barely significant. Only two of the seven subjects produced significant results, and the test of overall significance for the total formal series yielded a probability of 0.029.

The experiment, while nearly flawless, still had some problems as evidence for psi. For one thing, it was reported only in a technical report in 1980 and has never been published in a refereed scientific journal. Despite the admirable attention to details, all the control trials were taken when no human being was present. One might argue that this was not an ideal control for the experimental session, in which a subject was physically present in the room. The authors have assured us that their various attempts to bias the machine by physical means almost certainly rule out the possibility that the mere presence of a human being could have affected the output. However, a physicist who claims to have several years of experience in constructing and testing random number devices tells us that it is quite possible, under some circumstances, for the human body to act as an antenna and, as a result, possibly bias the output.

May and his colleagues at SRI, in the same technical report in which they claim successful results for their single experiment, surveyed all the RNG experiments known to them through the year 1979 and found that their combined significance was astronomically high. They add (May, Humphrey, and Hubbard, 1980:8):

This impressive statistic must, however, be evaluated with respect to experimental equipment and protocols. All the studies surveyed could be considered incomplete in at least one of the following four areas: (1) No control tests were reported in more than 44 percent of the references. Of those that did, most did not check for temporal stability of the random sources during the course of the experiment. (2) There were insufficient details about the physics and constructed parameters of the experimental apparatus to assess the possibility of environmental influences. (3) The raw data was not saved for later and independent analysis in virtually any of the experiments. (4) None of the experiments reported controlled and limited access to the experimental apparatus.

As far as we can tell, the same four points can be made with respect to the RNG experiments that have been conducted since 1980. The situation for the RNG experiments thus seems to be the same as that for remote viewing: over a period of approximately 15 years of research, only one successful experiment can be found that appears to meet most of the minimal criteria of scientific acceptability, and that one successful experiment yielded results that are just marginally significant.

RESEARCH ON THE GANZFELD

The Ganzfeld Experiments

The Ganzfeld psi experiments are named after the term used by Gestalt psychologists to designate the entire visual field. For theoretical purposes, the Gestalt psychologists wanted to create a situation in which the subject or observer could view a homogeneous visual field, one with no imperfections or boundaries. Psychologists later discovered that when individuals are put into a Ganzfeld situation they tend quickly to experience what they described as an altered state of mind.

In the early 1970s, some parapsychologists decided that the use of the Ganzfeld would provide a relatively safe and easy way to create an altered state in their experimental subjects. They believed that such a state was more conducive to picking up the elusive psi signals. In a typical psi Ganzfeld experiment, the subject, or percipient, has halved ping-pong balls taped over the eyes. The subject then reclines in a comfortable chair while white noise plays through earphones attached to his or her head. A bright light shines in front of the subject's face. When seen through the translucent ping-pong balls, the light is experienced as a homogeneous, foglike field. When so prepared, almost all subjects report experiencing a pleasant, altered state within 15 minutes.

While one experimenter is preparing the subject for the Ganzfeld state, a second experimenter randomly selects a target pool from a large set. The target pool typically consists of four possible targets, usually reproductions of paintings or pictures of travel scenes. One of the four is chosen at random to be the target for that trial. The target is given to an agent, or sender, who tries to communicate its substance psychically to the subject in the Ganzfeld state. After a designated period, the subject is removed from the Ganzfeld state and presented with the four candidates from the target pool. The subject then ranks the four candidates in terms of how well each matched the experience of the Ganzfeld period. If the actual target is ranked first, the trial is designated a hit. An actual experiment consists of several trials. In the example, the probability is that one of every four trials will produce a hit. If the number of hits significantly exceeds the expected 25 percent, then the result is considered to be evidence for the existence of psi.

Critique of the Ganzfeld Experiments

In a careful and systematic review of the Ganzfeld experiments undertaken in 1981 and published in the March 1985 issue of the *Journal of Parapsychology*, Hyman concluded that the data base exhibited flaws involving multiple testing, inadequate controls for sensory leakage, inadequate randomization, statistical errors, and inadequate documentation. These flaws, in his opinion, were sufficient to disqualify the Ganzfeld data base as evidence for psi. Of the 42 experiments, 39 (93 percent) used multiple analyses, which artificially inflated the chances of obtaining significant outcomes. Only 11 (26 percent) clearly indicated that they had adequately randomized the target selections. As many as 15 (36 percent) used inferior randomization, such as hand shuffling, or no randomization at all. The remaining 16 experiments did not supply sufficient information on how they had chosen the targets. As many as 23 of the experiments (55 percent) used only one target pool, which means that the subject was handed for judging not a copy of the target but the very same target that the percipient had handled, permitting the possibility of sensory cueing. Although the argument for psi is mainly a statistical one, the reports of 12 experiments (29 percent) revealed statistical errors. A number of other departures from optimal practice were also found.

The same issue of the *Journal of Parapsychology* contained a lengthy rebuttal by parapsychologist Charles Honorton, one of the pioneers of the Ganzfeld psi technique. Honorton disputed many of Hyman's opinions as to what constituted flaws; provided a reanalysis of the data base to overcome many of the statistical weaknesses of the original experiments; and argued that the flaws he agreed existed were not sufficient to have accounted for the findings. In this respect his analysis is consistent with Palmer's approach. He does not deny that the experiments depart from optimal design, but he argues that such departures are insufficient to account for the results.

Honorton and Hyman had the opportunity to discuss their differences about psi in general at the Parapsychological Association meetings in 1986; as a result, they agreed to draft a joint communiqué to emphasize those points on which they agree. That communiqué appeared in the December issue of the *Journal of Parapsychology* (Hyman and Honorton, 1986). They agree that the current data base is insufficient to support either the conclusion that psi exists or the conclusion that the results are due to artifacts. They further agree that the issue can be settled only by future experiments conducted according to the stated standards of parapsychology, which are also the accepted standards of psychological research.

Another important input to the committee's judgment on the Ganzfeld research was the systematic evaluation of the contemporary parapsychological literature by Charles Akers (1984), a former parapsychologist. Akers's critique used a methodological strategy different from that used by Hyman. Hyman undertook to evaluate the entire data base of a single research paradigm (Ganzfeld), including both successful and unsuccessful outcomes. Akers surveyed contemporary ESP experiments broadly, but confined his evaluation to those that had produced significant results with unselected subjects. Hyman assigned flaws to experiments without regard to whether each flaw, by itself, could have caused the observed outcome. Akers charged a flaw to a study only if he thought the flaw could have been sufficient to produce the observed result. He chose a sample of 54 parapsychological experiments from areas of research that had been previously reviewed by Honorton or Palmer; his intent was to choose experiments that could be viewed as the best current evidence for the existence of psi. As a result of this exercise, he concluded (Akers, 1984:160–161):

Results from the 54-experiment survey have demonstrated that there are many alternative explanations for ESP phenomena; the choice is not simply between psi and experimenter fraud. . . . The numbers of experiments . . . flawed on various grounds were as follows: randomization failures (13), sensory leakage (22), subject cheating (12), recording errors (10), classification or scoring errors (9), statistical errors (12), reporting failures (10). . . . All told, 85% of the experiments were considered flawed (46/54).

This leaves eight experiments where no flaws were assigned. . . . Although none of these experiments has a glaring weakness, this does not mean that they are especially strong in either their methods or their results. . . .

In conclusion, eight experiments were conducted with reasonable care, but none of these could be considered as methodologically ideal. When all 54 experiments are considered, it can be stated that the research methods are too weak to establish the existence of a paranormal phenomenon.

RESEARCH ON ELECTRICAL ACTIVITY AND EMOTIONAL STATES

The Backster Laboratory

In addition to examining parapsychological research in areas that have produced large literatures, the committee witnessed an example of experimental work at a far less developed stage. On February 10, 1986, committee members visited the Backster Research Foundation in San Diego and saw a demonstration of experimental procedures for detecting a correlation between the electrical activity of oral leukocytes and the emotional states of the donor.

Cleve Backster is a polygraph specialist who had at one time helped develop interrogation techniques for the Central Intelligence Agency and now runs his own polygraph school in San Diego. The school is housed in the same rooms that constitute the Backster Research Foundation, which is devoted to the study of what Backster refers to as primary perception. Backster's research on paranormal matters began in February 1966, when he recorded, from a philodendron plant that he had hooked up to a polygraph, a response he recognized as similar to that of human beings in emotional states. Backster believed he had demonstrated that the plant showed such emotional response when brine shrimp or other living organisms were either threatened or actually killed in an adjoining room. The notion of primary perception in plants became both a popular subject for research and a highly controversial concept during the late 1960s and early 1970s.

We were told that Backster has quietly continued his researches into this and related matters. He has now devised a technique for recording electrical activity in leukocytes taken from a donor's mouth. The advantage of this technique, we were told, is that the leukocytes respond mostly to emotional states of the donor.

One committee member volunteered to be the demonstration subject. Another member accompanied him to observe the techniques for obtaining the leukocytes and preparing them for recording. The sample was obtained by having the subject "chew" on a 1.2 percent saline solution and then spit it back into a centrifuge tube. Ten such samples were obtained in this way. The samples were then spun in a centrifuge for six minutes, and the particulate matter at the bottom of each tube was pipetted into the preparation tube. The preparation tube contained about one centimeter of particulate matter and was filled almost to the top with 1.2 percent saline solution. Two uninsulated wire electrodes were inserted into the bottom of the tube, which was then placed within a shielded cage and connected by leads to an EEG-type recording apparatus.

During the demonstration, the subject sat approximately two meters from the preparation. We were told that subjects usually sit about five meters from the preparation. A split-screen projection video display was provided: the lower portion of the screen recorded the movements of the polygraph paper and pen as they produced a record of the electrical activity presumably taking place in the leukocyte preparation. The upper portion of the screen recorded the behavior of the seated subject.

In his previous research using this arrangement, Backster reported that, when the subject revealed an emotional reaction, the electrical action of the leukocytes showed a corresponding reaction. During our demonstration, the polygraph record produced several strong deflections in both the control and the experimental series, but they did not obviously correlate with any corresponding thoughts or emotional states of the subject as various stimuli were presented. Backster suggested that this was probably because so many people were crowded into the laboratory that the leukocytes were responding to thoughts and feelings of other individuals in the room. Thus, a demonstration of results, as opposed to techniques, was not, after all, going to be possible during our visit.

Backster then showed us videotapes of the split-screen results he had obtained in his "formal" experiments. The results consisted of 12 examples of apparent correlations between an emotional response and a deflection of the polygraph record. The 12 examples came from 7 sessions with 7 different subjects. Although the information is not given in his written report, it appears that each session lasted for approximately half an hour. During this time, the donor is engaged in conversation or watches videotapes of television programs. The sessions are not standardized or planned. Backster's intent, apparently, is to elicit spontaneous emotional responses from a subject during the session. He believes that a stimulus that evokes an emotional response in one subject will not necessarily do so in another subject.

In one example, the subject was a young man who was looking at an issue of *Playboy* magazine. The polygraph tracing began to display large deflections soon after he encountered a nude photograph of an attractive young woman. The large deflections continued for approximately two minutes; the tracing slowly settled down to normal activity after the magazine was closed. Soon after, the young man reached for the closed magazine, and the record reveals a single deflection at that point. In another example, the subject was a retired police lieutenant. When discussing his approaching retirement, he was asked a question about his wife's attitude toward having him "underfoot." A large deflection of the polygraph tracing occurred soon after this question was asked. When asked, the donor confirmed that he was emotionally aroused at that moment in the session (see Backster and White, 1985).

Cleve Backster and his supporters apparently believe that he has successfully demonstrated that detached oral leukocytes respond to the emotions of their donor even when separated by as much as several miles. They also believe that these results are reliable and replicable.

Critique of the Backster Experiment

What we have read and observed about Backster's procedures does not justify the claim he is making. His answers to our questions made it clear that he has not considered using the appropriate controls needed to ensure that the obtained "correlations" are real and due to the causes he has assumed. To make adequate physiological recordings from a preparation of in vitro leukocytes and to demonstrate the correlation between emotional response and leukocyte activity requires experimental arrangements and procedures at a level of sophistication well beyond those we observed.

Committee members who are knowledgeable about the procedures and instrumentation of psychophysiological experiments expressed doubts about the adequacy of the setup to perform the tasks Backster has undertaken. Serious doubts were expressed about the possibility that the leukocytes were alive at the time of recording. Further doubts were expressed about the setup's ability to avoid contamination of the recording procedures by stray influences of various sorts. We do not discuss these drawbacks in detail here. We confine our discussion to Backster's method for establishing a correlation between the alleged activity of the detached leukocytes and the emotional state of the donor. When we consider how the existence of such correlations was established, we again see how inappropriate methodology can lead to very misleading conclusions.

Many problems exist with regard to Backster's procedures for detecting correlations. In trying to demonstrate a pattern of covariation between two records of behavior over time, one record is the tracing of amplified electrical activity coming from the electrodes and through the leads. Although this tracing can be quantified, Backster has apparently made no attempt to do so. Instead, he has relied on visual inspection of the polygraph record to pick out points at which the deflections of the pen from the baseline are noticeable. Although such subjective judgment is scientifically unacceptable, the deflections that he uses in his examples seem sufficiently marked that they probably can be considered to be real deviations from the baseline. At any rate, let us assume that responses on the polygraph record can be visually pinpointed with reasonable objectivity.

The deflections on the polygraph record are then compared with happenings on the concurrent videotaping of the conversation with the subject. Here we encounter very serious problems as to what constitutes an emotional response on this behavioral record. Backster believes he can identify categories of potentially emotionally arousing stimuli in the nonstandardized, qualitative, ongoing record of conversation. He then can determine if the subject was experiencing an emotional reaction to such a stimulus by simply replaying the record, pointing to the segment that corresponds to a place where the polygraph showed a deflection, and asking the subject if he or she recalls what was taking place at that moment as an emotionally arousing experience. If the subject agrees, this is said to confirm a "correlation" between the emotional state and the corresponding activity of the tracing.

Such a purely subjective determination of an emotional response opens the process to a variety of known biases, many of them discussed in the paper prepared for the committee by Griffin (Appendix B). The literature on "illusory correlation" (Alloy and Tabachnik, 1984; Griffin paper) makes it clear how subjective expectations and cognitive biases can lead to false impressions of correlation. Backster's method of searching for correlations compounds these inevitable biases: he does not independently determine moments of emotional response in the subject's behavioral record and moments of polygraph deflections and then look for a match between the two. Instead, he apparently looks for polygraph deflections and then tries to determine if an emotional response can be found that occurred in the vicinity of the polygraph activity. In other words, the determination of the emotional response is done with full knowledge of the fact that a polygraph deflection has occurred.

Under such circumstances, we would expect processes of subjective validation to operate. In addition, the method of verifying the emotional response, by asking the subject to acknowledge that he or she was in fact experiencing such a state at the moment the polygraph record indicated a leukocyte response, is itself suspect. This is the sort of circumstance in which demand characteristics (i.e., responses determined by the presumed intent of the experimenters) are known to operate.

Good science dictates that the moments of emotional response should be determined independently of the moments of polygraph response. Both the experimenter and the subject must be blind to the polygraph record when determining the moments of emotional response. Only when the determination of events on the two records has been made independently of each other can the records be compared to determine if the emotional responses and the polygraph activity are correlated.

Illusory correlations occur because our subjective judgments of covariation tend to use only a portion of the relevant information and because we tend to bias observed events in terms of our expectations. In particular, intuitive judgments of covariation tend to focus only on the co-occurrence of treatment of interest and successful outcomes, ignoring times when the treatment co-occurred with unsuccessful outcomes. Backster uses only those examples from his records in which an emotional response co-occurs with a polygraph deflection; the 12 such examples from the 7 experimental series represent a very small fraction of the total data collected.

Not only is a sample of just 12 co-occurrences probably too small for estimating whether a true correlation exists, but it is also impossible from this information alone to estimate whether any correlation exists. All the data are needed for this purpose. Almost certainly, more than 12 polygraph deflections must have appeared in the total record. In the brief demonstration for the committee, both the control and the experimental series yielded several deflections, so it is reasonable to assume that many more than 12 deflections were obtained in the complete record. It is likely that these unreported deflections were not preceded by any emotional responses.

Almost certainly, more than 12 emotional responses must have appeared in the total record. The point of conducting the sessions was to expose the subjects to a variety of emotional stimuli; therefore, it is essential to know the number of times that emotional responses occurred *without* the corresponding occurrence of polygraph responses. Finally, to determine correlation, it is essential to know the frequency of co-occurrence of the absence of emotional responses and the absence of polygraph responses.

All this information is needed to determine whether the claimed correlation exists. All the data must be used. From these data, one can compare the proportion of times that an emotional response is followed by a polygraph response with the proportion of times that the absence of an emotional response is followed by a polygraph response. Only if these two proportions are significantly different from one another can we assume that the data provide evidence for a correlation between emotional response and leukocyte activity. The fact that Backster was able to find 12 examples of the co-occurrence between emotional response and polygraph deflection, even if these correspondences had come from double-blind matching, provides us with absolutely no information about whether a correlation exists.

The stronger claim would be, of course, not that a correlation exists, but that a causal connection exists between the subject's emotional states and the responses of the detached leukocytes. As Chapter 3 on evaluation indicates, such a causal explanation requires much more than the demonstration of correlation between two series. Because Backster did not use double-blind procedures to determine emotional responses, and because the procedures he did use are known to be just those that facilitate the occurrence of a variety of subjective biases, he may well have obtained a correlation between his two series. However, his procedures for finding such correlations are sufficiently flawed that we do not know if in fact the suspected (and presumably biased) correlation actually does exist in his data. The Backster experiment indicates that the best intentions combined with scientific instrumentation and polygraphic records cannot, in themselves, guarantee data of scientific quality.

DISCUSSION OF THE SCIENTIFIC EVIDENCE

Both the parapsychologists cited in this report and the critics of parapsychology believe that the best contemporary experiments in parapsychology fall short of acceptable methodological standards. The critics conclude that such data, based on methodologically flawed procedures, cannot justify any conclusions about psi. The parapsychologists argue that, while each experiment is individually flawed, when taken together they justify the conclusion that psi exists.

Palmer's conclusion in this regard is unique. Although he agrees that the data do not justify the conclusion that a paranormal phenomenon has been demonstrated, he argues that the data, with all their drawbacks, do justify the conclusion that an anomaly of some sort has been demonstrated. It is this purported demonstration of an anomaly that, according to Palmer, further justifies the claim that parapsychologists do have a subject matter. The awkward aspect of Palmer's position is that, without an adequate theory, there is no way to know that the anomaly "demonstrated" in one experiment is the same anomaly "demonstrated" in another; indeed, there is no limit to the possible causes of the anomaly in a given experiment. Without an adequate theory, there is no reason to assume that the various anomalies constitute a coherent or intelligibly related class of phenomena.

The committee distinguishes among three types of criticism that can be leveled at a given parapsychological finding. The first is what we might refer to as the smoking gun. This type of criticism asserts or strongly implies that the observed findings were due not to psi but to factor X. Such a claim puts the burden of proof on the critic. To back up such a claim, the critic must provide evidence that the results were in fact caused by X. Many of the bitterly contested feuds between critics and proponents have often been the result of the proponent's assuming, correctly or incorrectly, that this type of criticism was being made.

The second type of criticism can be referred to as the plausible alternative. In this case, the critic does not assert that the result *was* due to factor X, but instead asserts that the result *could have been* due to factor X. Such a stance also places a burden on the critic, but one not so stringent as the smoking gun assertion. The critic now has to make a plausible case for the possibility that factor X was sufficient to have caused the result. For example, optional stopping of an experiment on the part of a subject can bias the results, but the bias is a small one; it would be a mistake to assert that an outcome was due to optional stopping if the probability of the outcome is extremely low. Akers's critique, which was previously discussed, is an example based on the plausible alternative.

The third type of criticism is what we have called the dirty test tube. In this case, the critic does not claim that the results have been produced by some artifact, but instead points out that the results have been obtained under conditions that fail to meet generally accepted standards. The gist of this type of criticism is that test tubes should be clean when doing careful and important scientific research. To the extent that the test tubes were dirty, it is suggested that the experiment was not carried out according to acceptable standards. Consequently, the results remain suspect even though the critic cannot demonstrate that the dirt in the test tubes was sufficient to have produced the outcome. Hyman's critique of the Ganzfeld psi research and Alcock's paper on remote viewing and random number generator research are examples of this type of criticism.

In the committee's view, it is in this latter sense, the dirty test tube sense, that the best parapsychological experiments fall short. We do not have a smoking gun, nor have we demonstrated a plausible alternative; but we imagine that even the parapsychological community must be concerned that their best experiments still fall far short of the methodological adequacy that they themselves profess.

Honorton and Hyman differ on whether to assign a flaw in randomization to a particular series of experiments. With Honorton's assignment, the studies with adequate randomization do not differ in significance of outcome from those with inadequate randomization. With Hyman's assignment, the experiments with inadequate randomization have significantly more successful outcomes than do those with adequate randomization. A simple disagreement on one experiment can thus make a huge difference as to whether we conclude that this flaw contributed or did not contribute to the observed outcomes. Several similar examples could be cited to illustrate the extreme sensitivity of this data base to slight changes in flaw assignments.

Even if Palmer is correct in asserting that in a particular case an anomaly has been demonstrated, serious problems remain. In astronomy and other sciences, an anomaly is a very precise and specifiable departure from a well-defined theoretical expectation. Neptune was discovered, for example, when Leverrier was able to specify not only that the orbit of Uranus departed from that expected by Newtonian theory, but also precisely in what way it departed from expectation. Nothing approaching such a specifiable anomaly has been claimed for parapsychology. A vague and unspecifiable departure from chance is a far cry from a well-described and systematic departure from a precise, theoretical equation. Leverrier's anomaly was consistent with only a very narrow range of possibilities. The sort of anomaly claimed for parapsychology is currently consistent with an almost infinite variety of possibilities, including artifacts of various kinds.

THE PROBLEM OF QUALITATIVE EVIDENCE

The committee continually encountered the distinction between qualitative and quantitative evidence for the existence of paranormal phenomena. Many proponents of the paranormal acknowledge such a difference in one way or another. Some realize that it is only quantitative evidence that will convince the scientific community. Although they themselves have relied on qualitative evidence for their own beliefs, they refer us to the RNG experiments of Robert Jahn or the remote viewing experiments at SRI as examples of supporting quantitative data.

Most proponents seem impatient with the request for scientific evidence. They have been convinced through their own experiences or the vivid testimonies of individuals whom they trust. Many argue that qualitative evidence can be as good as quantitative; indeed, they claim that in some circumstances it can be better.

The arguments for the superiority of qualitative evidence are based in many cases on such factors as ecological validity, conducive atmosphere, and holism. The ecological validity argument asserts that the artificial conditions required for laboratory experiments are so different from the natural settings in which paranormal phenomena typically occur that findings from such controlled studies are irrelevant. By removing the psychic from his or her natural domain or by arranging conditions to suit the needs of scientific observation, it is claimed, the scientist destroys the very phenomenon under question. The ecological validity argument is closely related to the other arguments. Proponents who emphasize the conducive atmosphere assert that the austere conditions of strict laboratory procedure create an atmosphere that is numbing or inimical to psychic functioning. Those who emphasize holism point out that the experimental procedures necessarily dissect and focus on restricted portions of a system. Such compartmentalization, it is claimed, makes it impossible to study the sorts of paranormal phenomena that operate only as a total system in a naturalistic context.

QUALITATIVE EVIDENCE AND SUBJECTIVE BIASES

What is meant by qualitative evidence? Roughly, it means any sort of nonscientific evidence that proponents find personally convincing. Typically, it involves personally experiencing or witnessing the phenomenon. Less compelling, but still effective, is the testimony of friends or trusted acquaintances who have personally experienced it. Even individuals who are intellectually aware of the pitfalls of personal observation and testimony find it difficult, even impossible, to disregard the compelling quality of such evidence in the formation of their own beliefs.

A major parapsychologist admitted to one committee member that the scientific evidence did not justify concluding that psi exists. "As a trained scientist," he said, "I know quite well that by scientific criteria there is no evidence for the existence of psi. In fact, I have always argued with my parapsychological colleagues that they are making a serious mistake in trying to get the scientific community to take their current evidence seriously. Before they do this, they first have to be able to collect the sort of repeatable and lawful data that constitute scientific evidence." This same parapsychologist then explained why, despite the current lack of evidence, he remained a parapsychologist. "When I was 16 I had some personal experiences of a psychic nature that were so compelling that I have no doubt that they were real. Yet, as a trained scientist, I know that my personal experiences and subjective convictions cannot and should not be the basis for asking others to believe me." This parapsychologist is unusual in that he makes the distinction within himself between beliefs that are subjectively compelling and beliefs that are scientifically justifiable. More typical is the proponent who, as a result of compelling personal experience, not only has no doubt about the reality of underlying paranormal cause, but also has no patience with the refusal of others to support that belief.

We see two problems regarding qualitative evidence. First, personal observation and testimony are subject to a variety of strong biases of which most of us are unaware. When such observations and testimony emerge from circumstances that are emotional and personal, the biases and distortions are greatly enhanced. Psychologists and others have found that the circumstances under which such evidence is obtained are just those that foster a variety of human biases and erroneous beliefs. Second, beliefs formed under such circumstances tend to carry a high degree of subjective certainty and often resist alteration by later, more reliable disconfirming data. Such beliefs become self-sealing, in that when new information comes along that would ordinarily contradict them, the believers find ways to turn the apparent contradictions into additional confirmation.

The committee asked Dale Griffin to describe many of the ways in which cognitive and social psychologists have documented that human subjective judgment can lead us astray. Griffin's paper emphasizes the cognitive biases termed *availability* and *representativeness*, but he also discusses motivational biases. Although most of these biases have been created under laboratory conditions, they are nonetheless quite powerful, and evidence has been mounting that, if anything, they are much more powerful in natural settings. Griffin points out that one vivid, concrete experience is usually sufficient to outweigh conclusions based on hundreds or thousands of cases based on abstract summary statistics. These and the other biases discussed by Griffin should make us wary of conclusions based on qualitative evidence.

Examples of Problematic Beliefs

In this section we discuss some examples of beliefs about paranormal phenomena that have been formed under conditions known to generate cognitive illusions and strong delusional beliefs. We attempt to make clear why we are skeptical of any evidence offered in support of the paranormal that does not strictly fulfill scientific criteria. We believe it is important to realize the power of such conditions to create strong but false beliefs.

In 1974 a group of distinguished physicists at the University of London observed renowned psychic Uri Geller apparently bend metallic objects and cause part of a crystal, encapsulated in a container, to disappear.

Impressed with what they saw, in 1975 these scientists contributed an article to *Nature* outlining their ideas about how to conduct successful parapsychological research (reprinted in Hasted et al., 1976). In their discussion they note that successful results depend on the relation among the participants and that phenomena are more likely to occur when all participants are in a relaxed state, all sincerely want the psychic to succeed, and "the experimental arrangement is aesthetically or imaginatively appealing to the person with apparent psychokinetic powers."

Hasted and his colleagues describe further desiderata. The psychic should be treated as one of the experimental team, contributing to an attitude of mutual trust and confidence that facilitates successful appearance of the allegedly paranormal effects. The slightest hint of suspicion on the part of the observers can stifle the occurrence of any phenomena. Observers should avoid looking for any particular outcome that interferes with the required relaxed state of mind and impedes paranormal powers. To help avoid the inhibiting effects of concentrated attention, participants should talk and think about matters irrelevant to the experiment at hand.

Acknowledging that these desiderata make it difficult to preclude trickery, Hasted and his colleagues express confidence that they can both create psi-conducive conditions and eliminate the possibility of being tricked (Hasted et al., 1976:194):

It should be possible to design experimental arrangements which are beyond any reasonable possibility of trickery, and which magicians will generally acknowledge to be so. In the first stages of our work we did in fact present Mr. Geller with several such arrangements, but these proved aesthetically unappealing to him.

Although we may sympathize with the British physicists' desire to create conditions conducive to the appearance of genuine psychic powers, if such powers exist, we cannot fail to note the quandary that their efforts produce. In their quest for psi-conducive conditions, they have created guidelines that play into the hands of anyone intent on deceiving them.

The very conditions that are specified as being conducive to the appearance of paranormal phenomena are almost always precisely those that are conducive to the successful performance of conjuring tricks. One of the first rules the aspiring conjuror learns is never to announce in advance the specific outcome that he or she is going to produce. In this way onlookers will not know where and on what they should focus their attention and consequently will be less apt to detect the method by which the trick was accomplished. The authors' advice to avoid focusing on a predetermined outcome greatly facilitates the conjuror's task.

The insistence that the arrangements meet with the psychic's approval is by far the most devastating of these conditions. Geller will perform only if the conditions are "aesthetically pleasing." This amounts to giving the alleged psychic complete veto power over any situation in which he or she feels that success is not ensured. This in turn means that the psychic being tested, not the experimenters, is controlling the experiment. Surely the British physicists ought to realize the irony of their admission that all their experimental arrangements designed to preclude trickery turned out to be aesthetically unacceptable to Uri Geller.

Another example of beliefs generated in circumstances that are known to create cognitive illusions is macro-PK, which is practiced at spoon-bending, or PK, parties. The 15 or more participants in a PK party, who usually pay a fee to attend and bring their own silverware, are guided through various rituals and encouraged to believe that, by cooperating with the leader, they can achieve a mental state in which their spoons and forks will apparently soften and bend through the agency of their minds.

Since 1981, although thousands of participants have apparently bent metal objects successfully, not one scientifically documented case of paranormal metal bending has been presented to the scientific community. Yet participants in the PK parties are convinced that they have both witnessed and personally produced paranormal metal bending. Over and over again we have been told by participants that they know that metal became paranormally deformed in their presence. This situation gives the distinct impression that proponents of macro-PK, having consistently failed to produce scientific evidence, have forsaken the scientific method and undertaken a campaign to convince themselves and others on the basis of clearly nonscientific data based on personal experience and testimony obtained under emotionally charged conditions.

Consider the conditions that leaders and participants agree facilitate spoon bending. Efforts are made to exclude critics because, it is asserted, skepticism and attempts to make objective observations can hinder or prevent the phenomena from appearing. As Houck, the originator of the PK party, describes it, the objective is to create in the participants a peak emotional experience (Houck, 1984). To this end, various exercises involving relaxation, guided imagery, concentration, and chanting are performed. The participants are encouraged to shout at the silverware and to "disconnect" by deliberately avoiding looking at what their hands are doing. They are encouraged to shout Bend! throughout the party. "To help with the release of that initial concentration, people are encouraged to jump up or scream that theirs is bending, so that others can observe." Houck makes it clear that the objective is to create a state of emotional chaos. "Shouting at the silverware has also been added as a means of helping to enhance the emotional level in a group. This procedure adds to the intensity of the command to bend and helps create pandemonium throughout the party."

A PK party obviously is not the ideal situation for obtaining reliable observations. The conditions are just those which psychologists and others have described as creating states of heightened suggestibility and implanting compelling beliefs that may be unrelated to reality. It is beliefs acquired in this fashion that seem to motivate persons who urge us to take macro-PK seriously. Complete absence of any scientific evidence does not discourage the proponents; they have acquired their beliefs under circumstances that instill zeal and subjective certainty. Unfortunately, it is just these circumstances that foster false beliefs.

DISCUSSION OF QUALITATIVE EVIDENCE

Our analysis of the evidence put before us indicates that even the most solidly based arguments for the existence of paranormal phenomena fall short of the currently accepted parapsychological standards. Even if the best evidence had been collected according to acceptable scientific standards, most proponents would have in fact remained convinced by personal experiences and data that clearly fall far short of scientific acceptability. We have looked at two examples to make clear why and in what ways such failures to meet acceptable standards render the corresponding arguments useless as evidence for the paranormal, even though they have created compelling and strongly held beliefs in those who have been exposed to them.

The examples illustrate how different ways of attempting to acquire evidence for paranormal phenomena can depart from adequate standards. These inadequacies become especially critical when we note that the conditions under which the alleged paranormal phenomena are supposed to occur are just those known to foster biases and false beliefs. The PK parties, while creating powerful beliefs in paranormal metal bending, clearly violate almost every principle for obtaining trustworthy data. These parties offer no standardization, no objective records, and no controls against self-deception or the deliberate deception of others. All participants, including the leader, are encouraged to achieve a peak emotional state, and general chaos is encouraged.

The suggestions of a group of British physicists for testing alleged psychics are aimed at somehow combining the desire to keep the psychic from feeling inhibited with the desire to obtain evidence of acceptable scientific quality. The observers' zeal for making the psychic feel trusted produces conditions that make scientific observation impossible: observers are instructed to refrain from focusing attention on any expected result, and the experimental arrangement must be aesthetically acceptable to the psychic, a condition that in effect puts the psychic in control of the experiment.

The search for psi-conducive conditions is understandable. Parapsychological research, even at its best, has been continually frustrated by the lack of robust, lawful, and repeatable outcomes, yet parapsychologists have experienced phenomena or have encountered data that have convinced them of the reality of the paranormal. When they try to put such evidence before their critics, however, the phenomena have a habit of disappearing. If one fervently believes that the phenomena are real, then it becomes easy to imagine a variety of reasons why they are elusive and hard to produce on demand.

When proponents encounter a new phenomenon or psychic, they are strongly motivated to create conditions that will not drive the phenomenon away. The special atmosphere of PK parties and the suggestions of the British physicists are just two examples of attempts to generate psi-conducive conditions that also seem to be deception-conducive and bias-conducive.

CONCLUSIONS

In drawing conclusions from our review of evidence and other considerations related to psychic phenomena, we note that the large body of research completed to date does not present a clear picture. Overall, the experimental designs are of insufficient quality to arbitrate between the claims made for and against the existence of the phenomena. While the best research is of higher quality than many critics assume, the bulk of the work does not meet the standards necessary to contribute to the knowledge base of science. Definitive conclusions must depend on evidence derived from stronger research designs. The points below summarize key arguments in this chapter.

1. Although proponents of ESP have made sweeping claims, not only for its existence but also for its potential applications, an evaluation of the best available evidence does not justify such optimism. The strongest

claims have been made for remote viewing and the Ganzfeld experiments. The scientific case for remote viewing is based on a relatively small number of experiments, almost all of which have serious methodological defects. Although the first experiments of this type were begun in 1972, the existence of remote viewing still has not been established. Furthermore, although success rates varying from 30 to 60 percent have been claimed for the Ganzfeld experiments, the evidence remains problematic because all the experiments deviate in one or more respects from accepted scientific procedures. In the committee's view, the best scientific evidence does not justify the conclusion that ESP—that is, gathering information about objects or thoughts without the intervention of known sensory mechanisms—exists.

2. Nor does scientific evidence offer support for the existence of psychokinesis—that is, the influence of thoughts upon objects without the intervention of known physical processes. In the experiments using random number generators, the reported size of effects is very small, a hit rate of no more than 50.5 percent compared with the chance expectancy of 50 percent. Although analysis indicates that overall significance for the experiments, with their unusually large number of trials, is probably not due to a statistical fluke, virtually all the studies depart from good scientific practice in a variety of ways; furthermore, it is not clear that the pattern of results is consistent across laboratories. In the committee's view, any conclusions favoring the existence of an effect so small must at least await the results of experiments conducted according to more adequate protocols.

3. Should the Army be interested in evaluating further experiments, the following procedures are recommended: first, the Army and outside scientists should arrive at a common protocol; second, the research should be conducted according to that protocol by both proponents and skeptics; and third, attention should be given to the manipulability and practical application of any effects found. Even if psi phenomena are determined to exist in some sense, this does not guarantee that they will have any practical utility, let alone military applications. For this to be possible, the phenomena would have to obey causal laws and be manipulable.

4. The committee is aware of the discrepancy between the lack of scientific evidence and the strength of many individuals' beliefs in paranormal phenomena. This is a cause for concern. Historically, many of the the world's most prominent scientists have concluded that such phenomena exist and that they have been scientifically verified. Yet in just about all these cases, subsequent information has revealed that their convictions were misguided. We also are aware that many proponents believe that the scientific method may not be the only, or the most

appropriate, method for establishing the reality of paranormal phenomena. Unfortunately, the alternative methods that have been used to demonstrate the existence of the paranormal create just those conditions that psychologists have found enhance human tendencies toward self-deception and suggestibility. Concerns about making the experimental situation comfortable for the alleged psychic or conducive to paranormal phenomena frequently result in practices that also increase opportunities for deception and error.

SOURCES OF INFORMATION

Two of the military officers who briefed us during our first meeting urged the committee to give serious consideration to paranormal phenomena and related parapsychological techniques. They described a variety of such phenomena that they felt had military potential, either as threats to security or as aids to defense. Site visits to leading laboratories and a paper prepared for the committee also contributed to the bases for the committee's work. Briefings were given to committee members by Robert Jahn, Cleve Backster, Helmut Schmidt, members of the staff of the Stanford Research Institute, and the U.S. Army Laboratory Command in Adelphi, Maryland. The paper prepared by James Alcock provided detailed reviews of the available evidence on random event generators and remote viewing. In addition, the committee benefited from a thorough review conducted for the Army Research Institute by John Palmer and from its own review of recent articles in the *Journal of Parapsychology* and other relevant periodicals and handbooks.

References

Aarons, L.
1976   Sleep assisted instruction. *Psychological Bulletin* 83:1–40.
Adams, J.A.
1980   *Learning and Memory: An Introduction*. Homewood, Ill.: Dorsey Press.
Akers, C.
1984   Methodological criticisms of parapsychology. In S. Krippner, ed., *Advances in Parapsychological Research*, vol. 4. Jefferson, N.C.: McFarland.
Alexander, L.
1982   Some preliminary experiments with SALT techniques: Music and exercises, paired-order and narrative word-types, and meaning checks. *Journal of the Society for Accelerative Learning and Teaching* 7:41–49.
Alloy, L.B., and A. Tabachnik
1984   Assessment of covariation in humans and animals: The joint influence of prior expectations and current situational information. *Psychological Review* 91:112–149.
American Psychiatric Association
1980   *Diagnostic and Statistical Manual of Mental Disorders*, 3d ed. Washington, D.C.: American Psychiatric Association.
Anderson, J.R., ed.
1981   *Cognitive Skills and Their Acquisition*. Hillsdale, N.J.: Erlbaum.
Annett, J.
1985   Motor learning: A review. In H. Heuer, ed., *Motor Behavior: Programming, Control, and Acquisition*. New York: Springer-Verlag.
Arnarson, E.O., and B. Sheffield
1980   Generalization of the effects of EMG and temperature biofeedback procedures in patients suffering from anxiety states. In *Proceedings of the 11th Annual Meeting of the Biofeedback Society of America*.
Aronson, R.M.
1981   Attentional and interpersonal factors as discriminators of elite and non-elite gymnasts. Ph.D. dissertation, Boston University.

Ausubel, D.P.
1960   The use of advance organizers in the learning of meaningful verbal material. *Journal of Educational Psychology* 51:267–272.

Back, K.W.
1973   *Beyond Words: The Story of Sensitivity Training and the Encounter Movement.* Baltimore: Penguin.
1987   *Beyond Words: The Story of Sensitivity Training and the Encounter Movement,* 2d ed. New Brunswick, N.J.: Transaction Books.

Backster, C., and S.G. White
1985   Biocommunications capability: Human donors and in vitro leukocytes. *The International Journal of Biosocial Research* 7(2):132–146.

Bancroft, W.J.
1976   Discovering the Lozanov method. *Journal of the Society for Accelerative Learning and Teaching* 14:263–277.

Bandler, R., and J. Grinder
1975   *The Structure of Magic.* Palo Alto, Calif.: Science and Behavior Books.

Bandura, A.
1977   Self-efficacy: Toward a unifying theory of behavior change. *Psychological Review* 84:191–215.

Barber, T.X.
1976   *Pitfalls in Human Research.* New York: Pergamon.

Basmajian, J.V.
1974   *Muscles Alive: Their Functions Revealed by Electromyography.* Baltimore: Williams and Wilkins.

Basmajian, J.V., and E.R. White
1973   Neuromuscular control of trumpeters' lips. *Nature* 241:70.

Bauer, H.
1984   Regulation of slow wave potentials affects task performance. In T. Elbert, B. Rockstroh, W. Lutzenberger, and N. Birbaumer, eds., *Self-Regulation of the Brain and Behavior.* New York: Springer-Verlag.

Baum, A., J.E. Singer, and C.S. Baum
1981   Stress and the environment. *Journal of Social Issues* 37:4–35.

Beach, J., H. Prince, and P.J. Klugman
1977   Stress management in two divergent military training settings. Paper presented at the 85th annual convention of the American Psychological Association, San Francisco, Calif.

Beatty, J.
1973   *Self-Regulation as an Aid to Human Effectiveness.* Annual progress report under contract NOOO14-70-0350, submitted to the San Diego State University Foundation. Los Angeles: University of California.

Beatty, J., A. Greensberg, W.P. Diebler, and J.F. O'Hanlon
1974   Operant control of occipital theta rhythm affects performance in a radar monitoring task. *Science* 183:871–874.

Beatty, J., and H. Legewie, eds.
1977   *Biofeedback and Behavior.* New York: Plenum.

Beatty, J., and J.F. O'Hanlon
1975   *EEG Theta Regulation and Radar Monitoring Performance of Experienced Radar Operators and Air Traffic Controllers.* UCLA technical report. Los Angeles: University of California.
1979   Operant control of posterior theta rhythms and vigilance performance: Repeated treatments and transfer of training. In N. Birbaumer and H.D. Kimmel, eds., *Biofeedback and Self-Regulation.* Hillsdale, N.J.: Erlbaum.

Beaumont, J.G., A.W. Young, and I.C. McManus
1984   Hemisphericity: A critical review. *Cognitive Neuropsychology* 1:191–212.
Beck, A.T.
1976   *Cognitive Therapy and the Emotional Disorders.* New York: International Universities Press.
Beck, A.T., and G. Emery
1985   *Anxiety Disorders and Phobias.* New York: Basic Books.
Beckhard, R.
1969   *Organizational Development: Strategies and Models.* Reading, Mass.: Addison-Wesley.
Benson, H.
1975   *The Relaxation Response.* New York: Morrow.
Benson, H., B.A. Dryer, and H.H. Hartley
1978   Decreased CO_2 consumption exercise with elicitation of the relaxation response. *Journal of Human Stress* 4:38–42.
Berkowitz, L.
1954   Group standards, cohesiveness and productivity. *Human Relations* 7:505–519.
Bever, T.G.
1975   Cerebral asymmetries in humans are due to the differentiation of two incompatible processes: Holistic and analytic. *Annals of the New York Academy of Sciences* 263:251–262.
Bilodeau, E.A., and I. McD. Bilodeau, eds.
1969   *Principles of Skill Acquisition.* New York: Academic Press.
Birbaumer, N., T. Elbert, B. Rockstroh, and W. Lutzenberger
1981   Biofeedback of event-related slow potentials of the brain. *International Journal of Psychology* 16:389–415.
Bisaha, J.P., and B.J. Dunne
1979   Multiple subject and long-distance precognitive remote viewing of geographical locations. In C.T. Tart, H.F. Puthoff, and R. Targ, eds., *Mind at Large.* New York: Praeger.
Blackburn, I.M., S. Bishop, A.I.M. Glen, L.J. Whalley, and J.E. Christie
1981   The efficacy of cognitive therapy in depression: A treatment trial using cognitive therapy and pharmacotherapy, each alone and in combination. *British Journal of Psychiatry* 139:181–189.
Blais, M.R., and R.J. Vallerand
1986   Multimodal effects of electromyographic biofeedback: Looking at children's ability to control precompetitive anxiety. *Journal of Human Stress* 8:283–303.
Borden, R.B., and D.H. Schuster
1976   The effects of suggestive learning climate, synchronized breathing and music on the learning and retention of Spanish words. *Journal of the Society for Accelerative Learning and Teaching* 1:27–39.
Bourne, P.G.
1970   *Men, Stress and Vietnam.* Boston: Little, Brown.
1971   Altered adrenal function in two combat situations in Vietnam. In B.E. Eleftheriou and J.P. Scott, eds., *The Physiology of Aggression and Defeat.* New York: Plenum.
Bradshaw, J., and L. Nettleton
1983   *Human Cerebral Asymmetry.* Englewood Cliffs, N.J.: Prentice-Hall.
Brady, J.V., A.H. Harris, D.H. Anderson, and J. Stephens
1974   Instrumental control of autonomic responses: Cardiovascular monitoring and performance interactions. In *Proceedings of the Fourth Symposium on Behavior Modification.* Mexico City.

Bush, B.J.
1985   A Study of Innovative Training Techniques at the Defense Language Institute Foreign Language Center. Monterey, Calif.

Campbell, D.T.
1975   On the conflicts between biological and social evolution and between psychology and moral tradition. *American Psychologist* 30:1103–1126.

Carroll, D., and M. McGovern
1983   Cardiac, respiratory and metabolic changes during static exercise and voluntary heart rate acceleration. *Biological Psychology* 17:121–130.

Charlesworth, E.A., and R.G. Nathan
1982   *Stress Management: A Comprehensive Guide to Wellness.* New York: Ballantine Books.

Cialdini, R.B.
1985   *Influence: Science and Practice.* Glenview, Ill.: Scott, Foresman.

Clemens, W.J., and R.J. Shattock
1979   Voluntary heart rate control during static muscular effort. *Psychophysiology* 16:327–332.

Coffey, B., and A.W. Reichow
1986   Vision Evaluation Program for the 1986 National Olympic Festival. Unpublished manuscript, College of Optometry, Pacific University, Forest Grove, Ore.

Cook, T.D., and D.T. Campbell
1979   *Quasi-experimentation: Designs and Analysis Issues for Social Research in Field Settings.* Boston: Houghton Mifflin.

Corbin, C.B.
1972   Mental practice. In W.B. Morgan, ed., *Ergogenic Aids and Muscular Performance.* New York: Academic Press.

Cowings, P.S.
1977   Combined use of autogenic therapy and biofeedback in training effective control of heart rate by humans. In *Proceedings of the 2nd International Symposium on Autogenic Training.* Rome: Ediz Pozzi.

Cowings, P.S., J. Billingham, and B.W. Toscano
1977   Learned control of multiple responses to compensate for the debilitating effects of motion sickness. *Therapy in Psychosomatic Medicine* 4:318–323.

Cowings, P.S., and W.B. Toscano
1977   Psychosomatic health: Simultaneous control of multiple autonomic responses in humans—a training method. *Therapy in Psychosomatic Medicine* 4:184–189.
1982   The relationship of motion sickness susceptibility to learned autonomic control for symptom suppression. *Aviation, Space, and Environmental Medicine* 53:570–575.

Cratty, B.J.
1973   *Movement Behavior and Motor Learning.* Philadelphia: Lea and Febiger.

Crowder, R.G.
1976   *Principles of Learning and Memory.* Hillsdale, N.J.: Erlbaum.

Cummings, M.S., V.E. Wilson, and E.I. Bird
1984   Flexibility development in sprinters using EMG biofeedback and relaxation training. *Biofeedback and Self-Regulation* 9:395–405.

Daniel, R.S.
1967   Alpha and theta EEG in vigilance. *Perceptual and Motor Skills* 25:697–703.

Daniels, F.S., and D.M. Landers
1981   Biofeedback and shooting performance: A test of disregulation and systems theory. *Journal of Sport Psychology* 4:271–282.

Danserean, D.F.
1986   Cooperative learning strategies. In C.E. Weinstein, E.T. Goetz, and P.A. Alexander, eds., *Learning and Study Strategies: Issues in Assessment, Instruction, and Evaluation.* New York: Academic Press.

Danskin, D.G., and M.A. Crow
1981   *Biofeedback: An Introductory Guide.* Palo Alto, Calif.: Mayfield.

Datel, W.E., and S. Lifrak
1969   Expectations, affect change, and military performance in the Army recruit. *Psychological Reports* 24:855–879.

Davidoff, J., J.C. Marshall, J.G. Beaumont, and A. Beaton
1985   *An Evaluative Review of Hemispheric Learning Potential.* Technical report no. 705. Alexandria, Va.: Army Research Institute.

Davison, G.C., and J.M. Neale
1986   *Abnormal Psychology: An Experimental Clinical Approach*, 4th ed. New York: John Wiley & Sons.

DeRenzi, E., P. Faglioni, and G. Scotti
1971   Judgment of spatial orientation in patients with focal brain damage. *Journal of Neurology, Neurosurgery, and Psychiatry* 34:489–495.

Dess, N.K., D. Linwick, J. Patterson, J.B. Overmier, and S. Levin
1983   Immediate and proactive effects of controllability and predictability on plasma cortisol responses to shocks in dogs. *Behavioral Neuroscience* 97:1005–1016.

Dewey, D., L.R. Brawley, and F. Allard
In   Does the test of attentional and interpersonal style (TAIS) really assess attention?
press *Journal of Sport Psychology.*

DeWitt, D.J.
1980   Cognitive and biofeedback training for stress reduction with university students. *Journal of Sport Psychology* 2:288–294.

Dilts, R.B.
1983   *Roots of Neuro-Linguistic Programming.* Cupertino, Calif.: Meta Publications.

Dilts, R.B., J. Grinder, R. Bandler, L.C. Bandler, and J. DeLozier
1980   *Neuro-Linguistic Programming: The Study of the Structure of Subjective Experience*, vol. 1. Cupertino, Calif.: Meta Publications.

Dobie, T.G., J.G. May, W.D. Fisher, S.T. Elder, and K. Kubitz
1986   A comparison of two methods of training resistance to visually-induced motion sickness. *Biofeedback and Self-Regulation.*

Donald, L.V., and J. Hovland
1981   Autoregulation of skin temperature with feedback assisted relaxation of the target limb and controlled variation in local air temperature. *Perceptual and Motor Skills* 53:799–809.

Druckman, D.
1971   The influence of the situation in inter-party conflict. *Journal of Conflict Resolution* 15:523–554.

Duffy, E.
1962   *Activation and Behavior.* New York: John Wiley & Sons.

D'Zurilla, T.J., and M.R. Goldfried
1971   Problem-solving and behavior modification. *Journal of Abnormal Psychology* 78:107–126.

D'Zurilla, T.J., and A. Nezu
1982   Social problem solving in adults. In P.C. Kendall, ed., *Advances in Cognitive-Behavioral Research and Therapy*, vol. 1. New York: Academic Press.

Easterbrook
1959   The effect of emotion on cue utilization and the organization of behavior. *Psychological Review* 1:183–201.
Ebon, M.
1983   *Psychic Warfare: Threat or Illusion?* New York: McGraw-Hill.
Eich, E.
1984   Memory for unattended events: Remembering with and without awareness. *Memory and Cognition* 12:105–111.
Elbert, T., N. Birbaumer, W. Lutzenberger, and B. Rockstroh
1979   Biofeedback of slow cortical potentials: Self-regulation of central-autonomic patterns. In N. Birbaumer and H.D. Kimmel, eds., *Biofeedback and Self-Regulation*. Hillsdale, N.J.: Erlbaum.
Elbert, T., B. Rockstroh, W. Lutzenberger, and N. Birbaumer
1980   Biofeedback of slow cortical potentials. *Journal of Electroencephalography and Clinical Neurophysiology* 48:293–301.
Ellis, A.
1962   *Reason and Emotion in Psychotherapy*. New York: Lyle Stuart.
Elton, R.M.
1984   Cohesion and unit pride aims of the new manning system. *Army Magazine* October:218–228.
Erlichman, H., and A. Weinberger
1978   Lateral eye movements and hemispheric asymmetry: A critical review. *Psychological Bulletin* 85:1080–1101.
Feltz, D.L., and D.M. Landers
1983   The effects of mental practice on motor skill learning and performance: A meta-analysis. *Journal of Sport Psychology* 5:25–57.
Finley, W.
1984   Biofeedback of very early potentials from the brain stem. In T. Elbert, B. Rockstroh, W. Lutzenberger, and N. Birbaumer, eds., *Self-Regulation of the Brain and Behavior*. New York: Springer-Verlag.
Finley, W.W., D. Karimian, and G. Alberti
1979   Sensory modification through biofeedback of brainstem auditory far-field potentials. In *Proceedings of the 10th Annual Meeting of the Biofeedback Society of America*.
Finley, W.W., R.A. Musicant, S.D. Billings, and M. Rosser
1978   Biofeedback and auditory far-field potentials from the brainstem: Implications for sensory modification. In *Proceedings of the 9th Annual Meeting of the Biofeedback Society of America*.
Fitts, P.M.
1964   Perceptual-motor skill learning. In A.W. Melton, ed., *Categories of Human Learning*. New York: Academic Press.
Fitts, P.M., and M.I. Posner
1967   *Human Performance*. Belmont, Calif.: Brooks Cole.
Fitzgerald, D., and J.A. Hattie
1983   An evaluation of the "Your Style of Learning and Thinking" inventory. *British Journal of Educational Psychology* 53:336–346.
Fleishman, E.A., and M.K. Quaintance
1984   *Taxonomies of Human Performance*. New York: Academic Press.
Ford, M., B.L. Bird, F.A. Newton, and D. Sheer
1980   Maintenance and generalization of 40 Hz EEG biofeedback effects. *Biofeedback and Self-Regulation* 5:193–205.

Frederiksen, N.
1972   Toward a taxonomy of situations. *American Psychologist* 27:113–115.
Fredrikson, M., and B.T. Engel
1985   Learned control of heart rate during exercise in patients with borderline hypertension. *European Journal of Applied Physiology* 54:315–320.
French, S.N.
1978   Electromyographic biofeedback for tension control during gross motor skill acquisition. *Perceptual and Motor Skills* 47:883–889.
1980   Electromyographic biofeedback for tension control during fine motor skill acquisition. *Biofeedback and Self-Regulation* 5:221–228.
Friedlander, F., and D. Brown
1974   Organizational development. *Annual Review of Psychology* 313–341.
Gale, A., and J.A. Edwards
1983   The EEG and human behavior. In A. Gale and J.A. Edwards, eds., *Physiological Correlates of Human Behavior: Attention and Performance,* vol. 2. New York: Academic Press.
Gannon, L., and R.A. Sternbach
1971   Alpha enhancement as a treatment for pain: A case study. *Journal of Behavior Therapy and Experimental Psychiatry* 2:209–213.
Gasser-Roberts, S.
1985   SALT, Suggestopedia and other accelerative learning methods in Japan and Europe. *Journal of the Society for Accelerative Learning and Teaching* 10:131–146.
Gasser-Roberts, S., and P. Brislan
1984   A controlled, comparative and evaluative study of a suggestopedic German course for first year university students. *Journal of the Society for Accelerative Learning and Teaching* 9:211–233.
Gazzaniga, M.S., and R.W. Sperry
1966   Simultaneous double discrimination response following brain bisection. *Psychonomic Science* 4:261–262.
Gillette, D.L.
1983   The effect of synchronized, multichannel EEG biofeedback and "open focus" training upon the performance of selected psychomotor tasks. *Dissertation Abstracts International* 44(3):910-B.
Glaser, E., C. Suter, R. Dasheiff, and A. Goldberg
1976   The human frequency following response: Its behavior during continuous tone and tone burst stimulation. *Electroencephalography and Clinical Neurophysiology* 40:25–32.
Glass, G.V.
1977   Integrating findings: The meta-analysis of research. *Review of Research in Education* 5:351–379.
Glass, A.L., and K.J. Holyoak
1986   *Cognition.* 2d ed. New York: Random House.
Goldfried, M.R., and G.C. Davison
1976   *Clinical Behavior Therapy.* New York: Holt, Rinehart and Winston.
Goldstein, D.S., R.S. Ross, and J.V. Brady
1977   Biofeedback heart rate training during exercise. *Biofeedback and Self-Regulation* 2:107–126.
Gordon, H.
1986   The cognitive laterality battery: Tests of specialized cognitive functions. *International Journal of Neuroscience* 29:223–244.

Gordon, H.W., R. Silverberg-Shalev, and J. Czernilas
1982   Hemispheric asymmetry in fighter and helicopter pilots. *Acta Psychologica* 52:33–40.

Green, E.E., A.M. Green, and E.D. Walters
1969   Self-regulation of the internal states. In J. Rose, ed., *Progress of Cybernetics: Proceedings of the International Congress of Cybernetics*. New York: Gordon and Breach.

Griffiths, T.J., D.H. Steel, S.P. Vaccaro, and M.B. Karpman
1981   The effects of relaxation techniques on anxiety and underwater performance. *International Journal of Sport Psychology* 12:176–182.

Grinker, R.R., and J.P. Spiegel
1945   *War Neuroses*. New York: Arno Press.

Groll, E.
1966   Central nervous system and peripheral activation variables during vigilance performance. *Zeitschrift fur Experimentelle und Angewandte Psychologie* 13:248–264.

Gumm, W.G., M.K. Walker, and H.D. Day
1982   Neurolinguistic programming: Method or myth? *Journal of Counseling Psychology* 29:327–330.

Haaga, D.A., and G.C. Davison
In   Outcome studies in rational-emotive therapy. In M.E. Bernard and R. DiGiuseppe,
press   eds., *Inside Rational-Emotive Therapy* New York: Academic Press.

Hale, B.D.
1981   The effects of internal and external imagery on muscular and ocular concomitants. Ph.D. dissertation, Pennsylvania State University.

Haley, S.A.
1978   Treatment implications of post-combat stress response syndromes for mental health professionals. In C.R. Figley, ed., *Stress Disorders Among Vietnam Veterans*. New York: Brunner/Mazel.

Hammer, A.L.
1983   Matching perceptual predicates: Effect on perceived empathy in a counseling analogue. *Journal of Counseling Psychology* 30:172–179.

Hardyck, C., and L. Petrinovich
1977   Left handedness. *Psychological Bulletin* 84:385–404.

Harris, A.H., J. Stephens, and J.V. Brady
1974   *Self-Regulation of Performance-Related Physiological Processes*. Annual progress report under contract NOOO14-70-C-0350, submitted to the San Diego State University Foundation. Baltimore: The Johns Hopkins University.

Harris, D.V., and W.J. Robinson
1986   The effects of skill level on EMG activity during internal and external imagery. *Journal of Sport Psychology* 8:105–111.

Hasted, J.B., D. Bohm, E.W. Bastin, and B. O'Regan
1976   Experiments on psychokinetic phenomena. In C. Panati, ed., *The Geller Papers*. Boston: Houghton Mifflin.

Hatfield, B.D., T. Spalding, T. Mahon, E.B. Brody, and P. Vaccaro
1986   Ventilatory economy as a function of attentional self-focus during treadmill running. *Psychophysiology* 23:440–441 (abstract).

Hayduk, A.W.
1980   Increasing hand efficiency at cold temperatures by training hand vasodilation with a classical conditioning-biofeedback overlap design. *Biofeedback and Self-Regulation* 5:307–326.

1982   The persistence and transfer of voluntary hand-warming in natural and laboratory cold settings after one year. *Biofeedback and Self-Regulation* 7:49–52.

Hedges, L.V., and I. Olkin
1985   *Statistical Methods for Meta-Analysis.* New York: Academic Press.

Hegge, F.W., C.F. Tyner, and S. Genser
1983   *Evaluating Human Technologies: What Questions Should We Ask?* Washington, D.C.: Walter Reed Army Institute for Research.

Henderson, W.D.
1985   *Cohesion: The Human Element in Combat.* Washington, D.C.: National Defense University Press.

Henry, F.M.
1968   Specificity vs. generality in learning motor skill. In R.C. Brown and G.S. Kenyon, eds., *Classical Studies on Physical Activity.* Englewood Cliffs, N.J.: Prentice-Hall (originally published 1958).

Hillyard, S.A., and M. Kutas
1983   Electrophysiology of cognitive processes. *Annual Review of Psychology* 34:33–61.

Hink, R., K. Kodera, O. Yamada, K. Kaga, and J. Suzuki
1980   Binaural interaction of a beating frequency following response. *Audiology* 19:36–43.

Holmes, T.H., and R.H. Rahe
1967   The social readjustment rating scale. *Journal of Psychosomatic Research* 11:213–218.

Holmes, T.S., and T.H. Holmes
1970   Short-term instrusions into the life style routine. *Journal of Psychosomatic Research* 14:121–132.

Honorton, C.
1985   Meta-analysis of psi ganzfeld research: A response to Hyman. *Journal of Parapsychology* 49:51–91.

Hord, D., A. Lubin, M.L. Tracy, B.W. Jensma, and L.C. Johnson
1976   Feedback for high EEG alpha does not maintain performance or mood during sleep loss. *Psychophysiology* 13:58–61.

Hord, D., M.L. Tracy, A. Lubin, and L.C. Johnson
1975   Effect of self-enhanced EEG alpha on performance and mood after two nights of sleep loss. *Psychophysiology* 12:585–590.

Horner, S.O., B.M. Meglino, and W.H. Mobley
1979   *An Experimental Evaluation of the Effects of a Realistic Job Preview on Marine Recruit Affect, Intentions, and Behavior.* TR-9. Columbia, S.C.: Center for Management and Organizational Research, University of South Carolina.

Hornstein, H.A., B.B. Bunker, W.W. Burke, M. Gindes, and R.J. Lewicki, eds.
1971   *Social Intervention: A Behavioral Science Approach.* New York: Macmillan.

Houck, J.
1984   PK party history. In C.B. Scott Jones, ed., *Proceedings of a Symposium on Applications of Anomalous Phenomena.* Alexandria, Va.: Kaman Tempo.

Hussian, R.A., and P.S. Lawrence
1980   Social reinforcement of activity and problem solving training in the treatment of depressed institutionalized elderly patients. *Cognitive Therapy and Research* 5:57–69.

Hyman, R.
1979   Psychics and scientists: A review of R. Targ and H. Puthoff, *Mind Reach. Humanist* 37(May/June):16–20.

1984– Outracing the evidence: The muddled 'Mind Race.' *Skeptical Inquirer* 9:125–
1985 145.
1985 The Ganzfeld psi experiment: A critical appraisal. *Journal of Parapsychology* 49:3–49.

Hyman, R., and C. Honorton
1986 A joint communique: The psi Ganzfeld controversy. *Journal of Parapsychology* 50:351–364.

Irion, A.L.
1969 Historical introduction. In E.A. Bilodeau and I. McD. Bilodeau, eds., *Principles of Skill Acquisition*. New York: Academic Press.

Jackson, G.M.
1978 Facilitation of performance on an arithmetic task with the mentally retarded as a result of the application of a biofeedback procedure to decrease Alpha wave activity. *Dissertation Abstracts International* 38(2):933-B.

Jackson, C.W.
1980 The relationship of swimming performance to measures of attention and interpersonal style. Ph.D. dissertation, Boston University.

Jacobson, E.
1938 *Progressive Relaxation*. Chicago: University of Chicago Press.
1932 Electrophysiology of mental activities. *American Journal of Psychology* 44:677–694.

Jacoby, L.L.
1983 Remembering the data: Analyzing interactive processes in reading. *Journal of Verbal Learning and Verbal Behavior* 22:485–508.

Jacoby, L.L., and M. Dallas
1981 On the relationship between autobiographical memory and perceptual learning. *Journal of Experimental Psychology: General* 110:306–340.

Jacoby, L.L., and D. Witherspoon
1982 Remembering with and without awareness. *Canadian Journal of Psychology* 36:300–324.

Jahn, R.G.
1982 The persistent paradox of psychic phenomena: An engineering perspective. *Proceedings of the IEEE* 70:136–170.

Jammott, J.B., III, J.Z. Borysenko, M. Borysenko, D.C. McClelland, R. Chapman, D. Meyer, and H. Benson
1983 Academic stress, power motivation, and decrease in salivary secretory immunoglobin A secretion. *Lancet* 1:1400–1402.

Janis, I.L.
1951 *Air War and Emotional Stress*. New York: McGraw-Hill.
1971 *Stress and Frustration*. New York: Harcourt Brace Jovanovich.
1972 *Victims of Group Think*. Boston: Houghton Mifflin.

Johnson, L.C.
1977 Learned control of brain wave activity. In J. Beatty and H. Legewie, eds., *Biofeedback and Behavior*. New York: Plenum.

Johnson, P.
1982 The functional equivalence of imagery and movement. *Quarterly Journal of Experimental Psychology* 34A:349–365.

Kahneman, D.
1973 *Attention and Effort*. Englewood Cliffs, N.J.: Prentice-Hall.

Kamiya, J.
1969 Operant control of the EEG alpha rhythm and some of its reported effects on consciousness. In C.T. Tart, ed., *Altered States of Consciousness: A Book of Readings*. New York: John Wiley & Sons.

1972   *Self-Regulation as an Aid To Human Effectiveness.* Annual progress report under contract NOOO14-70-C-0350 submitted to the San Diego State University Foundation. San Francisco: Langley Porter Neuropsychiatric Institute.

Kappes, B.M., and S.J. Chapman
1984   The effect of indoor versus outdoor thermal biofeedback training in cold weather sports. *Journal of Sport Psychology* 6:305–311.

Kappes, B.M., S.J. Chapman, and W. Sullivan
1986   Thermal biofeedback training in cold environments. Effects on pain and dexterity. *Biofeedback and Self-Regulation* 11:63 (abstract).

Kappes, B.M., and W.J. Mills
1985   Thermal biofeedback training with frostbite patients. *Circumpolar Health* 84:83–84.

Katz, D., and R.L. Kahn
1966   *The Social Psychology of Organizations.* New York: John Wiley & Sons.

Kelman, H.C.
1968   *A Time to Speak: On Human Values and Social Research.* San Francisco: Jossey-Bass.

Kennedy, J.E.
1979   Methodological problems in free-response ESP experiments. *Journal of the American Society for Psychical Research* 73:1–15.

Kitching, J.A., A.N. Bentley, and E. Page
1942   *New R.C.A.F. Flying Gloves.* National Research Council of Canada, report no. C-2216.

Klockner, K.
1984   Suggestopedia applied to an English-as-a-second-language setting. *Journal of the Society for Accelerative Learning and Teaching* 9:61–77.

Knibbeler, W.
1982   A closer look at Suggestopedia and the silent way. *Journal of the Society for Accelerative Learning and Teaching* 7:330–340.

Kobasa, S.C., S.R. Maddi, and S. Kahn
1982   Hardiness and health: A prospective study. *Journal of Personality and Social Psychology* 42:168–177.

Kohl, R.M., and D.L. Roenker
1983   Mechanism involvement during skill imagery. *Journal of Motor Behavior* 15:179–190.

Kreuter, C., M. Kinsbourne, and C. Trevarthen
1972   Are deconnected cerebral hemispheres independent channels? A preliminary study of the effect of unilateral loading on bilateral finger tapping. *Neuropsychologia* 10:453–461.

Lacey, J.I., J. Kagan, B.C. Lacey, and H.A. Moss
1963   The visceral level: Situational determinants and behavioral correlates of autonomic response patterns. In P.H. Knapp, ed., *Expressions of the Emotions of Man.* New York: International Universities Press.

Lakein, A.
1973   *How To Get Control of Your Time and Your Life.* New York: Peter W. Wyden.

Landauer, T.K., and R.A. Bjork
1978   Optimal rehearsal patterns and name learning. In M.M. Grunebert, P.E. Morris, and R.M. Sykes, eds., *Practical Aspects of Memory.* London: Academic Press.

Landers, D.M., S. Boutcher, and M.Q. Wang
1986   A psychobiological study of archery performance. *Research Quarterly for Exercise and Sport* 57:236–244.

Landers, D.M., and R.W. Christina
1986   Notice in *Journal of Sport Psychology* 8:144.

Landers, D.M., M.O. Wilkinson, B.D. Hatfield, and H. Barber
    1982   Causality and the cohesion-performance relationship. *Journal of Sport Psychology* 4:170–183.

Lawrence, G.H.
    1984   *Biofeedback and Performance: An Update.* Technical report 658. Alexandria, Va.: U.S. Army Research Institute for the Behavioral and Social Sciences.

Lawrence, G.H., and L.C. Johnson
    1977   Biofeedback and performance. In G.E. Schwartz and J. Beatty, eds., *Biofeedback: Theory and Research.* New York: Academic Press.

Lazarus, R.S.
    1966   *Psychological Stress and the Coping Process.* New York: McGraw-Hill.

Lazarus, R.S., and J.P. Cohen
    1977   Environmental stress. In I. Altman and J.F. Wohlwill, eds., *Human Behavior and the Environment: Current Theory and Research.* New York: Plenum.

Lerner, R.M.
    1984   *On the Nature of Human Plasticity.* Cambridge: Cambridge University Press.

LeShan, L.
    1942   The breaking of a habit by suggestion during sleep. *Journal of Abnormal and Social Psychology* 37:406–408.

Levi, A.H.
    1976   EEG biofeedback and its effects on psychological functioning. *Dissertation Abstracts International* 36(7):3614-B.

Levine, S., J. Madden IV, R.L. Conner, J.R. Moskal, and D.C. Anderson
    1973   Physiological and behavioral effects of prior aversive stimulation (preshock) in the rat. *Physiology and Behavior* 10:467–471.

Lifton, R.J.
    1976   Advocacy and corruption in the healing profession. In N.L. Goldman and D.R. Segal, eds., *The Social Psychology of Military Service.* Beverly Hills: Sage Publications.

Lo, C.R., and D.W. Johnston
    1984   Cardiovascular feedback during dynamic exercise. *Psychophysiology* 21:199–206.

Lockhart, J.M.
    1968   Extreme body cooling and psychomotor performance. *Ergonomics* 11:249–260.

Lozanov, G.
    1978   *Suggestology and Outlines of Suggestopedy.* New York: Gordon and Breach.

Luria, A.R.
    1969   *The Mind of a Mnemonist.* London: Cape.

Lutzenberger, W., T. Elbert, B. Rockstroh, and N. Birbaumer
    1979   Effects of slow cortical potentials on performance in a signal detection task. *International Journal of Neuroscience* 9:175–183.
    1982   Biofeedback of slow cortical potentials and its effects on the performance in mental arithmetic tasks. *Biological Psychology* 14:99–111.
    1985   Lateral asymmetries of event related brain potentials during tactile tasks. *International Journal of Psychophysiology.*

Lynch, J.J., and D.A. Paskewitz
    1971   On the mechanisms of the feedback control of human brain wave activity. *Journal of Nervous and Mental Disease* 153:205–217.

McCroskery, J.M., B.T. Engel, S.M. Gottlieb, and E.G. Lakatta
    1978   Operant conditioning of heart rate in patients with angina pectoris. *Psychosomatic Medicine* 40:89–90.

McGlone, J.
1980   Sex differences in human brain asymmetry: A critical survey. *Behavioral and Brain Sciences* 3:215–263.
McGuire, W.J.
1985   Attitudes and attitude change. In G. Lindzey and E. Aronson, eds., *The Handbook of Social Psychology*, 3d ed., vol. 2. New York: Random House.
Mackay, D.G.
1981   The problem of rehearsal or mental practice. *Journal of Motor Behavior* 13:274–285.
McRae, R.M.
1984   *Mind Wars: The True Story of Government Research into the Military Potential of Psychic Weapons*. New York: St. Martin's Press.
Magnusson, E.
1976   The effects of controlled muscle tension on performance and learning of heart-rate control. *Biological Psychology* 4:81–92.
Malinowski, B.
1948   *Magic, Science, and Religion*. New York: Free Press of Glencoe.
Marks, D., and R. Kammann
1978   *The Psychology of the Psychic*. Buffalo: Prometheus Books.
Marks, D., and C. Scott
1986   Remote viewing exposed. *Nature* 319:444.
Mason, J.W.
1968   A review of psychoendocrine research on the pituitary-adrenal-cortical system. *Psychonomic Medicine* 30:576–607.
May, E.C., B.S. Humphrey, and G.S. Hubbard
1980   *Electronic System Perturbation Techniques*. Final report. Menlo Park, Calif: SRI International.
Mayer, R.E.
1979   Can advanced organizers influence meaningful learning? *Review of Educational Research* 49:371–383.
Meichenbaum, D.H.
1977   *Cognitive-behavior Modification: An Integrated Approach*. New York: Plenum.
Meichenbaum, D.H., and R. Cameron
1983   Stress inoculation training. In D. Meichenbaum and M.E. Jaremko, eds., *Stress Reduction and Prevention*. New York: Plenum.
Melzack, R., and C. Perry
1975   Self-regulation of pain: The use of alpha-feedback and hypnotic training for the control of chronic pain. *Experimental Neurology* 46:452–469.
Mercier, M.A., and M. Johnson
1984   Representational system predicate use and convergence in counseling: Gloria revisited. *Journal of Counseling Psychology* 31:161–169.
Morasky, R.L., C. Reynolds, and G. Clarke
1981   Using biofeedback to reduce left arm extensor EMG of string players during musical performance. *Biofeedback and Self-Regulation* 6:565–572.
Morasky, R.L., C. Reynolds, and L.E. Sowell
1983   Generalization of lowered EMG levels during musical performance following biofeedback training. *Biofeedback and Self-Regulation* 8:207–216.
Morgan, B.B., and G.D. Coates
1975   Enhancement of Performance During Sustained Operations Through the Use of EEG and Heart-Rate Autoregulation. Annual Progress Report under contract N00014-70-0350 submitted to San Diego State University Foundation. Old Dominion University, Norfolk, Va.

Morris, S.E.
1985   The facilitation of learning. Unpublished paper, the Monroe Institute, Faber, Va.
Moruzzi, G., and H.W. Magoun
1949   Brainstem reticular formation and activation of the EEG. *EEG and Clinical Neurophysiology* 1:455–473.
Moscovici, S.
1985   Social influence and conformity. In G. Lindzey and E. Aronson, eds., *The Handbook of Social Psychology*. 3d ed. Vol 2, New York: Random House.
Moses, J., W.J. Clemens, and J. Brener
1986   Bidirectional voluntary heart rate control during static muscular exercise: Metabolic and respiratory correlates. *Psychophysiology* 23:510–520.
Moskos, C.C.
1975   The American combat soldier in Vietnam. *Journal of Social Issues* 31:27.
Mowday, R.T., L.W. Porter, and R. Steers
1982   *Employee-Organization Linkages*. New York: Academic Press.
Mulholland, T.
1962   The electro-encephalogram as an experimental tool in the study of internal attention gradients. *Transactions of the New York Academy of Sciences* 24:664–669.
Murphy, P., W. Lakey, and P. Maurek
1976   Effects of simultaneous divergent EEG feedback from both cerebral hemispheres on changes in verbal and spatial tasks. In *Proceedings of the 11th Annual Meeting of the Biofeedback Society of America*.
Nelson, R.D., B.J. Dunne, and R.G. Jahn
1984   Operator related anomalies. In *An REG Experiment with Large Data Base Capability*. Princeton, N.J.: School of Engineering/Applied Science, Princeton University.
Newell, A., and P.S. Rosenbloom
1981   Mechanisms of skill acquisition and the law of practice. In J.R. Anderson, ed., *Cognitive Skills and Their Acquisition*. Hillsdale, N.J.: Erlbaum.
Nideffer, R.M.
1976   Test of attentional and interpersonal style. *Journal of Personality and Social Psychology* 34:394–404.
1979   The role of attention in optimal athlete performance. In P. Klavora and J.V. Daniels, eds., *Coach, Athlete and the Sport Psychologist*. Toronto: University of Toronto Press.
1981   *The Ethics and Practics of Applied Sport Psychology*. Ithaca, N.Y.: Movement Publications.
1985   *An Athlete's Guide to Mental Training*. Champaign, Ill.: Human Kinetics Publishers.
1986   Concentration and attention control training. In J. Williams, ed., *Applied Sport Psychology*. Palo Alto, Calif.: Mayfield.
Nisbett, R., and L. Ross
1980   *Human Inference: Strategies and Shortcomings of Social Judgment*. Englewood Cliffs, N.J.: Prentice-Hall.
Novaco, R.W., T.M. Cook, and I.G. Sarason
1983   Military recruit training: An arena for stress-coping skills. In D. Meichenbaum and M.E. Jaremko, eds., *Stress Reduction and Prevention*. New York: Plenum.
Nowlis, D.P., and J. Kamiya
1970   The control of electroencephalographic alpha rhythms through auditory feedback and the associated mental activity. *Psychophysiology* 6:476–484.

Orne, M., F. Evans, S. Wilson, and D. Paskewitz

1975 *The Potential Effectiveness of Autoregulation as a Technique to Increase Performance Under Stress.* Final summary report under contract NOOO14-C-0350 submitted to the San Diego State University Foundation. Philadelphia: University of Pennsylvania.

Oster, G.

1973 Auditory beats in the brain. *Scientific American* 229.

Ostrander, S., and L. Schroeder

1979 *SuperLearning.* New York: Dell.

Paivio, A.

1971 *Imagery and Verbal Processes.* New York: Holt, Rinehart and Winston.

1975 Imagery and long-term memory. In A. Kennedy and A. Wilkes, eds., *Studies in Long-Term Memory.* New York: John Wiley & Sons.

Paivio, A., and A. Desrochers

1979 Effects of an imagery mnemonic on second language recall and comprehension. *Canadian Journal of Psychology* 33:17–27.

Palmer, J.

1985 An evaluative report on the current status of parapsychology: draft final report. U.S. Army Research Institute for the Behavioral and Social Sciences, Alexandria, Va.

Palmer, L.L.

1985 Suggestive Accelerative Learning and Teaching (SALT): With learning disabled and other special needs students. *Journal of the Society for Accelerative Learning and Teaching* 10:99–130.

Paskewitz, D.A., and M. Orne

1975 Visual effects on alpha feedback training. *Science* 181:360–363.

Paul, G.L.

1966 *Insight vs. Desensitization in Psychotherapy.* Stanford, Calif.: Stanford University Press.

Peper, E., and A. Schmid

1983 Mental preparation for optimal performance in rhythmic gymnastics. In *Proceedings of the 14th Annual Meeting of the Biofeedback Society of America.*

Perski, A., and I. Dureman

1979 Voluntary control of heart rate: An extended replication study. *Scandanavian Journal of Behavior Therapy* 8:83–96.

Perski, A., and B.T. Engel

1980 The role of behavioral conditioning in the cardiovascular adjustment to exercise. *Biofeedback and Self-Regulation* 5:91–103.

Perski, A., S.P. Tzankoff, and B.T. Engel

1985 Central control of the cardiovascular adjustments to exercise. *Journal of Applied Physiology, Respiratory, Environmental and Exercise Physiology* 58:431–435.

Peters, T.J., and R.H. Waterman

1982 *In Search of Excellence.* New York: Harper & Row.

Plotkin, W.B.

1976 On the self-regulation of the occipital alpha rhythm, control strategies, states of consciousness, and the role of physiological feedback. *Journal of Experimental Psychology: General* 105:66–99.

Porras, J.I., and P.O. Berg

1978 The impact of organization development. *Academy of Management Review* 3.

Porter, L.W., E.E. Lawler, and J.R. Hackman

1975 *Behavior in Organizations.* New York: McGraw-Hill.

Posner, M.I.
1975   Psychobiology of attention. In M.S. Gazzaniga and C. Blakemore, eds., *Handbook of Psychobiology*. New York: Academic Press.

Powers, C.J.
1980   The psychophysiological effects of biofeedback OPEN FOCUS self-regulation training upon homeostatic efficiency during exercise. *Dissertation Abstracts International* 41:3927-B.

Pribram, K.H., A. Sharafat, and G.J. Beekman
1984   Frequency encoding in motor systems. In H.T.A. Whiting, ed., *Human Motor Actions: Bernstein Reassessed*. Amsterdam: North-Holland.

Puthoff, H.E., and R. Targ
1976   A perceptual channel for information transfer over kilometer distances: Historical perspectives and recent research. *Proceedings of the IEEE* 64:329–354.

Radin, D.I., E.C. May, and M.J. Thomson
1985   Psi-experiments with random number generators: Meta-analysis part I. Unpublished manuscript. SRI International, Menlo Park, Calif.

Rahe, R.H., and E. Lind
1971   Psychosocial factors and sudden cardiac death: A pilot study. *Journal of Psychosomatic Research* 15:19–24.

Rasmussen, T., and B. Milner
1975   Clinical and surgical studies of the cerebral speech areas in man. In K.J. Zulch, O. Creutzfeldt, and G. Galbraith, eds., *Cerebral Localization*. New York: Springer-Verlag.

Reder, L.M., and J.R. Anderson
1980   A comparison of text and their summaries: Memorial consequences. *Journal of Verbal Learning and Verbal Behavior* 19:121–134.
1982   Effects of spacing and embellishment on memory for the main points of a text. *Memory and Cognition* 10:79–102.

Reder, L.M., D. Charney, and K. Morgan
1986   The role of elaborations in learning a skill from instructional text. *Memory and Cognition* 14:64–78.

Regestein, Q.R., G.H. Buckland, and G.V. Pegram
1973   Effect of daytime alpha rhythm maintenance on subsequent sleep. *Psychosomatic Medicine* 35:415–418.

Reis, J., and A.M. Bird
1982   Cue processing as a function of breadth of attention. *Journal of Sport Psychology* 4:64–72.

Renold, A.E., T.B. Quingley, H.E. Kennard, and G.W. Thorn
1951   Reaction of the adrenal cortex to physical and emotional stress in college oarsmen. *New England Journal of Medicine* 244:754–757.

Revien, L., and M. Gabor
1981   *Sports-Vision*. New York: Workman.

Richardson, A.
1967   Mental practice: A review and discussion. *Research Quarterly* 38:95–107, 263–273.

Richardson-Klaveher, A., and R.A. Bjork
1988   Measures of memory. *Annual Review of Psychology*. Palo Alto, Calif.: Annual Reviews.

Robbins, T.W., and B.J. Everitt
1982   Functional studies of the central catecholamines. *International Review of Neurobiology* 23:303–365.

Rockstroh, B., N. Birbaumer, T. Elbert, and W. Lutzenberger
1984   Operant control of EEG and event-related and slow brain potentials. *Biofeedback and Self-Regulation* 9:139–160.
Rockstroh, B., T. Elbert, W. Lutzenberger, and N. Birbaumer
1980   Slow cortical potentials and response speed. In H.H. Kornhuber and L. Deecke, eds., *Motivational, Motor and Sensory Processes of the Brain. Electrical Potentials, Behavioral and Clinical Use.* New York: Elsevier.
1982   The effect of slow cortical potentials on response speed. *Psychophysiology* 19:211–217.
Roger, M.
1984   Operant control of evoked potentials: Some comments on the learning characteristics in man and the conditioning of subcortical reponses in the curarized rat. In T. Elbert, B. Rockstroh, W. Lutzenberger, and N. Birbaumer, eds., *Self-Regulation of the Brain and Behavior.* New York: Springer-Verlag.
Roger, M., and G. Garland
1983   Operant conditioning of visual evoked potentials in man. *Psychophysiology* 18:477–482.
Roland, P.
1985   Cortical organization of voluntary behavior in man. *Human Neurobiology* 4:155–167.
Roland, P.E., B. Larsen, N.A. Lassen, and E. Skinhoj
1980   Supplementary motor area and other cortical areas in organization of voluntary movements in man. *Journal of Neurophysiology* 43:118–136.
Roland, P.E., E. Skinhoj, N.A. Lassen, and B. Larsen
1980   Different cortical areas in man in organization of voluntary movements in extrapersonal space. *Journal of Neurophysiology* 43:137–150.
Rosenfield, J.P., R. Dowman, R. Silvia, and M. Heinricher
1984   Operantly controlled somatosensory brain potentials: Specific effects on pain processes. In T. Elbert, B. Rockstroh, W. Lutzenberger, and N. Birbaumer, eds., *Self-Regulation of the Brain and Behavior.* New York: Springer-Verlag.
Rosenthal, R., and L. Jacobson
1968   *Pygmalion in the Classroom.* New York: Holt, Rinehart and Winston.
Rubl, R.
1983   Assessment of attentional style. Master's thesis, University of Washington.
Rumelhart, D.E., and J.L. McClelland
1986   *Parallel Distributed Processing.* Cambridge, Mass.: Bradford Books, MIT Press.
Rush, A.J., A.T. Beck, M. Kovacs, and S.D. Hollon
1977   Comparative efficacy of cognitive therapy and pharmacotherapy in the treatment of depressed outpatients. *Cognitive Therapy and Research* 1:17–37.
Ryan, E.D., and J. Simons
1983   What is learned in mental practice of motor skills: A test of the cognitive-motor hypothesis. *Journal of Sport Psychology* 5:419–426.
Sabourin, M., and S. Rioux
1979   Effects of active and passive EMG biofeedback training on performance of motor and cognitive tasks. *Perceptual and Motor Skills* 49:831–835.
Sackett, R.S.
1934   The influences of symbolic rehearsal upon the retention of a maze habit. *Journal of General Psychology* 10:376–395.
Schachter, D.L., and E. Tulving
1982   Memory, amnesia, and the episodic/semantic distinction. In R.L. Isaacson and N.E. Spear, eds., *The Expression of Knowledge.* New York: Plenum.

Schachter, S., N. Ellertson, D. McBride, and D. Gregory
1951   An experimental study of cohesiveness and productivity. *Human Relations* 4:229–239.

Schein, E.H.
1985   *Organizational Culture and Leadership*. San Francisco: Jossey-Bass.

Schlitz, M., and E. Gruber
1980   Transcontinental remote viewing. *Journal of Parapsychology* 44:305–317.

Schlitz, M., and J.M. Haight
1984   Remove viewing revisited: An intrasubject replication. *Journal of Parapsychology* 48:39–49.

Schmid, A., and E. Peper
1986   Techniques for training concentration. In J. Williams, ed., *Applied Sport Psychology*. Palo Alto, Calif.: Mayfield.

Schmidt, R.A.
1982   *Motor Control and Learning: A Behavioral Emphasis*. Champaign, Ill.: Human Kinetics.

Schultz, J.H., and W. Luthe
1969   *Autogenic Therapy*. Vol. 1, *Autogenic Methods*. New York: Grune & Stratton.

Schuster, D.H.
1976a   A preliminary evaluation of the suggestive accelerative Lozanov method of teaching beginning Spanish. *Journal of the Society for Accelerative Learning and Teaching* 1:41–47.

1976b   The effects of the alpha mental state, indirect suggestion, and associative mental activity on learning rare English words. *Journal of the Society for Accelerative Learning and Teaching* 1:116–123.

1985   The effect of background music on learning words. *Journal of the Society for Accelerative Learning and Teaching* 10:21–37.

Schuster, D.H., and C.E. Gritton
1986   *Suggestive Accelerative Learning Techniques*. New York: Gordon and Breach.

Schuster, D.H., and D.J. Martin
1980   The effects of biofeedback-induced tension or relaxation, chronic anxiety, vocabulary easiness, suggestion and sex of subjects on learning rare vocabulary words. *Journal of the Society for Accelerative Learning and Teaching* 5:275–288.

Schuster, D.H., and D. Mouzon
1982   Music and vocabulary learning. *Journal of the Society for Accelerative Learning and Teaching* 7:82–108.

Schuster, D.H., and R.A. Prichard
1978   A two-year evaluation of the Suggestive Accelerative Learning and Teaching (SALT) method in a central Iowa Public School. *Journal of the Society for Accelerative Learning and Teaching* 3:108–121.

Schuster, D.H., and Wardell
1978   A study of Suggestopedia features that can be omitted once students learn how to learn. *Journal of the Society for Accelerative Learning and Teaching* 3:9–15.

Schwartz, G.E., and J. Beatty, eds.
1977   *Biofeedback: Theory and Research*. San Francisco: Academic Press.

Scott, C.
1982   No "remote viewing." *Nature* 298:414.

Seashore, S.
1954   *Group Cohesiveness in the Industrial Organization*. Ann Arbor: Institute of Social Research, University of Michigan.

Seiderman, A., and S. Schneider
1983   *The Athletic Eye.* New York: Hearst Books.
Seligman, M.E.P.
1975   *Learned Helplessness: On Depression, Development and Death.* San Francisco: W.H. Freeman.
Selye, H.
1936   A syndrome produced by diverse nocuous agents. *Nature* 138:32.
Sharpley, C.F.
1984   Predicate matching in NLP: A review of research on the preferred representational system. *Journal of Counseling Psychology* 31:238–248.
Sheer, D.E.
1977   Biofeedback training of 40 Hz EEG and behavior. In J. Kamiya, ed., *Biofeedback and Self-Control.* Chicago: Aldine.
1984   Focused arousal, 40 Hz EEG, and dysfunction. In T. Elbert, B. Rockstroh, W. Lutzenberger, and N. Birbaumer, eds., *Self-Regulation of the Brain and Behavior.* New York: Springer-Verlag.
Sheldon, W.H.
1942   *Varieties of Human Temperament: A Psychology of Constitutional Differences.* New York: Harper.
Silver, B.V., and E.B. Blanchard
1978   Biofeedback and relaxation training in the treatment of psychophysiological disorders: Or are the machines really necessary? *Journal of Behavioral Medicine* 1:217–238.
Simkins, L., and M. Funk
1979   Acquisition of skin temperature control in a cold pressor stress test situation. *Biofeedback and Self-Regulation* 4:290.
Simon, C.W., and W.H. Emmons
1955   Learning during sleep? *Psychological Bulletin* 52:328–342.
Slamecka, N., and P. Graf
1978   The generation effects: Delineation of a phenomenon. *Journal of Experimental Psychology, Human Learning and Memory* 14:592–604.
Slavin, R.E.
1983   When does cooperative learning increase student achievement? *Psychological Bulletin* 94:429–445.
Smith, R.W.
1975   *Self-Regulation as an Aid to Human Effectiveness.* Final report under contract N00014-70-C-0350, submitted to the San Diego State University Foundation. Denver: University of Colorado Medical Center.
Springer, S.P., and G. Deutsch
1985   *Left Brain, Right Brain.* New York: W.H. Freeman.
Stamm, J.S.
1984   Performance enhancement with cortical negative slow potential shifts in monkey and human. In T. Elbert, B. Rockstroh, W. Lutzenberger, and N. Birbaumer, eds., *Self-Regulation of the Brain and Behavior.* New York: Springer-Verlag.
Stein, A.
1976   Conflict and cohesion: A review of the literature. *Journal of Conflict Resolution* 20:143–172.
Stephens, J.H., A.H. Harris, and J.V. Brady
1972   Large magnitude heart rate changes in subjects instructed to change their heart rates and given exeroceptive feedback. *Psychophysiology* 9:283–285.

Stephens, J.H., A.H. Harris, J.V. Brady, and J.W. Shaffer
1975 Psychological and physiological variables associated with large magnitude voluntary heart rate changes. *Psychophysiology* 12:381–387.

Stevens, J.O., ed.
1979 *Frogs into Princes: Richard Bandler and John Grinder Live.* Moab, Utah: Real People Press.

Stine, C.D., M.R. Arterburn, and N.S. Stern
1982 Vision and sports: A review of the literature. *Journal of the American Optometric Association* 53(8):627–633.

Stockwell, T.
1986 Discussion of Suggestopedia in Liechtenstein. Paper presented at the annual meeting of the International Society for Accelerated Learning, West Palm Beach, Fla.

Stoffer, G.E., J.S. Jensen, and B.L. Nesset
1977 Cold stress tolerance as a function of biofeedback temperature training and internal-external locus of control. *Biofeedback and Self-Regulation* 2:295–296.

Stokes, J.P.
1983 Components of group cohesion: Intermember attraction, instrumental value, and risk taking. *Small Group Behavior* 14:163–173.

Stouffer, S.A.
1949 *The American Soldier.* Princeton, N.J.: Princeton University Press.

Stoyva, J., and T. Budzynski
1973 *Biofeedback Training in the Self-Induction of Sleep.* Annual progress report under contract NOOO14-70-C-0350, submitted to the San Diego State University Foundation. Denver: University of Colorado Medical Center.

Suarez, A., R.J. Kohlenberg, and R.R. Pagano
1979 Is EMG activity from the frontalis site a good measure of general bodily tension in clinical populations? In *Proceedings of 10th Annual Meeting of the Biofeedback Society of America.*

Tajfel, H.
1982 Social psychology of intergroup relations. *Annual Review of Psychology* 33:1–39.

Talen, M.I., and B.T. Engel
1986 Learned control of heart rate during dynamic exercise in nonhuman primates. *Journal of Applied Physiology* 61:545–553.

Targ, R., and K. Harary
1984 *The Mind Race: Understanding and Using Psychic Abilities.* New York: Villard Books.

Targ, R., and H. Puthoff
1974 Information transfer under conditions of sensory shielding. *Nature* 251:602–607.
1977 *Mind Reach: Scientists Look at Psychic Ability.* New York: Delacorte.

Targ, R., H.E. Puthoff, and E.C. May
1979 Direct perception of remote geographical locations. Pp. 13–76 in C.T. Tart, H.E. Puthoff, and R. Targ, eds., *Mind at Large.* New York: Praeger.

Tart, C.T., ed.
1969 *Altered States of Consciousness.* New York: John Wiley & Sons.

Tart, C.T., H.E. Puthoff, and R. Targ
1980 Information transmission in remote viewing experiments. *Nature* 284:191.

Taub, E.
1977 Self-regulation of human tissue temperature. In G.E. Schwartz and J. Beatty, eds., *Biofeedback: Theory and Research.* New York: Academic Press.

Tebbs, R., R. Eggleston, D. Prather, T. Simond, and T. Jarboe
1974 Stress Management Through Scientific Muscle Relaxation Training and Its Relation to Simulated and Actual Flying Training. Final report prepared under ARPA Order 2409 submitted to the Defense Advanced Research Projects Agency.

Teng, E.L., and R.W. Sperry
1973 Interhemispheric interaction during simultaneous bilateral presentation of letters in commissurotomized patients. *Neuropsychologia* 11:131–140.
1974 Interhemispheric rivalry during simultaneous bilateral task presentation in commissurotomized patients. *Cortex* 10:111–120.

Terborg, J.R., C. Castore, and J.A. DeNinno
1976 A longitudinal field investigation of the impact of group composition on group performance and cohesion. *Journal of Personality and Social Psychology* 34:782–790.

Tilley, A.J.
1979 Sleep learning during stage II and REM sleep. *Biological Psychology* 9:155–161.

Torrance, E.P.
1954 Some consequences of power differences on decision-making in permanent and temporary three-man groups. *Research Studies of the State College of Washington* 22:130–140.

Torrance, E.P., and C. Reynolds
1980 *Norms—Technical Manual for Your Style of Learning and Thinking.* Athens, Ga.: Department of Educational Psychology, University of Georgia.

Toscano, W.B., and P.S. Cowings
1982 Reducing motion sickness: A comparison of autogenic-feedback training and an alternative cognitive task. *Aviation, Space, and Environmental Medicine* 53:449–453.

Tulving, T.
1985 How many memory systems are there? *American Psychologist* 40:385–398.

Turner, R.G., and L. Gilliland
1977 Comparisons of self-report and performance measures of attention. *Perceptual and Motor Skills* 45:409–410.

Tversky, A., and D. Kahneman
1973 Availability: A heuristic of judging frequency and probability. *Cognitive Psychology* 5:207–232.

Tyerman, A., and C. Spencer
1983 A critical test of the Sherifs' Robber's Cave experiments: Intergroup competition and cooperation between groups of well-acquainted individuals. *Small Group Behavior* 14:515–531.

Ursin, H., E. Baade, and S. Levine, eds.
1978 *Psychobiology of Stress: A Study of Coping Men.* New York: Academic Press.

Vallerand, R.J.
1983 Attention and decision making: A test of the predictive validity of the Test of Attentional and Interpersonal Style (TAIS) in a sport setting. *Journal of Sport Psychology* 5:449–459.

Van Maanen, J.
1983 Golden passports: Managerial socialization and graduate education. *Review of Higher Education* 6:435–455.

Van Schoyck, R.S., and A.F. Grasha
1981 Attentional style variations and athletic ability: The advantage of a sport-specific test. *Journal of Sport Psychology* 3:149–165.

Varela, J.A.
  1971   *Psychological Solutions to Social Problems: An Introduction to Social Technology.* New York: Academic Press.
Wagner, M.J., and G. Tilney
  1983   The effects of "SuperLearning Techniques" on the vocabulary acquisition and alpha brainwave production of language learners. *TESOL Quarterly* 17(1): 5–17.
Warrington, E.K., and P. Rabin
  1970   Perceptual matching in patients with cerebral lesions. *Neuropsychologia* 8:475–487.
Weinberg, R.S.
  1982   The relationship between mental preparation strategies and motor performance: A review and critique. *Quest* 33:195–213.
Weinstein, C.E.
  1986   Assessment and training of student learning strategies. In R.R. Schmech, ed., *Learning Styles and Learning Strategies.* New York: Plenum.
Weiss, J.M.
  1971a   Effects of coping behavior in different warning signal conditions on stress pathology in rats. *Journal of Comparative and Physiological Psychology* 77:1–13.
  1971b   Effects of coping behavior with and without a feedback signal on stress pathology in rats. *Journal of Comparative and Physiological Psychology* 77:22–30.
  1971c   Effects of punishing the coping response (conflict) on stress pathology in rats. *Journal of Comparative and Physiological Psychology* 77:14–21.
Welford, A.T.
  1976   *Skilled Performance.* Glenview, Ill.: Scott, Foresman.
Wenger, W.
  1983   Toward a taxonomy of methods for improving teaching and learning. *Journal of the Society for Accelerative Learning and Teaching.* 8:75–90.
Williams, H.L., A.M. Granada, R.C. Jones, A. Lubin, and J. Armington.
  1962   EEG frequency and finger pulse volume as predictors of reaction time during sleep loss. *Electroencephalography and Clinical Neurophysiology* 14:64–70.
Wilson, V.E., and E.I. Bird
  1981   Effects of relaxation and/or biofeedback training upon hip flexion in gymnasts. *Biofeedback and Self-Regulation* 6:25–34.
Wilson, V.E., E. Willis, and E. Bird
  1981   Effects of relaxation response upon oxygen consumption during treadmill running. In *Proceedings of the 12th Annual Meeting of the Biofeedback Society of America.*
Wold, D.A.
  1968   The adjustment of siblings to childhood leukemia. Medical thesis, University of Washington.
Wolpe, J.
  1958   *Psychotherapy by Reciprocal Inhibition.* Stanford, Calif.: Stanford University Press.
Wolpe, J., and A.A. Lazarus
  1966   *Behavior Therapy Techniques.* New York: Pergamon.
Yates, A.J.
  1980   *Biofeedback and the Modification of Behavior.* New York: Plenum.
Yerkes, R.M., and J.P. Dodson
  1908   The relationship of strength of stimulus to rapidity of habit formation. *Journal of Comparative Neurological Psychology* 18:458–482.

Zaichkowsky, L.D.
 1984   Attentional style. In W.F. Straub and J.M. Williams, eds., *Cognitive Sport Psychology*. Lansing, N.Y.: Sport Science Associates.
Zaichkowsky, L.D., C. Jackson, and R. Aronson
 1982   Attentional and interpersonal predictors of elite athletic performance. In T. Orlick and J. Partington, eds., *Mental Training*. Champaign, Ill.: Human Kinetics.
Zaidel, E.
 1978   Auditory language comprehension in the right hemisphere following cerebral commisurotomy and hemispherectomy: A comparison with child language and aphasia. In A. Caramazza and E. Zurif, eds., *Language Acquisition and Language Breakdown*. Baltimore: Johns Hopkins University Press.
Zander, A.
 1979   The psychology of group processes. In M.R. Rosenzweig and L.W. Porter, eds., *Annual Review of Psychology* 30:417–451.
Zeiner, A.R., and M.H. Pollack
 1981   Bidirectional changes in digital skin temperature using biofeedback in a cold room. *Journal of Clinical Psychology* 36:514–519.
Zeiss, P.A.
 1984   A comparison of the effects of superlearning techniques on the learning of English as a second language. *The Journal of the Society for Accelerative Learning and Teaching* 9:93–102.

APPENDIXES

A

Summary of Techniques: Theory, Research, and Applications

This appendix is a summary of the techniques covered in the committee's report. For each technique we summarize the theory and assumptions on which it is based, key elements, the types of evaluations that have been employed, the kinds of performance to which it is relevant, results from relevant research, potential applications, and additional comments.

SLEEP-ASSISTED INSTRUCTION

Theory and Assumptions

There is no well-developed theory for sleep-assisted instruction. Theoretical guidance is provided, however, by models of such basic psychological processes as attention and information processing. Conceptualizations are proposed that take into account cognitive organization intrinsic to the natural state of sleep.

Key Elements

An individual's need to learn (motivation) and configuration of procedures (stimulus intensity, speech quality) as related to the task (learning or memory).

Tasks and Designs

Laboratory tasks, control-group designs.

Performances Assessed

Recall, recognition, and relearning of paired associates, nonsense syllables, or sentences.

Examples of Results

(1) Sleep-assisted instruction effects are stronger for certain sleep stages (EEG activation containing alpha frequencies) and learning tasks (recognition more than recall); (2) presleep set (need to learn specific material) may be essential for sleep-assisted instruction; (3) stronger effects occur with lengthy training sessions, self-motivated subjects, and material presented before, during, and after sleep; (4) retention of material (recall) is facilitated by repetition of the material during stage II but not REM sleep.

Applications

Extra time for learning for those who spend most of the day on operational tasks.

Comments

Different results obtained by Western and Soviet investigators are attributed to different emphases; Western EEG-stage studies focus on memory, whereas Soviet suggestibility studies focus on attention.

SUGGESTIVE ACCELERATIVE LEARNING AND TEACHING TECHNIQUES (SALTT)

Theory and Assumptions

The techniques permit content material to bypass traditional emotional blockages and antisuggestive barriers and go directly into long-term memory areas of the brain. The same information is routed simultaneously to different regions of the brain, producing information gain rather than the information losses of the forgetting curve. In fact, it is claimed that retention is greater over time.

Key Elements

Relaxation, guided (pleasant) imagery, concentration, and suggestion combined—the package is what counts.

Tasks and Designs

Classroom instruction in conjunction with courses and foreign language training institutes. Omnibus evaluation experiments involve treatment versus no-treatment packages.

Performances Assessed

Classroom learning, including reading comprehension, course content (emphasizes gain scores in before-after designs), foreign language learning.

Examples of Results

(1) Pretest-to-posttest improvements in science performance; (2) increases in pleasantness ratings, self-motivation ratings, and task-commitment appraisals; and (3) no significant differences on foreign language proficiency between SALTT and the standard Defense Language Institute Foreign Language Course instructional methods.

Applications

A relaxed approach to new materials, overcoming learning blocks in foreign languages.

Comments

Weak experimental designs are used to evaluate the effects of packages; further analytical work to "unpack" the parts is needed.

GUIDED IMAGERY OR REHEARSAL

Theory and Assumptions

Mental practice is beneficial because it serves either to give the performer a chance to rehearse the sequence of movements as symbolic task components or to provide a preparatory set by focusing attention and lowering sensory thresholds: the former theory is likely to be more appropriate to cognitive tasks, the latter to motor or strength tasks. Other hypotheses deal with effects of prior experience, type of imagery, and low-gain innervation of muscles.

Key Elements

Practice performance, imagined outcomes, focused attention, symbolic learning, and preset arousal levels.

Tasks and Designs

Laboratory tasks usually related to a sport; control-group designs, meta-analysis.

Performances Assessed

Motor skills that may emphasize motor, cognitive, or strength elements, depending on the task, which is usually related to a sport.

Examples of Results

(1) Mental practice of a motor skill enhances performance somewhat more than no practice; (2) practice or rehearsal produces larger effects on tasks with more symbolic elements (cognitive) than on those that are primarily motor; (3) performance imagery combined with negative outcome imagery produces a decrement in performance; and (4) vivid imagery (strong visual or kinesthetic imagery) or more practice sessions, or both, improves performance, irrespective of preferred cognitive style.

Applications

Improved performance on tasks for which the visual component is important, such as surface navigation; for other tasks, it may not be better than physical practice.

Comments

A common conceptual paradign and many studies make this literature suitable for meta-analysis. An updated meta-analysis by Feltz et al. (see Appendix B) takes into account the relative effects of physical and mental rehearsal. SyberVision® is a popular technique based on mental practice.

BIOFEEDBACK

Theory and Assumptions

This is an external form of feedback that is intended to bring the autonomic system into a regulated homeostatic balance. For example, heart rate or muscle tension levels may be inappropriate for the demands of the task. Such "disregulations" are adjusted through the use of biofeedback.

Key Elements

Control over internal events related to specific performance, self-regulation.

Tasks and Designs

Laboratory tasks with a variety of populations (e.g., football players, people prone to motion sickness), control-group designs.

Performances Assessed

General ability to relax in skilled motor tasks, specifically, riflery, playing stringed instruments, manual dexterity, and problem solving.

Examples of Results

(1) More effective for improving well-defined, specific performances in which subjects control discrete internal events (e.g., marksmanship, signal response and detection); (2) less effective in reducing general arousal levels, such as antistress training; and (3) learned suppression of a conditioned emotional response may be effective in developing an antistress response.

Applications

Assist in rehabilitation following injury, refinement of performance through fine tuning.

Comments

Promising work in two related areas are identifying internal events linked to specific task performances and training in self-regulation for performers. Additional control groups are needed to separate biofeedback effects from expectancy of positive outcomes resulting from sophisticated gadgetry.

Hemi-Sync™

Theory and Assumptions

Assumes a binaural beat phenomenon resulting from presenting two tones of slightly different frequency simultaneously, one to each ear. Binaural beats result in an alteration of the main frequency components of the EEG such that a frequency following response occurs. The EEG states produced improve performance.

Key Elements

Production of binaural beats, extending the duration of the period of theta activity (4 to 7 hertz), extended exposure to Hemi-Sync™ (for example, three days with an experienced staff administering the treatments), and music combined with Hemi-Sync™ may further enhance effectiveness.

Tasks and Designs

Laboratory tasks, clinics with controlled presentation of tones, classrooms (open-field presentation of tones). Testimonials, self-reports, small-sample experiments.

Performances Assessed

Purports to enhance receptivity to learning, more efficient sensory integration, more focused attention, deep relaxation, and expectations for unlimited learning.

Examples of Results

(1) In one study, about 78 percent of a class reported improvement in mental and motor skills; (2) more positive self-reports of feelings, ability to relax, increased energy levels, and so on when compared with no Hemi-Sync™ and guided imagery only (see comments below).

Applications

Relaxation, induced sleep for jet lag, receptivity to learning.

Comments

The evidence supporting the hypothesized effects of Hemi-Sync℠ on performance is based largely on testimonials and self-reports from small samples. The research designs to date are not adequate in terms of subject assignment to conditions or possible confounding effects of the atmosphere; moreover, the focus to date has been on feelings rather than skilled performances.

STRESS MANAGEMENT

Theory and Assumptions

High or inappropriate levels of stress reduce effectiveness in both cognitive and motor tasks. Various techniques are effective in reducing stress or in inducing relaxation. Each technique addresses one or all of the following: sources of stress, the environment (background music), and physiology (tranquilizing drugs).

Key Elements

Atmosphere and related expectations; specific treatments, including meditation or rest, biofeedback, drugs.

Tasks and Designs

Laboratory tasks, clinics, in situ (battlefield, sports competition), correlational designs.

Performances Assessed

Tension reduction per se (physiological and cognitive indicators), coping skills, learning.

Examples of Results

(1) The prospect of receiving treatment for tension in the near future may be as effective as active treatment techniques for reducing tension; (2) decreases in tension are reflected more strongly on

cognitive (self-rating scales) than on physiological (EMG) measures; and (3) reduced tension may enhance performance involving drawing inferences from materials but not simple recall of passages.

Applications

Enhancing coping skills, better physical and mental health, increased chances for a peak performance.

Comments

It is useful to distinguish between techniques for managing stress (organizations) and techniques for treating stress (relaxation therapies, tranquilizing drugs).

NEUROLINGUISTIC PROGRAMMING

Theory and Assumptions

Cognitive processes are represented by sensory systems or imagery that is visual, auditory, or kinesthetic. These are referred to as a client's preferred representational system (PRS). The PRS is the "deep structure" of a client's thought processes and is reflected in such "surface structure" clues as eye movements and predicate use. Knowledge about a client's PRS enables a counselor to speak the client's language, a process that enhances empathy and influence.

Key Elements

Matching on verbal (preferred predicates) and nonverbal (eye movements) dimensions.

Tasks and Designs

Interviews, counseling, analogue counseling interviews. Experiments designed to evaluate the PRS and effects of matching on perceptions.

Performances Assessed

Language style, perceptions of interviewer or counselor, relaxation and rapport, accommodative behaviors.

Examples of Results

(1) Evidence for a PRS is weak; correlations among alternative measures are low; (2) evidence for matching on preferred predicates only is weak; and (3) matching on all predicates produces significant effects on perceptions.

Applications

Potentially more effective vertical (and horizontal) communication, modeling experts as a training strategy.

Comments

Empathic verbal responding may underlie effects obtained for matching per se. Two parts of this technique are matching and modeling: the former is one of several influence strategies that may well produce effects; the latter is a possible basis for enhanced motor or cognitive performance.

COHESION

Theory and Assumptions

Cohesion is an aspect of the relation between a group and its members: it consists of affective (attraction among members), cognitive (goal satisfaction), and process (risk-taking behavior) elements. Cohesion is stronger in groups that provide for member needs and whose influence over member behavior is the result of perceived legitimacy rather than enforced sanctions. High group cohesion is associated with positive outcomes for group members.

Key Elements

Procedures (e.g., the COHORT system) and group properties (e.g., relation of group to members) that serve to increase intermember attraction, a sense of belonging, instrumental value of the group, risk taking, and teamwork.

Tasks and Designs

Work with sports teams, organizations (e.g., Army reservists), camps, personal change groups. Attitude surveys of soldiers in COHORT and non-COHORT units.

Performances Assessed

Win-loss percentages in interacting (basketball, hockey) and coacting (track and field) sports, organizational commitment, intergroup competition or cooperation, goal achievement, satisfaction.

Examples of Results

(1) Group-serving patterns of attribution (diffusing responsibilty to entire group and attributing more responsibility to self for failure and no more than equal responsibility to self and others for success) enhance team cohesion; (2) cohesion is a stronger correlate of organizational commitment than such factors as quality of training, increased communications, and compensation or tenure; (3) early and midseason cohesion is a significant predictor of late-season performance (win-loss record); and (4) team cohesion is functional for interacting sports but may be dysfunctional for coacting sports.

Applications

New Manning System of regiment or company stability across assignments and locations.

Comments

This literature can be divided into three parts: components of cohesion, factors that influence cohesion, and effects of cohesion on unit performance. Army studies document benefits of unit stability: for example, COHORT units have higher reenlistment rates, positive self-image, and psychological readiness for combat, including an ability to withstand more stress.

PARAPSYCHOLOGY

Theory and Assumptions

Psi phenomena exist and can be demonstrated; they are sensitive to aspects of the situation and moods of the percipient. An appropriate explanation is assumed to derive from an understanding of the role of consciousness in the physical world.

Key Elements

Elusive effects (rarely replicated) are explained in terms of a variety of phenomena including the nature of human consciousness, quantum mechanics, attitudes and laboratory ambiance, experimenter communications, and statistical (random) processes.

Tasks and Designs

Laboratory demonstrations and experiments (although anecdotal reporting of experiences in situ appear also).

Performances Assessed

Experience of state or event without sensory contact (extrasensory perception), prediction of future events the occurrence of which cannot be inferred from present knowledge (precognition), direct mental influence on an external physical process or object (psychokinesis).

Examples of Results

(1) Success rates for psi effects in Ganzfeld experiments range from an alleged 55 percent to a critically evaluated 30 percent; (2) psychokinesis effects demonstrated for very large data bases as small deviations from theoretical distributions (random event generator experiments); and (3) statistically significant remote perception effects reported over many trials with different stimulus materials.

Applications

Intelligence gathering, if demonstrated.

Comments

The key issues in this literature are whether psi effects are replicable and whether a certain configuration of circumstances is needed to produce them.

B

Background Papers

The committee commissioned 10 papers on specialized topics in order to broaden its perspective and knowledge on human performance. Each of these papers is available from the National Academy Press through the Publication-on-Demand program.

Evaluation Issues

INTERPERSONAL EXPECTANCY EFFECTS AND HUMAN PERFORMANCE RESEARCH
Monica J. Harris and Robert Rosenthal, Harvard University
INTUITIVE JUDGMENT AND THE EVALUATION OF EVIDENCE
Dale Griffin, Stanford University

Learning

LEARNING DURING SLEEP
Eric Eich, University of British Columbia
PRINCIPLES OF EFFECTIVE INSTRUCTION
Robert E. Slavin, The Johns Hopkins University

Strategies to Improve Performance

A REVISED META-ANALYSIS OF THE MENTAL PRACTICE LITERATURE ON MOTOR SKILL LEARNING
  Deborah L. Feltz, Michigan State University, Daniel M. Landers, Arizona State University, and Betsy J. Becker, Michigan State University

Stress Management

STRESS AND PERFORMANCE
  Seymour Levine, Stanford University
STRESS REDUCTION AND THE MILITARY
  Raymond W. Novaco, University of California, Irvine

Social Processes

MATCHING AND OTHER INFLUENCE STRATEGIES
  Dean G. Pruitt, Jennifer Crocker, and Deborah Hanes
  State University of New York, Buffalo
CULTURE AND MILITARY PERFORMANCE
  Boaz Tamir and Gideon Kunda, Massachusetts Institute of Technology

Parapsychological Techniques

A COMPREHENSIVE REVIEW OF MAJOR EMPIRICAL STUDIES IN PARAPSYCHOLOGY INVOLVING RANDOM EVENT GENERATORS AND REMOTE VIEWING
  James E. Alcock, York University, Toronto

C

Committee Activities

The committee met six times: on July 23–24, 1985, in Washington, D.C.; on November 20–21, 1985, in Cambridge, Mass.; on February 10–11, 1986, in La Jolla, Calif.; on May 12–14, 1986 in Columbus, Ga.; on August 18–22, 1986, in Woods Hole, Mass.; and on November 11–12, 1986, in Williamsburg, Va. In conjunction with the meeting in Georgia, the committee received briefings and a tour of Fort Benning. The following Army representatives made presentations to the committee at one or more of these meetings:

Colonel John B. Alexander, Manager, Technology Integration Office, Army Material Command
Dr. Edgar Johnson, Director, Army Research Institute
Dr. LaVerne Johnson, Chief Scientist, Naval Health Research Center
Mr. Robert A. Klaus, Organizational Effectiveness Consultant, Army Material Command
Dr. George Lawrence, Research Psychologist, Army Research Institute
Dr. Bruce Sterling, U.S. Army Soldiers Support Center
Major General Albert N. Stubblebine III, U.S. Army (retired)
Dr. Robert Sulzen, Research Psychologist, Army Research Institute
General Maxwell R. Thurman, Vice Chief of Staff, U.S. Army

In order to examine in greater detail the techniques under study, the committee organized itself into subcommittees, which carried out information-gathering activities specific to individual techniques. These activities included site visits to laboratories and other locations where the techniques are being developed, and briefings, interviews, and presentations by Army representatives and persons familiar with the techniques. We list below the subcommittees and the details of their activities.

SUBCOMMITTEE ON EVALUATION ISSUES

Thomas D. Cook, *Chair*

Lloyd B. Humphreys   John A. Swets

SUBCOMMITTEE ON SLEEP LEARNING

Robert A. Bjork, *Chair*   Walter Schneider

Presentation: LaVerne Johnson, Naval Health Research Center, San Diego, Calif., February 1986.

SUBCOMMITTEE ON ACCELERATED LEARNING

Walter Schneider, *Chair*   Robert A. Bjork

Site visit: Army Research Institute Conference on Research in Progress, March 1986.
Site visit: National Suggestive Accelerative Learning and Teaching Techniques (SALTT) Conference, West Palm Beach, Fla., April 1986.

SUBCOMMITTEE ON GUIDED IMAGERY

Daniel M. Landers, *Chair*   Robert A. Bjork

Briefing: Jim Forbes, Army Research Institute, on project on peak performance, February 1986.
Interview: Ray Reilly and Bill Harrison on Concentrix, May 1986.
Site visit: SyberVision®, Newark, Calif., August 1986.
Site visit: Vic Braden Tennis Academy, Trabuco Canyon, Calif., October 1986.
Briefing: Craig Farnsworth, Concentrix-type programs, October 1986.
Briefing: Leon Revien, ProVision, U.S. Olympic Committee, Colorado Springs, Colo., October 1986.

SUBCOMMITTEE ON BIOFEEDBACK

Richard F. Thompson, *Chair*

Daniel M. Landers   Sally P. Springer

Presentation: LaVerne Johnson, Naval Health Research Center, February 1986.

Subcomittee on Split-Brain Effects

Sally P. Springer, *Chair*   Richard F. Thompson

Site visit: Monroe Institute, Faber, Va., May 1986.

Subcommittee on Stress Management

Gerald C. Davison, *Chair*

Daniel M. Landers   Richard F. Thompson
Jerome E. Singer

Site visit: Fort Benning, Columbus, Ga., March 1986.

Subcommittee on Cohesion

Lyman W. Porter, *Chair*

Daniel Druckman   Jerome E. Singer
Sandra Ann Mobley

Briefing: Owen Jacobs, Army Research Institute, October 1985.
Briefing: Colonel William Darryl Henderson, Army Research Institute,
    March 1986.
Briefing: Colonel Kearns, Unit Manning Division, U.S. Army, April 1986.

Subcommittee on Influence

Jerome E. Singer, *Chair*

Gerald C. Davison   Sandra Ann Mobley
Daniel Druckman   Lyman W. Porter

Interview: Richard Bandler on neurolinguistic programming, July 1986.
Presentation: Workshop on NLP techniques by Robert Klaus, July 1986.

Subcommittee on Parapsychology

Ray Hyman, *Chair*

Lloyd G. Humphreys   Paul Horwitz, consultant

Site visit: Princeton University laboratory of Robert Jahn, November
    1985.
Site visit: Backster Research Foundation, San Diego, Calif., February
    1986.
Site visit: Mind Science Foundation laboratory of Helmut Schmidt, San
    Antonio, Tex., June 1986.

Site visit: Stanford Research Institute, Stanford, Calif., June 1986.
Briefing: U.S. Army Laboratory Command, Aldelphi, Md., November 1986.

SPECIAL BRIEFINGS

The committee met twice with the Army's Resource Advisory Group, which was appointed to monitor the progress of the study. On August 8, 1986, the Resource Advisory Group was briefed by the committee on its charge, planned activities, and schedule for completion. On November 10, 1986, the Research Advisory Group was briefed on the committee's progress in each of the areas being investigated. Listed below are the members of the Research Advisory Group, who also provided input to the committee's work:

Lieutenant General Robert M. Elton, *Chair,* Deputy Chief of Staff for Personnel
Dr. Louis M. Cameron, Director of Army Research and Technology
Dr. Phillip C. Dickinson, Assistant Secretary of the Army
Major General Maurice O. Edmunds, Commander, U.S. Army Soldier Support Center
Mr. Walter W. Hollis, Deputy Under Secretary of the Army for Operations
Lt. General Robert M. RisCassi, Deputy Chief of Staff for Operations and Plans
Major General Philip K. Russell, Commander, U.S. Army Medical Research and Development Command
Lieutenant General Louis C. Wagner, Jr., Deputy Chief of Staff for Research, Development, and Acquisition
Lieutenant General Sidney T. Weinstein, Assistant Chief of Staff for Intelligence

In addition, the committee's study director provided information about the study to several groups. On January 12, 1987, Army intelligence staff were briefed about the committee's findings at a technology seminar hosted by the Army's assistant chief of staff for intelligence. In February 1987 the committee's chair and study director attended briefings by Lloyd R. Roberts, U.S. Army Foreign Science and Technology Center, and Dale E. Graff, Defense Intelligence Agency, on technologies in the Soviet Union. On April 10, 1987, the study director presented the committee's findings and conclusions to the governing board of the National Research Council.

D

Key Terms

The following are key terms used often in the literatures related to the technologies examined by the committee. These terms will be especially useful to readers who wish to examine the literature more closely. The terms are arranged alphabetically within a topic heading.

BIOFEEDBACK AND STRESS MANAGEMENT

Alpha and theta producers: EEG patterns reflecting reduced levels of electrocortical activity and explored often in studies on meditation and related forms of relaxation; found in some studies to correlate with various induced states of relaxation.

Autogenic training: Self-generated regulation of tension levels without specific biofeedback on recorded internal events. Instructions are presented to encourage relaxation.

Battle fatigue: Symptoms are similar to battle shock but are long-term and more insidious in their onset. The victim is usually unable to perform duties for over 72 hours. May require evacuation to nearby medical facilities.

Battle shock: The immediate onset of severe anxiety with symptoms that last up to 72 hours. Ideally managed at the lowest level of care possible.

Biofeedback: A class of techniques that provide information to subjects about a variety of internal events, including heart rate, electromyography, autonomic events, respiration, brain frequencies, finger temperature, and peripheral vasoconstriction. Learned control of these internal events is a possible path to performance enhancement.

Cognitive versus physiological measures: Two types of measures for assessing effects of treatments on tension reduction: cognitive measures are self-reports of tension, frequency of problems, anxiety, distress, ability to relax, severity of problem, and so on; physiological measures include EMG and finger temperature data.

Conditioned emotional response (CER): In the context of biofeedback, refers to learned responses (feelings) to stressful situations; learned suppression of a CER is one path to developing an effective antistress response.

EEG synchronization: Refers to hemispheric symmetry indicative of an integration of hemispheric functioning, for example, correlated alpha waves.

Electromyography (EMG): An electrical signal generated by muscle tension; a technique used to infer general muscle relaxation.

Hawthorne effect: Effects on behavior that result from merely being selected to participate in an experiment. Identified by investigators conducting studies on the effects of setting (lighting, music) on performance at the Hawthorne plant of General Electric, this effect has been used to account for findings in biofeedback and other tension-reduction studies.

Hemispheric laterality: Refers to the relative predominance of right or left hemisphere activity. Relaxation techniques may serve to inhibit either (or both) right (associated with intuitive cognitive styles) or left (associated with logical and analytical styles) hemisphere activity.

Meditation practice: Any of several groupings of attentional strategies, including a focus on the whole field, as in *mindfulness meditation;* a focus on a specific object within a field, as in *concentrative meditation;* or a shifting back and forth between the two, as in *integrated meditation.*

Placebo control group: Exposure to nonspecific treatment, such as a potpourri of soft, soothing music to induce relaxation.

Stress management: The techniques or structures designed for recognizing the signs of stress and for administering treatments in an organizational context (as distinguished from treatment per se). The plan is often guided by the principles of immediacy (quick administration of treatment), proximity (close facilities), and expectancy (expect to recover).

Three-echelon model: A flexible medical delivery system designed to take account of the severity of casualties: the first echelon is limited in scope, relying on "buddy care" provided in situ; the second echelon is a site some distance from hostilities where victims are treated by medical personnel; and the third echelon is a site with permanent facilities and staff to provide longer-term care.

Waiting-list control group: Designed to control for Hawthorne-type effects, subjects are told that they will be in the experiment but actually receive no treatment.

COHESION

Cohesion: Cohesion consists of three components: intermember attraction (sociometric choice, friendship), instrumental value of the group (value of membership for achieving common goals), and risk taking (willingness of members to express true feelings). Other components include a sense of belonging, interpersonal influence, and teamwork.

Cohort system: A set of procedures (used by the Army) designed to increase unit cohesion by strengthening friendship ties and a sense of belonging.

Cross-cutting loyalties: Refers to shared identifications (loyalties) held by members of competing groups. Hypothesized to moderate the intensity of competition.

Expert power: A source of leader influence that derives from perceptions of a leader as having superior knowledge in an area of importance to the members, notably in the context of a current or expected situation.

Group attributes or properties: Characteristics of groups that contribute to cohesion, including group composition (extent of homogeneity), relation of group to members (provision of benefits), channels of communication, ideological strength, and goal satisfaction.

Group-serving patterns: Attributions of responsibility for success or failure, namely, diffusing responsibility to the whole group and attributing more responsibility to self for failure and no more than equal responsibility to self and others for success; these patterns have been found to enhance cohesion.

Interacting versus coacting teams: This distinction is best reflected in the difference between basketball (requires coordination among members) and bowling (each member performs apart from other members).

Legitimate power: A source of leader influence that derives from attitudes of "correct" behaviors, of "oughtness."

Normative control system: A system designed to influence behavior through internalization of group values and norms. The objective of such systems is to enhance personal commitment to a unit and its objectives; contrast with coercive motivation (emphasizes negative consequences) and to utilitarian control (uses monetary reward or other tangible benefits).

Referent power: A source of leader influence, referent power is based on personal relationships and on intense identifications between the leader and his or her subordinates.

HEMISPHERIC LATERALITY

Apraxias: Disorders in the execution of skilled purposive movements in the absence of significant motor weakness, incoordination, or sensory loss.

Dichotic listening: A technique used to assess differences in function between the hemispheres; it entails simultaneous presentation of competing information to the left and right ears.

Dual-code theory: An approach to the mental representation of objects that states that memories are tied to sensory modalities and that information is represented as sensory or motor experiences.

Dual-task experiments: A technique that consists of asking the subject to do two tasks simultaneously that putatively involve both hemispheres.

Hemisphericity: A notion that recognizes that different areas of the brain are specialized for different sensory, motor, and cognitive functions; in its more extreme versions, it is claimed that independent "minds" are supported by each cerebral hemisphere of the brain. Evidence to date does not support this claim.

Hemispheric Synchronization (Hemi-Sync)™: A machine-aided process that is presumed to more closely align brain wave activity (frequency and amplitude) in both left and right hemispheres.

Lateral orientation: Refers to the hypothesis, largely unsupported to date, that lateral eye movements index lateral cerebral activity, which in turn indicates cognitive activity associated with a particular hemisphere.

Matching studies: Refers to a series of studies calling for judgments of "sameness" or "differences." Results are shown to have implications for the dual-code theory defined above; they hint at a verbal-visual dichotomy for memory representation.

Modes of processing: A distinction is made between serial (successive cognitive operations) and parallel (simultaneous operations) processing in relation to the left and right hemispheres; the two modes of processing have also been referred to as analytic versus gestalt, respectively.

Priming: Refers to a procedure used to call forth either a verbal or a visual representation, to wit, a cue given verbally would prime the verbal store, and a visual cue would prime the visual store.

Propositional theory: Another approach to the mental representation of objects, this argues that memories are stored as neither a visual nor a verbal code, but in an abstract propositional form.

Split-brain studies: Refers to research on the effects of disconnected hemispheres on memory, as well as on linguistic and visuospatial abilities. Split-brain patients appear to suffer a general impairment of memory functions after commissurotomy (a surgical procedure that separates the hemispheres). These findings suggest that the commissures play a role in both encoding and retrieval of memories by providing links between the hemispheres.

IMAGERY AND REHEARSAL

Attention-arousal set: An explanation for the enhancing effects of rehearsal on performance: rehearsal helps performers to set pretension levels and maintain their attention on task-relevant cues.

Concentrix: A training procedure used to acquire, improve, and sustain skills in concentrating on a specific target at the current time, for the correct length of time. Marketed by the Allen Corporation of America (Alexandria, Va.), Concentrix is considered to be useful for such tasks as marksmanship training.

Future- or past-oriented imagery: A distinction between projecting performance into the future, or an upcoming task, versus thinking about past performances and how these were done.

Meta-analysis: A way of statistically analyzing the findings of many individual analyses. It is especially appropriate for integrating a group of studies related by a common conceptual hypothesis or common operational definitions of independent and dependent variables. One area that lends itself to this approach is the work on mental practice.

Another is the subarea of parapsychology known as Ganzfeld psi experiments.

Outcome imagery: Imagining the outcome of a task that may be either positive or negative; for example, "imagine the ball rolling, rolling, right into the cup" or "rolling, rolling, toward the cup, but at the last second narrowly missing."

Performance imagery: Rehearsing the acts involved in performing a task; instructions to subjects usually consist of asking them to imagine a performance (e.g., putting) and to go through the steps in their minds without imaging an outcome (sinking or missing the putt).

Preferred cognitive style: Distinctions along a dimension of amount of imagery (imagers, nonimagers, occasional imagers) and types of imagery as visual or kinesthetic; combining these distinctions results in strong and weak visual or kinesthetic imagers.

Symbolic learning: An explanation for the enhancing effects of rehearsal on performance: mental practice gives the performer the opportunity to rehearse the sequence of movements as symbolic components of the task.

Type of rehearsal: A distinction is made between physical and mental rehearsal. The former consists of actually going through the motions, while the latter consists of performance imagery.

Type of task: Distinctions are made among cognitive, motor, and strength tasks along a dimension of amount of symbolic content; a distinction is also made between self-paced (closed skill) and reactive (opened skill) tasks, for example, foul shooting versus playing a game of basketball.

NEUROLINGUISTIC PROGRAMMING

Anchors: A term used by NLP practitioners referring to the tactics involved in pinning down an internal response as auditory, visual, kinesthetic, or olfactory.

Congruity: The extent to which there is a correspondence between nonverbal behavior (voice tone, body movements) and language; for example, "You're a great athlete" said with a smirk or a look of disgust.

Dimensions for matching: The part of speech or language, nonverbal communication channel, or other aspects of interaction (topics discussed) used for matching by one or both participants.

Eye movements: According to NLP theory, preferred representational systems (PRS) are indicated by the direction of eye movements: for example, eyes up and to the right indicates visual-constructed images, eyes down and to the right indicates kinesthetic feelings.

Mutual accommodation or convergence: Responding by participants in like manner, an observed phenomenon that highlights the dyadic nature of influence. (Compare with tracking, which emphasizes one party's influence over another.)

Predicate matching: The process of matching those verbs, adverbs, and adjectives that correspond to a client's PRS; words or phrases used by a client are categorized as visual, auditory, or kinesthetic.

Preferred representational system (PRS): One of three sensory modalities, visual, auditory, or kinesthetic, in which most cognitive events associated with day-to-day experiences are principally encoded.

Reframing: A technique used to identify the positive intention behind observed behavior; the NLP practitioner attempts to build a system inside a person, using the person's internal dialogue to communicate with his or her "unconscious" parts.

Response mode measures: The three categories of response mode are usually match, mismatch, and nonmatch. A *match* occurs when the first speaker uses a specific representational system (RS) and the second speaker uses one or more of the same systems; a match is also defined as a joint nonuse of specific systems. A *mismatch* occurs when the first speaker uses a specific RS and the second speaker uses a different RS. A *nonmatch* occurs when the first speaker uses a specific RS and the responder fails to use one or more of the same systems.

Tracking: Refers to the process of monitoring certain aspects of a speaker's language; it is used both to assess a PRS (frequencies of sensory modalities represented) and to match or mismatch predicates. This process implies a one-sided perspective, distinguishing between the *influencer* and the *influencee*.

Transactional perspective: Acknowledges the two-way nature of social influence, emphasizing mutual convergence or accommodation rather than distinguishing between an influencer and an influencee, as in the tracking process.

Two-step process: Procedure used to identify RS predicates; first, predicates are identified by part of speech (verbs, adverbs, etc.) and, second, the predicates are classified by RS (visual, auditory, etc).

PARAPSYCHOLOGY

Agent: The "sender" in tests for telepathy, the person whose mental states are to be apprehended by the percipient. In ESP tests, the person who looks at the target object.

Clairvoyance: Extrasensory perception of objects or objective events.

Effective error rate: The actual rate of success, taking into account ambiguities and inconsistencies in the definition of independent studies as well as reporting biases.

Einstein-Podolsky-Rosen paradox: Suggests that quantum mechanics does not so much describe the state of the physical system as describe our knowledge of the state of that system.

ESP (extrasensory perception): Experience of, or response to, a target object, state, event, or influence without sensory contact.

File drawer problem: Unreported studies tend to be those with lower effect sizes; this problem serves to reduce the success rate calculated on the basis of published data.

Majority vote technique: In ESP tests, a scoring method whereby the most frequent call, from a number of calls made for the same target, is defined as a single response to that target. In PK tests, an analogous technique, whereby the most frequently occurring target event, from a number of attempts on the same target, is defined as a single outcome for that target.

Percipient: The person experiencing ESP; also, one who is tested for ESP ability.

PK (psychokinesis): The extramotor aspect of psi; a direct (i.e., mental but nonmuscular) influence exerted by the subject on an external physical process, condition, or object.

Precognition: Prediction of random future events, the occurrence of which cannot be inferred from present knowledge.

Preferential matching: A method of scoring responses to free material. A judge ranks the stimulus objects (usually pictures in sets of four) with respect to their similarity to, or association with, each response; or ranks the responses with respect to their similarity to, or association with, each stimulus object; or both.

Psi: A general term to identify a person's extrasensorimotor communication with the environment. Psi includes ESP and PK.

Random event generator (REG): Devices that consist of four components: an electronic noise source; a sampling system; a system that analyzes the pulse train and prepares output for a feedback system, and the feedback display. Used widely for experimentation with low-level PK.

Singles test: A PK technique in which the aim of the subject is to try to influence dice to fall with a specified face up.

STM (screened touch matching): An ESP card-testing technique in which the subject indicates on each trial (by pointing to one of five key positions) what he or she thinks the top card is in the inverted pack held by the experimenter behind a screen. The card is then laid opposite that position.

Target: In ESP tests, the objective or mental events to which the subject is attempting to respond; in PK tests, the objective process or object which the subject tries to influence (e.g., as the face or location of a die).

Telepathy: Extrasensory perception of the mental state or activity of another person.

Trial: In ESP tests, a single attempt to identify a target object; in PK tests, a single unit of effect to be measured in the evaluation of results.

SLEEP LEARNING

Hypnopedia: A term used particularly by Soviet researchers to refer to sleep education; it emphasizes stimulus properties, suggestibility, set, and training.

Sleep-assisted instruction (SAI): Situations in which the learning of verbal material takes place or is enhanced through its presentation to a sleeping person.

Sleep stages: Defined by EEG activity as follows: Stage W (waking state) shows alpha or a low-voltage mixed-frequency EEG, or both; stage I is a low-voltage mixed-frequency EEG with much 2 to 7 hertz activity; stage II shows high-voltage negative-positive spikes and the absence of generalized high-amplitude waves; stage III is 20 to 50 percent with high-amplitude delta waves; stage IV is characterized by delta waves in more than 50 percent of the epoch; and stage REM is characterized by the concomitance of low-voltage mixed-frequency EEG activity and episodic rapid eye movement. A night's sleep shows four or five cycles of EEG activity with possible consecutive stages consisting of W, I, II, III, IV, II, REM, II, III, IV, III, II, REM.

SUGGESTIVE ACCELERATED LEARNING TECHNIQUES

Meta strategies: Groupings of types of methods used to improve teaching and learning, usually arranged into a taxonomy with such categories as methods to improve the learner, to improve the teacher, to improve the context or setting within which learning occurs, and to improve the content of learning.

Mind calming: Physical exercises designed to enhance concentration by decreasing external pressure and increasing an awareness of self.

Passive music session: Providing a background of classical music such as Vivaldi, Teleman, Bach, and Handel.

Pleasant experience imaging: Images evoked by background sounds and pictures of scenes that the teacher can remember well.

Pleasant learning restimulation: Recalling an early pleasant learning experience where the student was eager to learn and before his or her memory skills were stymied. The student is encouraged to return to that situation once again and "try to learn and enjoy today in the same way."

Suggestive accelerative learning and teaching techniques (SALTT): A combination of methods geared primarily toward classroom learning and cognitive tasks. Relaxation, guided imagery, concentration, and suggestive principles are woven into a package designed to enhance learning.

Suggestopedia: A method of intensive teaching developed in the mid-1960s by G. Lozanov of Bulgaria. It was designed originally to provide a short course in language learning for adults leaving the country. This method is often cited as a basis for a wide range of accelerated teaching techniques.

E

Military Applications of Scientific Information

JAMES E. SCHROEDER

The research and development process in a military environment is difficult to characterize; there are probably as many exceptions as there are rules. Nevertheless, it is important to put the committee's findings in the larger context. This appendix was prepared at the request of the committee to provide general knowledge based on the author's observations of how the process works. Many of the ideas expressed do not describe formal policy. Discussion is limited to the field of applied psychology and may or may not generalize to hardware development. Although the following discussion is centered around military research and development, there are probably meaningful parallels in other, nonmilitary research and development programs. The reader is advised to read Crawford (1970) and Drucker (1976) for other discussions of research, development, and utilization of psychological products in the Army.

One common representation of the ideal process is provided by the Department of Defense research and development funding taxonomy, which defines the process in terms of the four funding steps shown in Figure E-1. In this model, the research and development process is represented by a funding continuum ranging from basic science through engineering development. In the ideal case, a potentially useful scientific finding would emerge from the basic research laboratory. This information is then "picked up by" or "handed to" applications-oriented scientists in the military setting for applied research and exploratory development. If the resulting applied research findings are promising and there are potential applications, then a project would proceed to the advanced

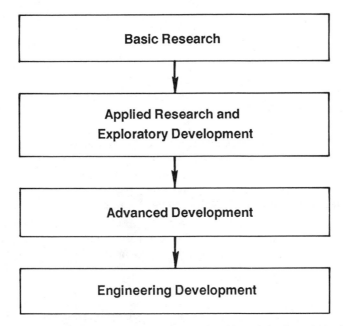

FIGURE E-1 Schematic representation of the transfer of knowledge from the basic science laboratory to a final product.

development stage for further enhancement and adaptation to a particular setting. In the engineering development stage, the specific engineering design requirements are made and actual delivery equipment or software is developed.

With the apparent logic and simplicity of this model, it is often difficult for people outside the system to understand why the transfer of new scientific information is slow or absent. Individuals and organizations within the development continuum complain of deficiencies in the other sectors. Basic scientists cannot understand why their theories or findings have not been applied, and applied scientists question why basic scientists don't work on topics with more application potential (Weinstein, 1986).

SOURCES OF "ERROR" IN THE RESEARCH AND DEVELOPMENT PROCESS

Most people who are familiar with military research and development would probably agree that the model just described, while presenting a useful ideal, is deceptively simple, and the actual process is tremendously more complex. For the sake of simplicity, consider two general classes of errors that can be made at a multitude of points along the research and development continuum. To borrow terms from hypothesis testing, let *Type I error* represent a class of errors that result in an invalid or inapplicable idea, procedure, theory, and so on, being inaccurately assessed as valuable and continuing in the development process. Let *Type II error* represent a set of errors in which a truly valuable potential application, for whatever reason, does not continue on the development path.

These two types of errors can occur at any point along the continuum represented in Figure E-1; however, it is worthwhile to divide the source of the error into two major categories. In this appendix, a *within-step* source of error refers to an error of either type that occurs as a result of the operations performed inside any of the boxes shown in Figure E-1; a *between-step* source of error refers to either type of error that occurs as a function of the procedures involved in handing off a project from one level to another level (represented by the arrows in Figure E-1).

WITHIN-STEP SOURCES OF ERROR

In general, these sources of error refer to traditional research design problems. While remaining troublesome issues that must be adequately dealt with in either basic or applied settings, many of these sources of error have already been identified. In addition, there is a substantial literature describing ways to eliminate, avoid, minimize, or measure most of these contaminating sources of error; Chapter 2 of the committee's report deals with some of these issues. It should be noted that these potential errors could occur in any of the boxes, since experimental evaluations presumably occur at all stages.

In summary, even if there is a potential and obtainable product that could evolve from some basic science finding, there are still many potential pitfalls within the steps taken along that path. While these pitfalls are clearly dangerous, they are widely known, and scientists have discovered and promulgated ways of recognizing, avoiding, and adjusting for most of them.

BETWEEN-STEP SOURCES OF ERROR

The arrows in Figure E-1 are deceptive. To the casual observer who is not familiar with the process, they would indicate a smooth flow of information from one step to the next. Indeed, this flow is often surprisingly smooth when one considers the multitude of issues involved in this evolution. As defined above, a between-step source of error is any condition that produces or contributes to one of two possible error states:

failure to continue an effort that actually could provide a significant improvement, or continuing an effort that actually has no significant fielded potential.

There is a great deal of activity which must occur between the steps identified in Figure E-1. Much of this activity involves complex decision making in which uncertainty, political considerations, readiness considerations, and cost considerations are often great. In the following section, Figure E-1 is revisited, with more careful attention paid to the transitions.

DECISIONS INVOLVED IN THE RESEARCH AND DEVELOPMENT PROCESS

Figure E-2 provides some information about the complexity of the decisions involved as an original idea is transformed into a meaningful product. Two additional stages—implementation and sustainment—have been added to the traditional steps shown in Figure E-1 because they are very important in ensuring that products are fully utilized. Implementation refers to the steps taken to successfully field a product, and sustainment refers to the steps taken to maximize the use of the product for its maximum life-cycle.

It is important to note that Figure E-2 and the following discussion are probably not complete. The purpose of this appendix is to provide the reader with a sample of the complexity involved in carrying an idea from conception to some useful military application, not to provide a complete documentary of the Army's research and development process for psychological products as it has emanated from Department of the Army regulation 10-7 (U.S. Department of the Army, 1981) or transfer of technology issues. For examples of this kind of documentation, see Morton, 1969; Gruber and Marquis, 1969; Seurat, 1979; Allen Corporation, 1985.

DECISIONS LEADING TO BASIC RESEARCH

An imperfect mechanism is involved in all of the transitions shown in Figure E-2: namely, human decision making. Although the basic research scientist, the applied scientist, and the evaluator all use techniques designed to eliminate, measure, or at least attempt to minimize various sources of error, it is nevertheless true that decisions about what ideas find their way to useful products are still based on human decision making and, consequently, are vulnerable to the imperfections and potential biases of that process (Tversky and Kahneman, 1974; Lichtenstein et al., 1978; Slovic, 1972; Kahneman and Tversky, 1979).

Ideally, applied military research programs benefit from the entire pool

1. What basic research gets funded?
2. Is the level of effort sufficient?
3. Does the applied scientist have input?
4. Does the potential user have input?
5. Is there a theoretical or empirical basis?
6. What is the history of success in the area?
7. Is there application potential?

_____V_____
Basic Research
_____

V
1. Is there sufficient empirical support in the literature?
2. Was the basic research conducted sufficiently high in quality and internal validity?
3. Are successes noticed by the right people?
4. Are there potential applications?
5. Are potential applications noticed?
6. Is there an "agent" (individual or organization)?
7. Is there a user who can profit?
8. Is there a sponsor with sufficient funds?
9. Does the basic scientist have input?

_____V_____
Applied Research and
Exploratory Development
_____

V
1. What applied research gets selected for development?
2. Are successes noticed?
3. Are failures reassessed?
4. Is the user still interested?
5. Is there still a sponsor with funds?

_____
Advanced Development
_____

V
1. What gets selected for engineering development:
2. How effective is the prototype?
3. What are the cost–benefit factors?

_____V_____
Engineering Development
_____

V
1. Who produces the final product?
2. How is it promulgated, distributed, maintained, replaced, and so on?
3. Is there command emphasis?
4. Who will oversee the implementation?
5. Is there flexibility in the product?
6. Is there flexibility in the system?
7. Does the targeted audience still want the product?

_____V_____
Implementation
_____

V
1. Is there a motive for using the product?
2. Is there still command emphasis?
3. Does the product have face validity?
4. Does the user feel the product works?
5. Is there a vehicle for updating the product?
6. Is the product available?
7. What has been done to insure continued use?
8. In the case of a psychological product, what is the vehicle for transfer?   V

_____
Sustainment
_____

FIGURE E-2 Schematic representation with more detail about the decisions involved in the research and development process.

of basic science research. Since there is a large pool of funding sources for basic science (e.g., universities, foundations, private companies, government scientific agencies, government military agencies), the comments in this section are relatively general and may be relevant to any funding agency. In contrast, comments in the rest of the appendix are limited to military research and development.

Although decisions about which ideas, concepts, and theories receive basic research funding are usually made by experts, they are still subject to sources of bias. In fact, experts may be susceptible to special sources of error because of their expertise (for the "mind snapping shut" phenomenon, see Perrin and Goodman, 1978; Zeleny, 1982; for overconfidence, see Lichtenstein and Fischhoff, 1977). The following are possible sources of bias that, whether leading to a correct or an incorrect decision, probably do affect the chances of a research proposal's getting through the initial gate:

1. Although many funding agencies attempt to conduct blind reviews, in practice this is often difficult, because information in the proposal provides the expert reviewer clues to the author's identity. Any hints of identity can produce other potential biases, such as the identity of the university or organization involved, the reputation of the investigator in the proposed field, the investigator's publications, and so on.

2. Even if the author is unidentified or the reviewer is able to discount the author's identity, there are inevitably references to theoretical positions and scientific philosophy that could provide identification and subtly bias a reviewer.

3. There may be subtle or not-so-subtle political pressures on reviewers to fund certain areas. For example, if the news media highlight some new procedure as promising (even though such claims may not be founded in data), there will almost certainly be some pressure (internal or external) placed on an agency or reviewer to give such proposals special attention.

4. There may be biases on the part of some reviewers to reject proposals that are radically different from the existing literature, have little or no empirical support, or are generated by nontraditional sources. While logically defensible, such a stance might stifle valuable new approaches.

5. Some reviewers might be subject to the influence of early results. Early results (positive or negative) may carry more weight than is justified, especially if popularized in the media. In addition, there may be a bias for positive results to be published in the literature (Sterling, 1959; Rosenthal, 1966).

6. Some research topics have acquired distinct reputations based on a history of findings in a given direction. This may produce a bias, leading

some reviewers to reject a proposal because a significantly different or novel approach may be involved in the proposed research.

7. There may be pressure on some agencies to fund new ideas, stay on the cutting edge, or be the first to discover something. This probably leads to a bias to fund different—as long as they are not too different—topics. While progressive, such biases could leave promising older approaches without funding and hence without progress. Psychological research appears to be novelty-oriented, with many investigators following the lead of a relatively small number of intellectual entrepreneurs. While the work of a few investigators receives great attention, the systematic and tedious investigations of traditional scientists may go without funding or appropriate recognition.

8. Decisions are often made on the basis of a small number of reviewers. Procedures that have been developed to minimize biases in group decision making (e.g., the Delphi or modified Delphi procedures, Linstone and Turoff, 1979) are often not used because of time or budget constraints.

9. Scientific reviewers have been trained to be critical. The critical review is, of course, an important and necessary part of the scientific process. Reviewers obtain and retain respect and credibility among their colleagues by identifying all possible faults. The danger is that a poorly written proposal, one that does not follow a prescribed professional format, or one that deviates significantly from the reviewers' expectations, may not be funded, even though a potentially valuable contribution might result.

10. Some reviewers tend to favor proposals that are founded in existing theory; of course, there are probably some reviewers who have the opposite bias. The potential danger is that, if proposals that offer to investigate simple empirical relationships are rejected because they lack a theoretical basis, many potentially useful and applicable research proposals may never be funded. Further exacerbating the problem, investigators submitting research proposals are asked to justify their research. Investigators offering proposals not based on theory may be more likely to examine and provide real-world applications as a justification for their work, while investigators whose proposals are based on theory may be more likely to offer refinement of the theory as a justification. If this is true, then any reviewer with a bias toward existing theory may inadvertently eliminate research that has been targeted for specific applications.

11. Scientists making decisions about funding for basic science are usually basic scientists and may not be application-oriented or trained in applied science. Basic science holds a higher place in many graduate education programs. As a result, there may be a lasting, and probably unintentional, bias toward pure science, a lack of familiarity with issues

involved in applied science, and a lack of understanding of applied issues. While applied scientists may have at least a minimal understanding of basic science in their field, basic scientists may never have been exposed to applied science. One potential result is that some reviewers of basic science proposals may neither recognize nor adequately weigh the potential application value of some research efforts. Application potential should not become the crucial criterion for funding; many important applications have come from basic research for which there were no known applications at the time (e.g., Boole's development of binary algebra). However, application potential should remain one of several criteria to be considered by all reviewers, especially when the sponsor is expecting a useful and usable product.

12. There is often a lack of communication between the basic scientist and the applied scientist or potential user. There is a need for more exchange of information between the two communities. Ongoing dialogue would help the applied scientist anticipate and plan applications based on promising basic research findings, would help the basic scientist target research for specific applications, and would help the basic science funding reviewer identify areas in which considerable needs and opportunities exist. It should be noted that, while such communication does exist, as evidenced by the work of this committee, more is needed.

The above considerations partly determine whether a given basic science research proposal is funded. From a funder's economic view, probably the worst error is funding an effort that leads to nothing. From an advancement of science view, probably the worst error is failure to fund a potentially valuable effort. Funding an invalid approach will usually be detected during the basic research efforts or later, during the applied research efforts. The rejection of a potentially valuable effort may mean its demise, unless the researcher is adaptive, devoted, and persistent.

DECISIONS LEADING TO APPLIED RESEARCH AND EARLY DEVELOPMENT

The first requisite for making the transition from basic to applied research is that there exists a substantial base of support for a given approach in the basic scientific literature. The major purpose of the committee's report is to provide the Army with facts and expert opinions about whether such support exists for the identified techniques and whether the research conducted was internally valid. The following general discussion of the process assumes that those essential criteria have been met.

While significant empirical support is a necessary condition for this transition, it is not a sufficient condition. The findings must be recognized by the "right people"—usually an applied scientist, a sponsoring research agency, or a potential user. Of course, there must be true application potential, and that potential must also be noticed.

One of the most important conditions is that there be a motivated agent. The agent must be a combination of entrepreneur, producer, director, motivator, broker, advocate, and salesperson. This individual or group usually provides the impetus for the move from basic to applied research and, if successful, into development. The agent could be an applied scientist, a research agency, a sponsor looking for projects with high potential, or an end user. In any case, the agent usually locates a potential end user, an applied research agency to conduct the work, and a sponsor with sufficient interest and funds.

There is a potential bias if the applied scientist becomes the agent, but this bias is probably no greater than the bias created when the basic scientist takes on similar roles when seeking funds, except that in the latter case an end user may not be identified. In addition, as in basic science, the results of applied research must stand up to the test of replicability by disinterested parties.

In summary, although the questions being addressed by the committee are important in determining whether the identified techniques offer significant potential applications for the Army, they are not sufficient conditions for entry to applied research. This thought is further developed in the following sections.

DECISIONS LEADING TO ADVANCED DEVELOPMENT

After a promising concept has been tested for application value and some initial development toward a target application has been made, there are two possible outcomes: either the results prove sufficiently promising to warrant consideration for early development, or they do not. Entering initial development is an important decision, because it means starting a machine that is hard to stop. Specifically, as more and more development money is spent, it becomes increasingly difficult for the decision makers to halt the effort and take responsibility for the "wasted" money.

As noted above, the validity of the applied research outcome is a function of many variables, including the quality of the design, control for experimental bias, and so on. In fact, the risk of inaccurate conclusions from applied research is much higher than in basic science, because the experimenter usually does not have the experimental control that is available to the basic scientist. Some of the many problems that plague design of applied research are discussed in Chapter 3 of the report. In addition to the difficulties of designing and carrying out high-quality applied research, there is another possible source of error in interpreting the outcome of such research.

Consider the decision matrix in Figure E-3, which depicts various outcomes from applied experiments based on sound or unsound basic research concepts. Ideally, only concepts with sound foundations would be selected for applied research. Nevertheless, consider the errors represented by *C*: such an error could be caused by flawed methodology (e.g., Hawthorne effect, nonrandom assignment, and experimenter bias). There is also a possibility that an effect actually due to the experimental manipulation was purely coincidental and was not a true function of the unsound basic science principle on which it was presumably based. Such an outcome would give false testimony to an unsound principle. In basic science, it would be tantamount to lending support to a false hypothesis, because inappropriate operational definitions have been accidentally confounded with causally important variables. In both cases, investigators are misled; however, the applied scientist may be less concerned about such an outcome (causality), because, after all, a functional relation has been demonstrated that has real-world effects.

Considering the outcomes of applied research that has been based on sound basic science principles, a parallel event could occur. Outcomes represented by *A* could in fact be the result of inappropriate applications of sound principles that accidentally happen to generate significant effects. Finally, *B* represents all failures that are due to methodological short-comings, plus all outcomes based on principles with low external validity, plus all instances in which inappropriate applications were made based on sound concepts. In summary, one important additional requirement

Application Outcome

		Success	Failure
Foundation			
In Basic	Sound	A	B
Science			
	Unsound	C	D

FIGURE E-3 Decision matrix depicting various outcomes from applied experiments based on sound or unsound concepts from basic science.

for applied research is that not only must the methodology be valid, but the application must also be valid. The biggest potential danger for the applied scientist who is seeking useful methods to help in real-world settings is represented by *B*, because such an outcome would reflect negatively on a sound, possibly applicable concept that simply was misapplied (assuming that basic scientists minimize the chances of *C* and *D*). Such an outcome may also incorrectly discourage other investigators from applying the concept.

Decisions about entering development early must address implementation issues, because even though there is still a long journey ahead, it is one that should not be initiated unless implementation is judged to be obtainable. Sustainment refers to keeping a given new approach in place. Like implementation, sustainment should be considered before entering development. In the following paragraphs, a sampling of implementation and sustainment issues is presented. Most of them have been included because they might partially determine the chances of survival for several of the techniques reviewed by the committee.

1. If the target user has not already been specified, it must be identified in this stage. In addition, it is important to ensure that the user understands what the product will and will not do. Users do not like surprises, and early expectations—especially for those unfamiliar with a new technology—are usually inaccurate. The user must be informed that the product has potential application value. The user's input must be continuously solicited and exploited. In this regard, it is most useful if the concept has face validity, empirical support, and a variety of other characteristics described in the following sections.

2. With notable exceptions, the Army system is not currently set up for enhancing human performance across the board. Rather, soldiers are trained to meet some standard of performance. One of the main concerns of trainers is to raise the performance level of all soldiers to some standard. Consequently, a disproportionate amount of training time is spent on poor performers, while less time is spent on polishing an excellent performer. Because trainers will use products that help them the most, the chances of implementation and sustainment are greatest if the product provides enhancement for the poorer performers.

3. The term *command emphasis* refers to substantial support from relatively high places and involves problems of allocation of time and resources. To implement and sustain new techniques often requires that something else be displaced. People may resist new techniques, not because they oppose them, but because they feel they must maintain their resources at the same level to continue doing a good job. Any resulting tough decisions about allocation of resources may escalate.

Consequently, the technique with the strongest support base will have the best chance of implementation and sustainment. This usually involves more than a commander's simply liking a new technique; it usually means that a technique must have empirical support compelling enough to justify cutting back on some other potentially valuable program.

4. The term *personnel turbulence* refers to the fact that there is significant personnel movement within the Army. Army officers can usually expect to stay in a given position no more than three to four years before moving on to another job. While potentially increasing general knowledge among officers, such movement can also be a source of disruption to the research and development process. For example, a sponsoring agency that was excited about a new technique last year may be indifferent to the same technique this year. New personalities bring new values, new priorities, and new objectives. In addition, some officers may feel that it is the innovators who get promoted, not the people who implement the last commander's innovation. Others may feel that the chance of failure (which inevitably accompanies innovation) represents a risk to their careers. Finally, much time is spent briefing and rebriefing key officials about ongoing work.

5. In addition to command emphasis, any new technique must have the support of the final user. In the Army, this probably means the cadre of noncommissioned officers. There are a number of issues involved here. First, as in any organization, there will probably be inertial resistance to new approaches (e.g., Schon, 1969). Consequently, the noncommissioned officers must be convinced that the new technique holds advantages that far exceed any possible additional work. Army leaders work hard and for long hours. They do not have time to spend familiarizing themselves with complex new techniques. Consequently, training the trainer or user and designing straightforward, easy-to-use techniques are important. Finally, certain personality and role-model characteristics of many Army personnel may go against successful implementation and sustainment of any techniques that are construed as nonmilitary, soft, or trivial, even if scientific evidence supports them. Consequently, even the personality of the user may be a significant consideration when figuring the chances of successful implementation and sustainment.

6. It may be useful for persons unfamiliar with the Army to conceptualize two armies: a peacetime Army and a wartime Army. This is an imprecise distinction at best, because elements of both probably exist in both conditions. Nevertheless, it is important for the applied scientist to distinguish which Army has been targeted. Development, implementation, and sustainment processes for a peacetime Army may be similar to those found in a large business; however, they may be substantially different from those targeted for wartime use.

7. In planning for implementation, it is important not to overlook practical considerations. For example, consider the applied scientist who takes a new weapon simulator to the range, only to find that there is no electricity; the investigator who asks the combat infantryman to carry the small (5-pound) electronic aid along with the 48- to 72-pound gear he is already carrying; or the researcher who provides a soldier with a fragile, battery-operated electronic device for improving land navigation.

8. It is also important to consider the organizational implications of presenting a new product. Is there time in an already busy schedule? Is there physical space available for using and storing the product? Are there security implications? Is there enough flexibility in the product to accommodate personnel surges, as in national mobilization? Is the product compatible with other currently existing approaches, products, doctrine, policies, and so on? Can the Army afford to implement this product in a way that would really have an impact? How, when, and where can the product be made accessible to the real user? These are all important organizational considerations that will partially determine the success of an implemented product.

9. Finally, it is important to consider the human implications of presenting a new product. What are the documentation requirements? What are the training implications? A common mistake made by developers is to assume that documentation will always be available, that any soldier is capable of using their product, that the system will absorb any new product, and that there is always a training cadre that is expert in the area of application. These assumptions may not always be true. It is far safer to start extensive communications with the target user and determine the human requirements (the Navy and the Army HARDMAN methods and the Army MANPRINT program are good examples of this approach).

In summary, although the above issues are related to implementing and sustaining developed products, they are also important considerations at the earlier stage. If there are any significant foreseen problems that cannot be overcome, then the development stages should not be entered. These points are raised in this context because it is possible that some of the techniques under review might contain elements that would be difficult to implement for various reasons.

DECISIONS LEADING TO ENGINEERING DEVELOPMENT

If the early development process is successful, the corresponding evaluations of effectiveness show significant effects, and the implementation path looks promising, then chances are high that a project will pass to the advanced development stage, at which an engineering design package is produced and the product to be implemented is finalized. More than ever, it is important to consider the needs and concerns of the target users. The user should be given detailed updates on different features of the product. It is useful to provide the target user with a prototype for informal test, evaluation, and comment. Until this stage, it is quite possible that the product has been developed in a vacuum, without much attention paid to the final context. While desirable at earlier stages, it is necessary at this stage of development to consider the context: environment, personnel, schedules, existing equipment, software, space, degree of hardening required, and transportability. The developers should always remember that what might seem to them to be an insignificant detail might be a very important feature to the user. It is also important to sell the user on the usefulness of the product and to help him or her sell others. Full-scale cost-effectiveness evaluations conducted by impartial parties should provide input to the final decision about whether to proceed with procurement. As in all steps, political and funding considerations can have an impact on a developing product.

Decisions Leading to Implementation

As noted by Pressman and Wildavsky (1973), there is a general lack of published analytic work dealing with implementation issues. For an excellent account of the implementation of Army products from different perspectives, see Drucker (1976).

There is a multitude of decisions to be made with regard to implementation. One important subset involves complex decisions about vendor selection. Another major subset involves complex decisions about logistics (e.g., how many are needed, how will they be distributed, how will they be maintained, replaced, and so on). These two major subsets of decisions are not discussed here, because they are very complex and not particularly relevant to the theme of this discussion. Because they are important, visible, and involve financial considerations, procurement and logistics have often overshadowed other issues in implementation, those dealing with whether purchased products are actually implemented in a useful way. One such subset of questions was presented above, in the section on decisions leading to applied science and early development. Also important are steps that must be taken at the time of implementation.

The implementation should be overseen. The ideal implementation team would include a member of the design team or at least someone familiar with the development process who knows how the product was intended to be implemented as well as answers to inevitable questions about why implementation is to proceed a certain way. Special demands, situations, and circumstances inevitably surface for different user groups; therefore, it is extremely advantageous to have noted these variables early in development rather than to try to adapt a finished product. In either case, a new technique has better chances of implementation if a certain degree of flexibility can be built into it without sacrificing quality.

Taken as a whole, the quality of the decisions discussed above sets the stage for implementation and determines the potential for the new product or technique. The critical issue still remains: Will the product be adopted by the real user, and will the user continue to use it? Army users are functional. If something works and causes little or no additional labor, they will adopt it and continue to use it. Consider the noncommissioned officer, for example, who is often the agent for implementing a change that has been decided on at a higher level. Noncommissioned officers are continuously bombarded with changes, some of which are not explained and some of which they may perceive as misguided. Nevertheless, they tend to become strong advocates and defenders of any techniques that are proven to be useful. Regardless of how carefully the stage is set, how well a product is implemented and sustained depends on whether the human users want it. If they perceive the product as satisfying a real need, reducing work, or increasing chances of survival, then implementation and sustainment take care of themselves. If not, no amount of planning and implementation will be sufficient.

DECISIONS LEADING TO SUSTAINMENT

There seems to be an intrinsic problem involved in implementing and sustaining psychological products. Conversely, there seems to be something about physical products that encourages their use and extends their survival, if they work. Possible explanations for this phenomenon are that the Army demands accountability for physical equipment (e.g., signatures in a property book) or that physical things are easier to brief people about and demonstrate.

Seward Smith and Art Osborne at the U.S. Army Research Institute's Fort Benning Field Unit tell stories based on decades of experience in implementing and sustaining marksmanship programs based on sound psychological principles of learning (Smith and Osborne, 1981; Osborne, 1981; Osborne and Smith, 1984). One of the stories is especially relevant to this appendix. Some time ago, decisions were made that virtually eliminated precise feedback about shot location. This was probably an unintended side effect of moving to more realistic "field fire" techniques, in which realistic targets are randomly raised and fall when hit. Hence, feedback on hits and misses is provided, but it is not meaningful feedback for the very good (all hits) or the very poor (all misses) shooters. Substantial efforts have been made by Smith, Osborne, and their colleagues at Fort Benning to increase the amount of feedback in marksmanship training.

One of many remedies included a downrange feedback exercise, in which soldiers fire rounds at fixed targets at real ranges. Next, after all the necessary safety precautions, soldiers move downrange to personally inspect shot location. The targets are large enough that they capture most rounds and represent realistic silhouette paper targets (black target on white background). Soldiers examine their shot groups and then put black markers on white paper (misses) and white markers on black paper (hits) and return to the firing line. The reverse markers help the training cadre and the soldiers detect any trends in overall grouping over cumulative groups. On the final trip downrange, soldiers cover the holes so that the next person has a fresh target.

This exercise remains one of the few opportunities for a soldier to get precise shot location at actual ranges. Notice that the soldier never receives feedback about a specific shot, only about a small group of shots (usually five). This is to be applauded as a simple, yet elegant solution to an existing problem. However, there have been occasions on which the range was visited only to find all black or all white markers on the targets because the range personnel ran out of one color, or worse, to find no markers because they ran out of both colors or did not understand the significance of the exercise.

The point is that, for a variety of possible reasons, the implemented technique was not properly sustained. Feedback is not an issue clouded by controversial and conflicting results from basic science laboratories. Feedback is not a politically charged issue. Feedback is recognized as very important even to the uninitiated. The feedback technique described above does not require significant funding or time, yet there have been problems in sustaining this relatively simple technique. This fact is potentially important when considering the various techniques described in this report.

One possible solution is to ride on the back of computer hardware technology. Computer-assisted training, instruction, performance aids, and so on allow psychological principles to be incoporated into hardware and software. That is why Smith, Osborne, and their colleagues are excited about new approaches made possible by microcomputers and other technological advances. Such technology may provide excellent transfer vehicles for various techniques. For example, rifle simulators allow safe, realistic practice with precise shot location and other kinds of feedback that were not possible previously (Schroeder, 1987). Location of misses and hits (LOMAH) technology provides precise shot location about real bullets at actual range. The computer allows psychological principles to become more demonstrable. It allows a way of standardizing information—by putting it in inaccessible computer code—thereby ensuring that there are no distortions in the delivery of the technique and avoiding the assumption that there will be experts in the field to deliver the technique.

Such technological advances are surely not the solution to all applications. Although they seem to be an excellent partial solution for many implementation and sustainment issues in a peacetime Army (e.g., training), they may not be appropriate in wartime applications (i.e., there is only so much equipment a soldier can carry into battle—see Vogel, Wright, and Curtis, 1987). Overdependence on technology by the system or the soldier is a real concern.

CONCLUSIONS

The purpose of this appendix is to provide the reader unfamiliar with the Army's research and development procedure a better context for the committee's work. Information about the scientific basis for new concepts and techniques is crucial for Army decision makers. Solid scientific support is a necessary condition; however, it is but one of several gates through which a technique must pass before it is utilized in a meaningful way.

The evolution from the basic science laboratory to a useful Army product was shown to be a relatively complex process. The major steps involved in Army research and development were identified in Figure E-1 to be basic research, applied research and exploratory development, advanced development, and engineering development. As scientists, we tend to concentrate on the research islands along the path and pay too little attention to the potentially dangerous waters in between. In this appendix, special attention was paid to the various decisions that must take place between the formalized research steps. The account presented is informal, based on personal experience with the system. While not a rigid procedure, the questions and transitions identified should be considered by scientists and engineers along the entire continuum.

The various techniques discussed by the committee fall at various points along this continuum. For example, sleep learning, brain asymmetry, and parapsychology appear to be having trouble clearing the first hurdle. Another cluster of techniques appears to have support or to contain elements that have support from basic science. These techniques are currently at various stages of applied research and early development, in which investigators are attempting to find the optimum combination of elements and target audiences to achieve a meaningful application (i.e., influence strategies, stress management, biofeedback, accelerated learning, and mental rehearsal). Finally, because of the Army's historic interest in group cohesion, work on cohesion can be considered in the advanced development or implementation stages. A recent instance of this interest is the Army's COHORT program.

Regardless of where a technique currently falls on the continuum, some of the questions posed are relevant to its future success. For example, user acceptance is seen as a problem for brain asymmetry, neurolinguistic programming, biofeedback, accelerated learning, and parapsychology.

It is recommended that scientists along the entire continuum become more familiar with all phases of research and development as generally discussed in this appendix. More communication is needed at all stages of development among the basic scientist, the applied scientist, the engineer, and the user. The reviews of scientific support for these techniques, which are provided in this report, are critical and necessary; however, given a scientifically defensible foundation, similar reviews by applied scientists and potential users are equally important.

While the current model of research and development as described above is a linear, sequential procedure, perhaps other models should be considered, for example, a parallel model. The current model implies little or no feedback to earlier stages and could partially explain the relative lack of communication that often exists among the parties. It is impossible for the basic scientist to anticipate all the questions that could become relevant to the applied version of his or her work. Similarly, it is impossible for the applied scientist to anticipate all the ways in which the product could be used. Finally, it is impossible for the user to recognize and identify all the uses or features of a product until he or she has become familiar with its early forms. I suggest that many excellent existing products have in fact resulted from a parallel research and development approach, which emerged when the user handed a product back to the applied scientist with suggestions, or when the applied scientist referred fundamental questions back to the basic scientist for clarification. Current knowledge about the techniques discussed and their potential applications is sufficiently limited that a parallel research and development approach may be a better strategy than the linear one.

REFERENCES

Allen Corporation of America
    1985   *Proceedings of Technology Transfer Workshop.* (Conducted under contract to the U.S. Office of Personnel Management.) Alexandria, Va.: Allen Corporation of America.

Crawford, M.P.
1970   Military psychology and general psychology. *American Psychologist* 25:328–336.
Drucker, A.J.
1976   *Military Research Product Utilization.* Research product review 76-15. Alexandria, Va.: U.S. Army Research Institute for the Behavioral and Social Sciences.
Gruber, W.H., and D.G. Marquis
1969   *Factors in the Transfer of Technology.* Cambridge, Mass.: MIT Press.
Kahneman, D., and A. Tversky
1979   Intuitive prediction: Biases and corrective procedures. In S. Makridakis and S.C. Wheelwright, eds., *Forecasting.* Vol. 12 of TIMS/North-Holland Studies in Management Sciences. Amsterdam: Elsevier, 313–317.
Lichtenstein, S., and B. Fischhoff
1977   Do those who know more also know more about how much they know? *Organizational Behavior and Human Performance* 20:159–183.
Lichtenstein, S., P. Slovic, B. Fischhoff, M. Layman, and B. Coombs
1978   Judged frequency of lethal events. *Journal of Experimental Psychology: Human Learning and Memory* 4:551–578.
Linstone, H.A., and M. Turoff
1979   *The Delphi Method: Techniques and Applications.* Reading, Mass.: Addison-Wesley.
Morton, J.A.
1969   From research to technology. In D. Allison, ed., *The R&D game.* Cambridge, Mass.: MIT Press, 213–235.
Osborne, A.D.
1981   The M16 rifle: Bad reputation, good performance. *Infantry* 71(5):22–26.
Osborne, A.D., and S. Smith
1984   *US Army FC 23-11: Unit Rifle Guide.* Research product 85-12. Alexandria, Va.: U.S. Army Research Institute for the Behavioral and Social Sciences.
Perrin, E.C., and H.C. Goodman
1978   Telephone management of acute pediatric illnesses. *New England Journal of Medicine* 298:130–135.
Pressman, J.L., and A.B. Wildavsky
1973   *Implementation: How Great Expectations in Washington Are Dashed in Oakland; or, Why It's Amazing that Federal Programs Work at All.* Berkeley: University of California Press.
Rosenthal, R.
1966   *Experimenter Effects in Behavioral Research.* New York: Appleton-Century-Crofts.
Schon, D.A.
1969   The fear of innovation. In D. Allison, ed., *The R&D game.* Cambridge, Mass.: MIT Press, 119–134.
Schroeder, J.E.
1987   Overview of the development and testing of a low-cost, part-task weapon trainer. In R.S. Stanley II, ed., *Proceedings of the 1987 Conference on Technology in Training and Education.* Colorado Springs: American Defense Preparedness Association, 200–209.
Seurat, S.
1979   *Technology Transfer: A Realistic Approach.* Houston: Gulf Publishing.

Slovic, P.
1972   *From Shakespeare to Simon: Speculations—and Some Evidence—About Man's Ability to Process Information.* Research Monograph 12, Oregon Research Institute.

Smith, S., and A.D. Osborne
1981   Troubleshooting rifle marksmanship. *Infantry* 71:28–34.

Sterling, T.D.
1959   Publication decisions and their possible effects on inferences drawn from tests of significance—or vice versa. *Journal of the American Statistical Association* 54:30–34.

Tversky, A., and D. Kahneman
1974   Judgement under uncertainty: Heuristics and biases. *Science* 185:1124–1131.

U.S. Department of the Army
1981   *Organization and Functions of the US Army Research Institute for the Behavioral and Social Sciences.* U.S. Army regulation 10-7.

Vogel, R.J., J.E. Wright, and G. Curtis
1987   Soldier load: When technology fails. *Infantry* 77(2):9–11.

Weinstein, L.F.
1986   The ivory tower and the real world: A graduate student's perspective. *Human Factors Society Bulletin* 29(12):8–9.

Zeleny, M.
1982   *Multiple, Criteria Decision Making.* New York: McGraw-Hill.

F

Biographical Sketches

JOHN A. SWETS is chief scientist of Bolt Beranek and Newman Inc. After receiving degrees from the University of Michigan, he was assistant and associate professor of psychology at the Massachusetts Institute of Technology and then senior vice-president and general manager of Bolt Beranek and Newman Inc. He is also lecturer in clinical epidemiology at the Harvard Medical School. He is a fellow of the American Psychological Association and a fellow as well as a current or former council member of the American Association for the Advancement of Science, the Acoustical Society of America, and the Society of Experimental Psychologists. In 1985 he received the latter society's Warren Medal. He has served on several advisory panels for the Department of Defense (including the Science Advisory Board of the Navy Personnel Research and Development Center), the National Institutes of Health (including the clinical evaluation group of the National Cancer Institute), and the National Research Council (including panels on intraservice standardization of audiometric tests, research to improve hearing aids, design of a standard emergency signal, and accuracy of polygraph lie detection). He is editor or author of four books and many journal articles. His recent research on enhancement and evaluation of human performance has focused on thinking skills in secondary education and diagnostic skills in the clinic.

ROBERT A. BJORK is professor of psychology at the University of

California, Los Angeles. He received a B.A. degree in mathematics from the University of Minnesota and a Ph.D. in psychology from Stanford University. He has been assistant, associate, and full professor at the University of Michigan and has been a visiting scientist at Bell Laboratories, the University of California, San Diego, and the Rockefeller University. His research interests center on human information processing, particularly human memory, and on the practical application of that research to instruction and the optimization of performance. He is the author of numerous publications and has presented lectures and seminars to many groups, such as corporate executives, college alumni, educators, lawyers, and physicians, in this country and in Europe. He served as editor of *Memory & Cognition* from 1981 to 1985 and has been on the editorial boards of several other journals. He is a fellow of the American Psychological Association and of the Society of Experimental Psychologists and is a member of the Psychonomic Society and the Cognitive Science Society.

THOMAS D. COOK is a professor of psychology at Northwestern University and a research fellow at its Center for Urban Affairs and Public Policy. He went to Northwestern after receiving degrees from Oxford University and Stanford University. He has been a visiting professor at the London School of Economics and a visiting scholar at both the Russell Sage Foundation and the General Accounting Office. He serves on the board of the American Evaluation Association, from which he received the Myrdal prize for science in 1982. He has served on panels for a number of federal agencies: the Department of the Army, the Department of the Treasury, the General Accounting Office, the Department of Education, the Department of Agriculture, the National Heart, Lung, and Blood Institute, the National Cancer Institute, and the National Science Foundation. He has served on panels for the MacArthur Foundation, the Russell Sage Foundation, the Police Foundation, and the World Bank, as well as on scientific advisory boards for many corporations doing evaluations for the federal government. He is editor or author of four books and many journal articles. His major research interests are theories of the practice of evaluation and the social psychological dynamics associated with poverty in the United States.

GERALD C. DAVISON has been professor of psychology at the University of Southern California since 1979. Until 1984 he was also director of clinical training and since then has been department chair. He received an A.B. from Harvard University and a Ph.D. from Stanford University and from 1966 to 1979 taught at the State University of New York at Stony Brook. He has published articles on cognitive behavior therapy and experimental personality research and is coauthor of three books. He is a fellow of the American Psychological Association and has served on the executive committee of the Division of Clinical Psychology, on the Board of Scientific Affairs, and on the Committee on Scientific Awards. He is also a past president of the Association for the Advancement of Behavior Therapy. He has served on the editorial board of several journals, including the *Journal of Consulting and Clinical Psychology*, *Behavior Therapy*, and *Cognitive Therapy and Research*. His current research is concerned with cognitive assessment, stress, and hypertension.

DANIEL DRUCKMAN is study director of the Committee on Techniques for the Enhancement of Human Performance. He received a Ph.D. in social psychology from Northwestern University and was a winner of the American Institutes for Research's best-in-field award for his dissertation. He is a member of the Society of Experimental Social Psychology. He was previously the Mathtech scientist at Mathematica, Inc., and senior scientist and program manager at Booz, Allen & Hamilton. He has also been a consultant to the U.S. Foreign Service Institute, the U.S. Arms Control and Disarmament Agency, and the U.S. delegation to the Vienna talks on force reductions. His primary research interests are in the areas of conflict resolution and negotiations, nonverbal communication, group processes, and modeling methodologies, including simulation. He has published four books and numerous articles on these topics, some of which have appeared in the *Journal of Conflict Resolution*, *Advances in Applied Social Psychology*, *A Handbook of Communication Skills: Comparative Regional Systems*, and *Corporate Crisis Management*.

LLOYD G. HUMPHREYS is professor emeritus of psychology and education at the University of Illinois. After receiving degrees from the University of Oregon, Indiana University, and Stanford University, he held postdoctoral appointments at Yale and Columbia universities and faculty appointments at Northwestern University, the University of Washington, and Stanford University prior to his long-time tenure at the University of Illinois. He also served in the Aviation Psychology Program of the Army Air Forces during World War II and headed the Air Force's Personnel Research Laboratory during and for several years following the Korean War. He is a member of the Psychonomic Society (one-time chairman of the governing board) and of the American Educational Research Association. He is a fellow of the American Association for the Advancemnet of Science (two-time chairman of the psychology section). For the federal government, he served a brief term as assistant director for science education in the National Science Foundation and has been on several advisory panels, including the Air Force's Scientific

Advisory Board. He was also associated with the Commission on Human Resources of the National Research Council for a number of years. He is the author of many book chapters and journal articles. In recent years his research has been concerned with individual differences in human abilities and theories of human intelligence.

RAY HYMAN is professor of psychology at the University of Oregon, where he has taught since 1961. He received a Ph.D. from The Johns Hopkins University and taught at Harvard University from 1953 to 1958. He has also been a consultant to the General Electric Company, a Fulbright-Hays research scholar (University of Bologna), a National Science Foundation faculty fellow, and a visiting professor of psychology at Stanford University. He serves on the editorial board of *The Skeptical Inquirer* and is an associate editor of the *Zetetic Scholar*. His numerous publications on topics related to parapsychology date back to 1957, appearing in both parapsychological and other journals. They include several books, encyclopedia chapters, and technical articles in such journals as *Proceedings of the IEEE* and the *Journal of Parapsychology*.

DANIEL M. LANDERS is professor in the Department of Health and Physical Education at the Arizona State University. After receiving degrees from the University of Illinois, he was on the faculty at Illinois University, the University of Washington, and the Pennsylvania State University. He is a member of the American Psychological Association, the Society for Psychophysiological Research, and the American College of Sports Medicine. He is a fellow in the Research Consortium of the American Alliance of Health, Physical Education, Recreation, and Dance; a fellow of the American Academy of Physical Education; and former president of the North American Society for the Psychology of Sport and Physical Activity. His advisory work has included membership on education and training committees for national sport governing bodies as well as membership on the Visual Performance and Enhancement and Sport Psychology committees of the U.S. Olympic Committee. He was the cofounder and editor of the *Journal of Sport Psychology* and has also edited or authored six books and many journal articles. His recent research has dealt with psychophysiological theory and methodology applied to sport and exercise, with a focus on understanding how athletes control arousal and focus concentration so as to maximize performance.

SANDRA ANN MOBLEY has been director of training and development for the Wyatt Company, an actuarial and benefit consulting organization, since October 1986. She has worked in the field of training and development in industry for the past seven years. Her previous position as manager of executive education at Hewlett Packard gave her broad experience in methods for organizational change and executive development. She has served on task forces to develop human resource systems for the National Red Cross and the California Youth Authority. In addition, she has consulted on organizational change, training, and development for both high-technology and service-oriented firms. She received bachelor's and master's degrees in mathematics and computer science from the University of Texas at Arlington and a master's in business administration from the Harvard Business School.

LYMAN W. PORTER is professor of management and psychology in the Graduate School of Management at the University of California, Irvine. He was formerly dean of the Graduate School of Management. Previously he served 11 years on the faculty of the University of California, Berkeley. During 1966–1967 he was a visiting professor in the Department of Administrative Sciences at Yale University. He is past president of the Academy of Management and in 1983 received that organization's award for scholarly contributions to management. He has also served as president of the Division of Industrial-Organizational Psychology of the American Psychological Association. His major fields of interest are organizational psychology and management. He is the author or coauthor of six books and many articles in these fields.

MICHAEL POSNER is professor of neuropsychology and psychology at Washington University in St. Louis. He received a Ph.D. from the University of Michigan and taught in the psychology department at the University of Oregon from 1968 to 1985. He has also been a visiting professor at Yale University, Cornell Medical College, and the University of Minnesota and served as director of the neuropsychology laboratory at Good Samaritan Hospital from 1979 to 1985. He has been an editor of the *Journal of Experimental Psychology,* a Guggenheim fellow, a fellow of the American Academy of Arts and Sciences, and the winner of the distinguished scientific contribution award of the American Psychological Association in 1980. His recent work has concentrated on problems of attention and performance, and he has published numerous journal articles and book chapters. He was elected to the National Academy of Sciences in 1981.

WALTER SCHNEIDER is senior scientist at the Learning Research and Development Center at the University of Pittsburgh. He received a Ph.D. in psychology from the University of California, Berkeley, and was a Miller research fellow there. He was both assistant and associate professor at the University of Illinois and associate professor at the University of

Pittsburgh. He is past president of the Society for Computers in Psychology. He has served on several panels of the National Research Council, studying such topics as flight simulator training and pilot performance models in computer-aided design. His current research involves skill acquisition and attention, modeling human performance, computer-based training, and neural modeling of attention.

JEROME E. SINGER is professor and chair of the Department of Medical Psychology at the Uniformed Services University of the Health Sciences in Bethesda, Md. He received a B.A. in social anthropology from the University of Michigan and a Ph.D. in psychology from the University of Minnesota, as well as a postdoctoral fellowship at Minnesota in histochemistry. He has taught at the Pennsylvania State University and the State University of New York at Stony Brook. He has been a visiting scholar at the Educational Testing Service, a guest researcher at the University of Stockholm, a staff associate at the Social Science Research Council, and study director at the National Research Council. He has been the recipient of the American Association for the Advancement of Science's sociopsychological prize and the outstanding contributor award of the Division of Health Psychology of the American Psychological Association. He is founding editor of the *Journal of Basic and Applied Social Psychology* and coeditor of two monograph series, *Advances in Environmental Psychology* and *Handbook of Psychology and Health.*

SALLY P. SPRINGER is visiting professor in the Program in Human Development at the University of California, Davis. She received a B.S. from Brooklyn College and a Ph.D. in experimental psychology from Stanford University and has done postdoctoral work in the Program in Hearing and Speech Sciences at the Stanford University School of Medicine. She was assistant and associate professor of psychology at the State University of New York at Stony Brook and also served as associate provost there. She is coauthor, with George Deutsch, of *Left Brain, Right Brain*, winner of the 1981 American Psychological Foundation distinguished contribution award. Her research and publications have been in the area of hemispheric asymmetry of function.

RICHARD F. THOMPSON is professor of psychology and Bing Professor of Human Biology at Stanford University. His previous positions include professor of psychobiology in the School of Biological Sciences at the University of California, Irvine, professor of psychology at Harvard University, and professor of medical psychology and psychiatry at the University of Oregon Medical School. His research is in the broad field of psychobiology, with a focus on the neurobiological substrates of learning and memory. He is a member of the National Academy of Sciences and the Society of Experimental Psychologists, councilor of the Society for Neuroscience, chair of the Psychonomic Society, and president of Division 6 of the American Psychological Association. He has received the distinguished scientific contribution award of the American Psychological Association and a research scientist career award from the National Institute of Mental Health. He received a B.A. degree from Reed College and a Ph.D. in psychobiology from the University of Wisconsin.

Index

M

Parapsychological Association, 176
Parapsychology
    experiments, *see* Ganzfeld psi
      experiments; Random number
      generator experiments; Remote
      sensing experiments
    file drawer problem in, 259
    laboratories, 175–176
    military R&D status on, 278
    preferential matching in, 259
    recommended research in, 22,
      207–208
    replication of experiments in, 8, 172,
      174, 178
    theory and assumptions, 244
    user acceptance, 279
Performance
    altering states of awareness and,
      20–21, 103–105
    biofeedback effects on, 8, 20, 21, 61,
      77, 86, 89–90, 239
    expert, model of, 133, 134, 143, 145,
      146–148
    group cohesion and, 152, 153–154,
      155, 157–158, 160–162
    hemispheric laterality and, 102, 105
    measures of, 153, 155, 161
    meditation and, 105
    mental concentration and, 104
    peak, 6, 20, 103–105
    satisfaction and, 136
    in sleep-deprived state, 46
    under stress, 20–21, 58, 89–90, 116
Persuasion, attitude change through,
    135–136
Physical exercise, concentration
    enhancement by, 261
Physical rehearsal, mental rehearsal
    contrasted with, 257
Posttraumatic stress disorder
    symptoms and diagnosis, 128–129
    treatment, 129–130
Precognition
    definition, 170, 245, 259
    military applications, 171
    random number generator
      experiments, 176
Preferred representational system
    characterization, 139–140, 242, 258
    EEG pattern correlated with, 140
    eye movement indicators of, 146, 258
    importance in neurolinguistic
      programming, 142

predicate matching, 258
    tracking to assess, 258
Pribam, Karl, 8, 67, 68, 141
Price, Pat, 177, 182
ProVision Training Program, approach
    and claims, 73–75
Psi
    conducive conditions for, 203–206
    definition, 173
    see also Extrasensory perception;
      Paranormal phenomena
Psychic warfare
    antimissile time warp, 170
    First Earth Battalion of warrior
      monks, 171
    hyperspatial nuclear howitzer, 171
    psychotronic weapons, 170–171
Psychokinesis
    definition, 170, 245
    evidence for, 190, 207, 245
    majority vote technique in tests, 259
    metal bending, 171, 203–206
    military applications, 171
    singles test, 260
    see also Random number generator
      experiments
Psychoneuroimmunology, 119

Q

Quantum physics
    Einstein-Podolsky-Rosen paradox,
      259
    imagery analysis, 69
    paranormal phenomena and, 172

R

Random number generator experiments,
    22, 172
    characterization of, 184–185, 259
    criticism of, 200, 201
    results, 185–186, 207
    scientific assessment, 186–190
    sites for, 175–176
    special requirements, 174
    well-controlled, 189–190
Reading skills, Hemi-Sync™ applied to, 7
Relaxation
    alpha and theta producers in, 252
    autogenic training and, 81, 252
    cognitive, 98